"This Gospel . . . Shall Be Preached":

A History and Theology of Assemblies of God Foreign Missions to 1959
Volume 1

Gary B. McGee

Gospel Publishing House
Springfield, Missouri

02-0511

D0057437

5th Printing 2001

Library of Congress Cataloging-in-Publication Data

McGee, Gary B., 1945–
  This Gospel—shall be preached, volume 1.

  Originally presented as the author's thesis
(doctoral—St. Louis University)
  Bibliography: p.
  Includes index.
  1. Assemblies of God—Missions—History.
2. Pentecostal churches—Missions—History. I. Title.
BV259.A8M36 1986   266'.99   86-80015
ISBN 0-88243-511-6 (v. 1: soft)
ISBN 0-88243-673-2 (v. 2: soft)
Printed in the United States of America

To the memory of Noel Perkin
Missionary statesman of the
Assemblies of God: 1927–1959

Contents

Foreword

On the pedestal of one of the statues outside the Pennsylvania Avenue entrance to the national Archives building in Washington, D.C., is this inscription: "What is past is prologue."

Unfortunately, when the title of a volume has in it the word *history,* it immediately is faced with certain barriers. To the young, it conjures up memories of dull classroom discussion, memorization of dates, attempts to pronounce difficult names, and the tracing of battles fought somewhere in the dim past. History is sometimes also given a low priority because of our penchant for living in the present— undoubtedly encouraged by the electronic media reporting the happenings of the moment almost instantaneously in our homes. The world has become a very small community.

However, this historical book by Dr. Gary B. McGee immediately catches the reader's attention. By a marvelous array of facts and figures, this history becomes interesting reading.

We never escape our past. In every sense, the past is prologue. What we have been constitutes very much what we are and will be. The concepts that gave rise to our present situation need to be thoroughly understood or we can never interpret the present. Every day our lives are touched by institutions and movements birthed out of principles and concepts now sometimes forgotten.

In 1989 the Assemblies of God will celebrate its 75th anniversary. From its earliest days it has been a great missionary movement. The spiritual stirrings of the early 20th century were at flood tide. Great lay movements had come into being, great revivals had swept campuses, and the YWCA and the YMCA and other such institutions had been formed to conserve the vision for missions that had come in the closing years of the 19th century.

However, by 1906 a common hunger was growing among spiritually minded missionaries, many of whom were already occupying stations in far-flung places of the world; they felt the task of world evangelism must be aided by a fresh tide of the Holy Spirit. It became a common feeling that "we are his witnesses of these things; and so is also the Holy Ghost, whom God hath given to them that obey him." When the revival came in Pentecostal dimension, it brought men and women from the far places of the world to Azusa Street to find out what this new revival was all about. The saga of how this all came into being, the tracing of the streams of diverse interests as they merged to form the Division of Foreign Missions and its outreach around the world, is interesting reading in this sequel to the Book of Acts.

The present missionary movement of the Division of Foreign Missions is the outgrowth of precise missionary concepts undoubtedly authored by the Holy Spirit and implanted in the hearts of early pioneers who knew the New Testament but were in no sense recognized as missiologists. However, the things they said, the papers they wrote, the concepts they adopted, the dreams they dreamed, are still being carried out today. The present worldwide movement and fraternal fellowship numbering in the millions are the product of a few principles announced by these pioneers and incorporated in the bylaws of the General Council of the Assemblies of God.

It is interesting to note that the administrative personalities that emerge in this history were indeed gifted men, but no one personality rises above the plain. To be sure, this volume is dedicated to the memory of Noel Perkin, who was a spiritual giant. But a host of sometimes unheralded and unmentioned leaders plowed the fields and sowed the seed, many never living to see the harvest of their labors. In a real sense, this is the story of "the wind blowing where it listeth." Above human instrumentality, the sovereignty of the Holy Spirit stands in bold relief.

This work is scholarly enough to attract anyone who wants to probe deeper into the history of foreign missions. At the same time it is popular enough to attract and hold the interest of anyone who simply wants to read another and different record of the moving of the sovereign harvest Master.

J. Philip Hogan
Executive Director
Division of Foreign Missions
Assemblies of God

Acknowledgments

The writer expresses appreciation to Dr. J. Philip Hogan, executive director of the Assemblies of God Division of Foreign Missions, for his encouragement in this project and generous permission to utilize the division's historical resources for research. A senior editorial assistant in the division and widow of a distinguished missionary, Mrs. Adele Flower Dalton, deserves special recognition for her painstaking labors in collecting and preserving valuable data about the history of the organization. Her achievements in accumulating such information on missionaries and the fields of foreign endeavor played a significant role in the preparation of this book.

The Assemblies of God Archives, located in Springfield, Missouri, proved to be especially helpful for historical research. Mr. Wayne Warner, director, and his staff graciously assisted the writer in his research there.

The doctoral program at Saint Louis University from which this study grew was completed during the writer's tenure as a faculty member at Central Bible College, Springfield, Missouri. A sabbatical leave of absence for the 1978–1979 academic year enabled him to begin graduate work at the university. The Central Bible College Library with its Assemblies of God Collection greatly assisted the writer in his study.

The writer is indebted to Dr. Belden C. Lane, associate professor of theological studies at Saint Louis University, for his skillful guidance in the progress and direction of the dissertation. Providing additional assistance were Dr. Richard L. Foley and Dr. Joan A. Range, A.S.C., respected professors in the department of theological studies.

Two esteemed colleagues at Central Bible College rendered valuable assistance by reading the dissertation during its various stages of development. Dr. Claude Black, associate professor of history and chairman of the division of general education, and Rev. Gerard J. Flokstra, Jr., associate professor of theology and former director of the library, offered many helpful criticisms and suggestions.

For the transition from unpublished dissertation to published book, Mr. Glen Ellard, book editor for the Gospel Publishing House, and his staff rendered valuable suggestions and assistance. James E. Richardson, associate professor of missions at the Assemblies of God Theological Seminary, prepared the index.

Finally, the project could not have been completed without the faithful support of my wife, Alice. Her interest in Assemblies of God history and recognition of the importance of this work were a never-failing source of encouragement.

Pictures have been graciously provided by the Assemblies of God Archives, Assemblies of God Division of Foreign Missions, A. B. Simpson Historical Library, Boys and Girls Missionary Crusade, Central Bible College Library, Women's Ministries Department, and the following individuals: Samuel and Ruth Beckdahl, Frances Bell, Sydney and Harriet Bryant, J. Kevin Butcher, George and Christine Carmichael, J. Philip and Virginia Hogan, Anabel Manley, Martha Nikoloff, Howard and Edith Osgood, Mildred Smuland, Louie W. Stokes, and Louise Jeter Walker.

The editors of the *Pentecostal Evangel* and *Mountain Movers* have generously allowed the author to quote at length from their publications.

Introduction

The story of the world mission of the Assemblies of God from its beginning through the mid-20th century is the adventure of a revival movement that took seriously the command of Christ to evangelize the world in "the last days." It was propelled by the expectancy that the Holy Spirit would accompany its gospel proclamation with the same "signs and wonders" that marked the triumphs and expansion of the Early Christian Church pictured in the Book of Acts and that when this message had reached the ends of the earth, God would bring the present age to a close.

This overseas effort appeared at a time when American Protestant missions, which previously had generated considerable enthusiasm and support, were confronted by unparalleled problems. The Assemblies of God missions endeavor, along with those of other Pentecostals, represented a fresh and vigorous effort in this century to fulfill the Great Commission of Christ.

The General Council of the Assemblies of God came into existence at its organizational meeting April 2–12, 1914, in Hot Springs, Arkansas, as a result of the worldwide Pentecostal movement that began at the turn of the century. Rejected by other Christian organizations for their Pentecostal beliefs and desiring closer fellowship with others of like mind, over 300 people gathered for this meeting. The delegates pledged themselves to work toward scriptural unity and fellowship, evangelism, dissemination of their Pentecostal theology, and coordination of overseas missionary activities. In the following months, approximately 27 missionaries affiliated with it. From these modest beginnings, the Assemblies of God spread rapidly across the United States. Its far-flung missions program grew to become one of the most significant and successful

Protestant missions agencies, having members and adherents numbering in the millions.

The organization's overseas venture is the story of many earnest believers who were willing to suffer enormous sacrifices to advance the cause of Christ. For some, this meant traveling to distant parts of the world to preach the gospel, learning new languages, caring for the needy, struggling to rear children in primitive surroundings, and trusting that God would supply their needs. The accounts of their ministries abroad, however, are not altogether notable. Some did not have a clear strategy for long-range development of indigenous, or national, churches, and mistakes were made that took years to correct. But most were guided by the organization's original ideal: to establish indigenous congregations abroad, which they believed would be empowered by the Holy Spirit to evangelize their own nations. To this end the missionaries prayed, preached, and planned. The astonishing success of Assemblies of God foreign missions in this century is a tribute to their vision.

For most Assemblies of God church members who remained at home, the missionary effort meant faithful prayer support and financial sacrifice. Pastors and evangelists preached that God had raised up the Assemblies of God to evangelize the world and called their hearers to prayer, local evangelism, and sacrificial support of the missions program. Letters from abroad, news reports in Council and non-Council periodicals, and stirring appeals at General Councils and local churches by visiting missionaries also contributed to the commitment to overseas evangelism, which has continued to the present.

This book was originally presented as a doctoral dissertation in the Department of Theological Studies of Saint Louis University, St. Louis, Missouri. It traces the historical and theological development of the parent organization: the Division of Foreign Missions of the General Council of the Assemblies of God, U.S.A., and analyzes the factors that led to its growth between 1914 and 1959. No attempt was made to record the histories of the various foreign mission fields of the Assemblies of God. Such an effort would have been well beyond the scope of this study. Information taken from available field histories was, however, utilized for its contributions toward a better understanding of the development of the Division of Foreign Missions.

The analysis of information on the division's historical and theological development laid the basis for this study. Such sources included minutes and reports, official histories and surveys of the division's expansion, biographies, autobiographies, theological and missiological studies, articles in independent and denominational publications, missionary manuals, and interviews with key personalities. It should be noted that the nomenclature of the missions program most recently underwent change in 1972, becoming the Division of Foreign Missions; before that time the program was variously referred to as the Missionary Department, the Foreign Missions Department, the Department of Foreign Missions, which is reflected in the primary documents incorporated into the text.

The publisher has generously allowed the book to retain its extensive endnotes and much of its lengthy bibliography to assist the student who may be interested in pursuing further the history of the Division of Foreign Missions. Some of the resources, however, are available only at the Assemblies of God Archives in Springfield, Missouri.

The division's development is best understood when theological factors are interpreted in light of their historical contexts. Thus the book is not a theology of mission or merely a chronicle of past events. It is an attempt to synthesize the historical and theological development of the program. In this way the influence of Biblical interpretation, important personalities, schools, strategies, and controversies on the objectives of the enterprise can be noted.

Before the development of the Assemblies of God missions enterprise can be properly understood, the general state of Protestant missionary endeavors must be considered. For this purpose, Part One presents the climate of American Protestant foreign missions by 1914 and focuses on motivations, missiology, and cooperation. It then addresses the rise of modern Pentecostalism and traces its beginnings to revivals in Topeka, Kansas, and Los Angeles, California. Subsequent revivals that influenced the Assemblies of God and its missions program are then considered.

Part Two discusses the administration of the foreign missions program from 1914 to 1926: leadership, personnel, and finances. Cooperative relationships and popular support are also considered. During those years, the Division of Foreign Missions struggled to maintain itself financially and provide a measure of direction to the efforts abroad. Instability reigned during the early part of this period. However, the later years reflect a steady growth and increasing maturity.

The development of the enterprise from the permanent appointment of Noel Perkin as missionary secretary in 1927 to the middle of World War II is traced in Part Three. At this point the agency was forced to consider what steps it would take when the conflict was over. The formulation of policies, increase in publications, and better means of raising home support figured prominently during these years.

The last period, which began in 1943 and ended with Perkin's retirement in 1959, is covered in Part Four. Great advances in organization, planning, training, and articulating indigenous church principles from a Pentecostal perspective occurred during this time. By 1959, the enterprise was achieving its goals and being ranked as a leader in the Christian world mission. The significant changes that began in that year and the spectacular increase in converts abroad must await another volume.

Among other factors since the 19th century, two contradictory developments have influenced Christendom. In the first place, the Christian faith achieved an unprecedented worldwide expansion through the work of foreign missionaries as the colonial powers carved out empires abroad. At the same time, various forms of skepticism assaulted the foundations of Christianity, questioning the ultimate claims of its beliefs. Significantly, this occurred in the very countries, Germany, Great Britain, and the United States among others, that had been bastions of the Christian faith. Before long the Protestant missionary enterprise felt the impact of this assault.

In the early part of the 20th century, the American fundamentalist/modernist controversy erupted in the major Protestant denominations with the attempts of conservative evangelicals to stem the tide of liberal theology. Their struggles partially resulted from concerns over the theological integrity of some missionaries and programs overseas. While not involved, the Pentecostals, nevertheless, shared the same concerns about the authority of the Bible and the ultimate claims of Christianity. Affirming that God's purposes would be fulfilled in history, that His Word is entirely trustworthy, and testifying to the Spirit's outpouring of power in their time for the evangelization of the world, the Pentecostals shrugged off the charges of the skeptics. Like other Pentecostals, Assemblies of God church members and missionaries believed that the words of Jesus in the Gospel of Matthew signaled the direction of the future: "This gospel of the kingdom shall be preached in all the world for a witness unto all nations; and then shall the end come" (Matthew 24:14).

Part One

Beginnings

1

American Protestant Missions by 1914

The End of the Great Century

The foreign missions program of the General Council of the Assemblies of God arose during the last year of what historian Kenneth Scott Latourette called the Great Century in Christian missions.[1] By the close of this epoch in 1914, the world had witnessed an unprecedented expansion of Christianity, making it the most widespread religious faith. Statistics reveal that 21,307 Protestant missionaries served overseas by 1910 and contributions had reached an all-time high of $39 million.[2]

The events in Protestant missions during the last decades of this epoch are especially important for understanding some of the major developments in Christendom following World War I. Indeed, one writer attested that these decades "were far more critical in shaping the Christian Church than those decades which culminated in the Peace of Augsburg (1555) and the Treaty of Westphalia (1648)" during the Reformation era.[3]

The year 1914 proved to be a pivotal year in world history. The Great War which began that year retarded the American missionary effort overseas and ushered the Protestant churches into a period of critical reflection over the nature of missionary efforts. In addition, tensions over Biblical authority, missionary motivation, and missionary strategy caused breaches in the unity that had characterized the movement before the war.

The unparalleled building of vast colonial empires by the major Western powers before 1914 allowed missionaries access to and privileges in many regions of the world that had been closed to Christian influence. America engaged in overseas expansionism and also played an increasingly prominent role in world affairs. In this context, the growing American missionary efforts were consequently fired by a blending of humanitarianism, patriotism, spiritual zeal, and imperialism.[4] R. Pierce Beaver, formerly a historian of missions at the University of Chicago Divinity School, observes that in the decade before 1914 "tremendous enthusiasm . . . carried American missions to first place in the total Protestant enterprise with respect to the number of missionaries, the amount of money raised and spent, and the diffusion of the work."[5] Several types of missions societies in the United States directed the vast American Protestant missions network. First, most major denominations developed agencies, committees, or societies, such as the American Baptist Missionary Union, that perpetuated and oversaw the missionary work. Second, some independently chartered societies, such as the American Board of Commissioners for Foreign Missions, relied heavily on one or two denominations for support. Third, there were independent or nondenominational societies that generally subscribed to a conservative evangelical or fundamentalist theology.[6] These independent societies often generated like-minded local congregations that provided them with support. Two agencies illustrate this last category: the China Inland Mission and, in its earlier days, the Christian and Missionary Alliance.

The missionary enterprise produced many different kinds of overseas activities besides preaching the gospel. By 1910, there were 180,000 students enrolled in secondary and higher educational institutions supported by Protestant missionary agencies. Over 1,000 missionary doctors practiced overseas during the same year. To assist the converts on the foreign field to read the Bible, translation work became a major concern. Consequently, "missionaries reduced hundreds of languages to writing . . . taught people how to read, and by 1910 had translated the Scriptures into more than five hundred tongues."[7]

Another major feature of Protestant missions in the last several decades of the Great Century was the service of women as missionaries. By 1914, about 21,500 missionaries served overseas. Women constituted half this number and single women one fourth. Apparently, as demands for missionaries increased, more opportunities arose for the services of single women. Because the wives of missionaries found they could inexpensively hire local people to help them with household tasks and childcare, they too assumed missions responsibilities. Nevertheless, the single women missionaries had the advantage of greater mobility and could approach their responsibilities with single-minded attention.[8]

After 1890, laymen played an increasingly important role in the missions movement. The Laymen's Missionary Movement enlisted persons of large and modest incomes in its attempt to finance the missions enterprise. Charles W. Forman, professor of missions at Yale Divinity School, observes that "the role of the lay person as distinct from the clergy was given greater importance by this emphasis. Laymen as well as ministers could be equal participants in mission activity and support."[9]

The above factors reflect the unparalleled zeal for Christian missions that coincided with the late 19th-century enthusiasm for empire building. With notable advances in science, technology, industry, and transportation, plus an unbridled confidence in the superiority of Western civilization, it appeared that the kingdom of God would shortly be established on earth marked by a universal peace and a spread of Western culture. One of the best known advocates of this perspective was James S. Dennis, a Presbyterian missionary to Syria and widely-read author on Christian progress overseas. In 1908, Dennis wrote of the current missionary challenge: "As if to emphasize and glorify the call of obligation, and magnify the significance of our opportunity, we find ourselves in many distant and perhaps obscure posts of missionary service, not only ambassadors of Christ, and bearers of His spiritual gifts to men, but the forerunners also of the material blessings of a higher civilization."[10]

Another influential writer of the period, John P. Jones, urged his readers to "mark how Christian nations, especially Protestant nations, are multiplying their political influence and showing their qualities of leadership and control in the world. . . . and . . . notice also the growing prevalence of the English language."[11]

Even President William McKinley, addressing the Ecumenical Missionary Conference at New York City in 1900, said: "I am glad of the opportunity to offer without stint my tribute of praise and respect to the missionary effort which has wrought such wonderful triumphs for civilization. . . . The services and sacrifices of the missionaries for their fellow men constitute one of the most glorious pages in the world's history."[12]

At this point it is important to review the origins of the modern missions movement. The spiritual awakenings in some Protestant churches in the 17th and 18th centuries fueled the new effort in missions in the 19th century. Kenneth Scott Latourette, an authority on the expansion of Christianity, attributed the growth in Protestant missions work to the evangelical strain within Western Christendom that had also produced Pietism, Moravianism, the Great Awakenings, and the Wesleyan revival in England. Characteristically, this evangelical strain "made much of the transformation of the individual through the Christian Gospel and it also gave rise to many efforts for the elimination of social ills and for the collective betterment of mankind."[13] The revivals of Dwight L. Moody and other evangelists also influenced the growing missionary movement. Moody's revivals on campuses and at conference centers influenced students and fired them with the idealism of winning the world for Christ.

A major agency for recruiting college and university students for foreign missions came into existence in 1886 with the formation of the Student Volunteer Movement for Foreign Missions. Undenominational in character, it channeled thousands of students into the denominational and independent missions societies for overseas ministry. John R. Mott, a graduate of Cornell University and a Methodist layman, served as its dynamic leader for many years.

The watchword for the above organization was, The evangelization of the world in this generation. In spite of controversy surrounding the meaning of this expression in some quarters, Mott defined it as providing all men "an adequate opportunity to know Jesus Christ as their Saviour and to become His real disciples. . . . It does not mean the conversion of the world within the generation. Our part consists in bringing the Gospel to bear on unsaved men."[14]

Such an ideal appeared possible because of the available resources, the favorable political climate overseas for the colonial powers, including the United States, and the unity of the Protestant missionary agencies in their efforts for evangelization abroad.

In spite of the optimistic assessments of the future of Christian missions and "Christian" civilization made by such writers as Dennis and Jones and illustrated by some speakers at conferences of the Student Volunteer Movement, more cautious observers became alarmed by the evils arising from the linkage of the missionary enterprise and colonial expansion. Mott warned a student gathering in 1914 that the world situation "is more urgent than ever because of the rapid spread of the corrupt influences of so-called western civilization. The blush of shame has come to my cheeks as I have seen how these influences from North America and the British Isles and Germany, not to mention other countries, are eating like gangrene into the less highly organized peoples of the world."[15]

Other observers had long questioned the opinion held by many that the preaching of the gospel and the advance of Western civilization would usher in the kingdom of God on earth. These writers, distinctly viewing the Kingdom's establishment as an eschatological event preceded by the second coming of Christ, became increasingly vocal. They perceived that eschatological views affect one's missionary motivation. By 1914, theological tensions over the necessity and role of Christian missions reached the breaking point.

Motivational Tensions

Missionary motivation in the 19th century was complex. The predominant motives in this period were (1) concern for the promotion of the glory of God, (2) love for Christ through obedience to the Great Commission (Matthew 28:19,20), and (3) an ardent desire "to pluck brands from the burning."[16] Toward the close of the century, motivation for missionary service underwent major changes because of the new perspectives on Biblical authority, colonial expansion, and the study of comparative religions, which often altered the old perspectives on "heathenism."

In the latter part of the century, rescuing the perishing from eternal damnation began to diminish in importance. Beaver contends that

> the salvation of the perishing heathen . . . became less and less prominent as a motive in mainstream missionary vocation and support, and while salvation through Christ was vigorously affirmed, the fate of the unbeliever was no longer faced. . . . Christians became uncomfortable about assigning noble, righteous, humanitarian unbelievers to eternal damnation. By the second decade of the twentieth century it was widely agreed that God can be known fully only in Christ, but that men are saved by God's gracious response to their reverent, positive attitude toward the best they know, since Christ is the "light which lighteth every man."[17]

Under the outward unity of the missions movement, several schools of thought vigorously disagreed over one pivotal issue of the time: the nature of the kingdom of God. An individual's or an organization's understanding of the kingdom of God inevitably determined the nature of their missionary motivation. This issue was closely linked to millennialism.

Millennialism, while diminishing in the mainstream missionary societies, still found active promotion in some conservative evangelical ranks. Two positions, premillennialism and postmillennialism, became especially important during the period. The premillennialists believed that the second coming of Christ would usher in an eschatological Kingdom. The postmillennialists anticipated that the positive effects of the preaching of the gospel to the nations would eventually precipitate the appearance of the Kingdom.

William Owen Carver, an influential Southern Baptist theologian of missions early in this century, identified four major schools of thought in missions theology. The first two schools represented different brands of premillennialism. By virtue of being premillennial, both emphasized the present era as the age of the Church or the time of "outgathering," that is, witnessing.

Dispensational premillennialism made up the first school. According to his interpretation of Acts 15:14 and other passages, C. I. Scofield, a well-known dispensationalist, concluded that "the Gospel has never anywhere converted all, but everywhere has called out some."[18] After this age, evangelization will continue during the Millennium when the kingdom of God is established on the earth. Carver strongly condemned this view for its pessimistic expectation of evangelism in this present age.[19]

Carver identified a second school representing a larger segment of premillennialists who maintained that all the work of missions would occur before the return of Christ and the Millennium. Thus the kingdom of God would continue to expand during this present age "until that time when the results of the age of witnessing, together with the effects of a cataclysmic demonstration, will be gathered together under the personal reign of Christ."[20]

However, according to Timothy P. Weber, professor of church history at Denver's Conservative Baptist Theological Seminary, many conservative evangelicals and advocates of the social gospel[21] "who envisioned a more Christian world through the spread of the gospel

and a more consistent application of Christian principles to all of
life were generally appalled by the apparent pessimism and de-
featism of the premillennial outlook."[22] Indeed, with such a dismal
view of human history, how could anyone be motivated for Christian
service abroad? In spite of such criticisms, premillennialism, particularly the second school of thought identified by Carver, offered
a strong motive for missions since it vigorously contended that all
who died without Christ were eternally doomed. Weber continues
by stating: "When this concern for the lost was joined with the belief
that Christ's imminent return might cut short opportunity to save
them, premillennialists were given a strong drive toward missionary
activity."[23] At the same time, premillennialists also believed that
the proclamation and acceptance of the gospel would lead to a better
quality of life in this present age.[24]

The premillennialists ardently prayed for the conversion of the
world and believed that an unusual work of the Holy Spirit would
be needed to accomplish this goal. Hopes were stirred by the development of the remarkable Welsh Revival in 1904. In a short
period of time, this awakening claimed over 100,000 converts. Its
influence spread around the world and many prayed that this divine
work would continue.[25]

Premillennialism, which eventually dominated the arena among
conservative evangelicals, grew in an atmosphere of Biblical liter-
alism. To understand the connection between this view of Biblical
interpretation and the missionary enterprise, the role of the Bible
institute movement must not be overlooked. Early Bible institutes
included the Missionary Training Institute at Nyack, New York,
founded in 1882 by A. B. Simpson; the Chicago (later Moody) Bible
Institute founded in 1889 by Dwight L. Moody; and the Boston
Missionary Training School founded in 1889 by A. J. Gordon. Each
of these schools, stressing a premillennial interpretation of the Scripture, attempted "to produce a well-trained, biblically literate, and
spiritually mature corps of lay people to meet the changing conditions in the nation and the world. Along with training urban workers
and evangelists, the Bible institutes were committed to preparing
young men and women for foreign service."[26] These institutions also
steadfastly resisted the growing influences of Biblical criticism and
liberal theology.

The third school of thought in missions theology identified by

Carver was postmillennialism. This view, harmonizing the evolutionary theories of the day with the preaching of the gospel, held that society would be transformed, thus ushering in the kingdom of God. Carver observed that "no effort is made to sustain this view by specific texts of Scripture, though the claim would be made by many that the spirit of the Bible is at least not out of harmony with such a view."[27] James S. Dennis, a missionary to Syria and prolific writer who reflected this perspective, assessed the future:

> The situation is one which calls for serious and devout attention; it should stir us to a holy and fervent passion for the coming of Christ's kingdom. "Thy Kingdom come," we pray daily, and behold here it is, in all its potential promise; here it is as a possible reality, if we are true to our duty. It is quite within the bounds of reason, and in harmony with already demonstrated facts, to say that we have it fully within our power to secure a larger, finer, sweeter, and nobler life to the world. The triumphs of the Gospel over individual lives will insure this; since the multiplication of citizens in the spiritual commonwealth of God means the sure establishment of a kingdom of righteousness among men.[28]

Although this was the dominant view at the time, missionary personnel became less and less interested in millennial expectations.

A fourth school of thought expressed a skepticism about all millennial expectations and their relationship to the missionary enterprise. With little effort made to analyze any detailed scheme of coming eschatological events or their relationship to the present work of missions, the attention focused on evangelism in this age. Great results, however, were expected in the moral and religious transformation of society.

Conservative evangelicals grew uneasy with the assertions of many representatives of the last two schools of thought. It is apparent that the new theological liberalism, or modernism, that became popular in the late 19th century had made a major imprint.

Questions over the nature of Biblical authority, the integrity of the other major religions of the world, and the role of Christian missions overseas at the turn of the century traumatized missionary theology instead of merely challenging it. William R. Hutchinson, professor of the History of Religion in America at Harvard University, summarizes the essentials of this redefinition of traditional Protestant theology when he writes that

> the crux of the liberal theory lay in its attempt to preserve, and at the same time considerably revise, the Christian claims to finality and indispensability. Leading elements in the theory were its conversion of the idea of Christian finality into an almost purely ethical concept, its search for a quintessential Christianity suitable for export, a professed devotion to the ideal of establishing native churches free of Western control, a questioning of the right of Western Christendom to lecture the rest of the world, and a steady assertion that it was the old theology, not the new, that threatened to "cut the nerve of missions."[29]

After 1914, bitter controversies developed over theological liberalism on the mission field and they played a major part in the coming fundamentalist/modernist controversy in the United States. Following an extensive tour of mission fields overseas, Augustus H. Strong, president emeritus of Rochester Theological Seminary and a prominent theologian, complained in 1918 that "our lack at home of the right interpretation of Scripture, and our fading knowledge in experience of the presence and power of Christ, have gone from us around the world. Some boards are sending out as missionaries young men who lack definite views of doctrine."[30] He further condemned the seminaries for their failure to teach traditional Protestant theology and labeled them as "organs of Antichrist." In his opinion "this accounts for the rise, all over the land, of Bible schools, to take the place of the seminaries. The evil is coming in like a flood, and the Spirit of the Lord will surely raise up a standard against it. But oh the pity! that money given by godly men to provide preachers of the gospel should be devoted to undermining the Christian cause."[31]

Despite the growing controversies, unity remained on the surface. Two major factors made this possible. First, even though theological tensions rose before World War I, the issues had not hardened as they did later in the fundamentalist/modernist controversy of the twenties.[32] Second, the leaders of the missions movement viewed themselves as Christian statesmen "who could rise above political, sectarian, or even national ties."[33] Such leaders as John R. Mott, Robert E. Speer, and Robert Wilder were conservative theologically, but tolerant of other views. According to Robert T. Handy, an authority on American religious history, "as laymen deeply devoted to the Christian cause . . . they were not concerned with theological minutae, and were able to a remarkable degree to bridge the gap between those oriented to the older theology and those informed by the new."[34] Thus the dynamic leadership of the enterprise postponed the parting of the ways until the beginning of a new era (post-1914) in Christian missions.

Missiological Tensions

Missiology, the science of missions, deals with the theory and strategy of the enterprise; it is therefore tied closely with theology. Accordingly the methods of Christian missionaries, their goals and attitudes toward their foreign audiences, are all "based on theories or theologies whether these are fully articulated or not."[35]

The Anderson/Venn formula for Christian missions served as the accepted strategy in the 19th century. Rufus Anderson (1796–1880), foreign secretary of the American Board of Commissioners for Foreign Missions, and Henry Venn (1796–1873), general secretary of the Church Missionary Society in London, directed two of the largest missionary agencies. Anderson, a Congregationalist, and Venn, an Anglican, arrived at the same basic principles independently of each other.

To them, the chief goal of the Protestant missions enterprise focused on establishing the Christian Church on foreign fields through preaching the gospel and developing indigenous churches. The famous "three-self" formula that they articulated describes the indigenous church as self-governing, self-supporting, and self-propagating.[36]

Concerns such as educational plans, medical facilities, and programs designed to advance Western civilization on a foreign field were all downplayed by these men. They believed that social consequences would gradually develop over the years as the indigenous church matured. Forman credits Anderson with being "well ahead of his time in seeing the confusion involved in the identification of Christianity with Western culture and seeing the long term incompatibility of the Christian faith with Western imperialism."[37]

Anderson was the first American to see the importance of the indigenous church. The missions societies could not expand their works endlessly. Therefore, this limited objective directed all attention toward building a strong indigenous church with trained leadership that could support itself and continue the evangelization of the region, freeing the missionaries to proceed to "the regions beyond" (in the phrase of A. B. Simpson's song). According to this perspective, the role of the missionary was "to preach the gospel and gather the converts into churches. He was always to be an evangelist and never a pastor or ruler. Churches were to be organized at once out of converts who showed a change of life towards Christ without waiting for them to reach the standard expected of American Christians with two thousand years of Christian history behind them."[38] Anderson also promoted education in the vernacular as a means of serving the church for the raising up of a mature laity and an adequately trained clergy.

Despite the official allegiance to the Anderson/Venn formula, a notable shift in missionary thought, representing another approach to missions work, occurred after the death of these two men; this new approach gained ground in the latter part of the century. Under Venn's leadership, for example, British missionaries in West Africa had tried to build a strong indigenous church with its own clergy. But shortly after Venn's administration ended,

> missions executives and field missionaries took the view that the African was of inferior quality and could not provide ministerial leadership which consequently would be furnished indefinitely by Europeans. The African middle class businessman and intellectual was despised. This imperialist viewpoint was an ecclesiastical variant of "the white man's burden," and it reduced the native church to a colony of the foreign planting church.[39]

After Anderson's time, American Protestant missions came increasingly under the spell of Social Darwinism and its doctrine of progress. Education in English became more and more important as institutions of secondary and higher education were set up on the mission field. Philip Schaff, the renowned 19th-century church historian, contended that the English language was superbly equipped to disseminate Christianity and Western civilization.[40]

James E. Wood, Professor of Religion at Baylor University, remarks that

> Britons and Americans freely expressed a faith in the destiny and mission of their common culture, civilization, language, and institutions. The purpose of Christian missions was to "Christianize," and this inevitably involved the transmission of culture as well; for God had called the Anglo–Saxon nations not only to take the Gospel to the ends of the earth, but also to spread a civilization which "betters the condition of every race it conquers, rules or touches."[41]

As interest in millennial eschatology subsided or was redefined among theological progressives, many looked for the establishment of the kingdom of God through the influence of schools and other Christian institutions. Apparently they felt that the language of the coming "heaven-on-earth" would be English.

The ideal of the Anderson/Venn formula, however, did not fade away. As the century drew to a close, more and more missionary spokesmen pressed for its application. One of the best known, John Livingston Nevius (1829–1893), served as an American Presbyterian missionary to China. Addressing the Presbyterian missionaries in Korea, he proposed a slightly modified version of the Anderson/Venn Formula. The "Nevius Plan" accordingly emphasized the three selfs, Bible study, and missionary itineration. It enjoyed considerable success in Korea, but was not followed widely elsewhere.[42] Nevertheless, Nevius' publication of *The Planting and Development of Missionary Churches* in 1886 stirred up a great deal of controversy and gained widespread acceptance among some missions executives and theologians. Robert E. Speer, a contemporary of Nevius and for many years the secretary of the Board of Missions for the Presbyterian Church in the United States, remarked at a convention of the Student Volunteer Movement that Nevius' methods were both scriptural and rational and advised every aspiring missionary to study them.[43]

A host of writers at the turn of the 20th century strongly advocated the adoption of the principles laid down by Anderson, Venn, and Nevius. A sizable number of books appeared promoting this perspective. Edward A. Lawrence, a Baltimore pastor who had traveled extensively overseas among missions works, wrote before his death in 1893 that "the primary aim of missions is to preach the gospel in all lands, the ultimate aim is to plant the church in all lands. When they have done that, their work is accomplished. Then the church of each land thus planted must win its own people to Christ."[44]

Edward Pfeiffer, a Lutheran, declared in 1908 that if establishing the indigenous church constituted the ultimate aim of missions, then "it should be kept in view from the outset, and the methods of work shaped accordingly."[45] Roland Allen, a missionary with the Church Missionary Society (Anglican), author of *Missionary Methods: St. Paul's or Ours?* first published in 1912, stressed the need of the missionary to serve as an elder brother while the Holy Spirit leads the new church on the field in developing its own form of leadership, polity, and worship.[46]

John R. Mott, a Methodist, maintained in 1900 that the ultimate aim of evangelism was "planting and developing in all non-Christian lands self-supporting, self-directing, and self-propagating churches which shall become so thoroughly rooted in the convictions and hearts of the people that if Christianity were to die out in Europe and America, it would abide in purity and as a missionary power in its new homes and would live on through the centuries."[47] Other writers such as Arthur Judson Brown[48] and Edwin Munsell Bliss[49] also spoke eloquently in favor of the indigenous church principles articulated decades before by Rufus Anderson and Henry Venn.

At the turn of the century and continuing for several decades, the indigenous church principles appeared to be the talk of the town in missions circles. At the Ecumenical Missionary Conference at New York City in 1900, missionaries of various theological persuasions debated the issue at a session called "Self-Support of Native Churches."[50] The World Missionary Conference at Edinburgh, Scotland, in 1910 endorsed the indigenous church principles as the proper mission strategy for the missions agencies to follow.[51] Roman Catholic missions were also moving in this direction.[52]

When the Great Century came to a close in 1914, sober reflection began when it became apparent that the ideal of the Anderson/Venn formula had not been widely achieved. Kenneth Scott Latourette lamented that

> of all the major features of its program, the one in which the
> missionary enterprise of the age just passing advanced most

slowly was in bringing to birth Christian communities which could continue into the next age. In translating the Scriptures, in broadcasting the Christian message, and in pioneering in the introduction and adaptation of greatly needed features and methods of Western origin, modern Protestant missions have been phenomenally successful. In helping to build the Christian Church they have not made such rapid strides. In none of the major areas to which missionaries have gone do the younger churches include more than one percent of the population. Only a minority of these younger churches are financially self-supporting. In few of them is there emerging sufficient leadership, lay or clerical, of ability and training adequate to insure permanence without financial aid. Of the various types of education conducted by missionaries the theological colleges and Bible training schools are, as a class, the least satisfactory. . . .

Indeed, in their emphases, Protestant missions of the era just closing have differed from anything previously known in history. Never in any period in the spread of Christianity have missionaries paid relatively so little attention to building the Christian Church and devoted so much effort to broadcasting the Christian message and to meeting, in a Christian fashion, the educational and physical needs of peoples as a whole. Never, indeed, in the spread of any religion, have the propagating agencies given themselves so much to activities which were believed to be of help to the entire community, including those not belonging to the faith, but only indirectly, if at all, leading to an increase in the professed adherents of the religion.[53]

What could have sidetracked the initiatives to implement the Anderson/Venn formula? As early as 1893, Edward A. Lawrence cited four reasons:

> (1) The necessary inexperience of the early missionaries; (2) the failure to see that the aim of mission work is not simply the conversion of souls, but the founding of the native church; (3) an exaggerated estimate of the poverty of the people and of the difficulty of their supporting their religious leaders; (4) the unconscious growth, in some cases, of a spirit of domination, which leads the mission too often to exalt itself above the native church.[54]

Roland Allen, a former missionary to North China writing in 1912, described the overseas church as a colonial institution transplanted by the sending church. Furthermore, he concluded that "we have maintained it by supplying a large number of European officials who carry it on."[55] Allen predicted that under the present arrangement, an indigenous church supported, governed, and evangelizing by itself would never come into being.

It would not be until after the World Missionary Conference in 1910, the passing of the Great Century, and the fading of the great colonial empires that the younger churches would slowly be allowed to chart their own courses.

Cooperation and Ecumenicity

For many years before the World Missionary Conference in 1910 at Edinburgh, Scotland, a measure of unity and cooperation had existed among Protestant missionaries. Many missionaries found a common bond with others who were obeying the Great Commission and "were usually ready to accept each other's message as 'evangelical' if its foundation was the doctrine of the Trinity and the Incarnation. Beyond this there was at most a desire for explicit acceptance of the ecumenical creeds."[56] The term *evangelicals* in the 19th century did not carry a sectarian meaning and included most Protestant groups; Roman Catholics and Orthodox Catholics were excluded.

The practice of comity represented an important item of missionary strategy during this era. *Comity* has been called "denominationalism by geography." It was designed to make some missionary society responsible for the evangelization of every part of the globe. This, of course, prevented and discouraged the unnecessary practice of overlapping missionary activities. Many hoped that denominational differences that would confuse converts on the foreign field and create obstacles for evangelism would be eliminated.

As missions agencies began to recognize each other as valid members of the one universal church of Christ, cooperation accelerated among them, which included membership transfers/baptismal recognition, Bible translation projects, regional boards to enhance cooperation and understanding, educational institutions, medical schools, famine relief, and other joint ventures. As time went on, city, regional, and national missionary conferences were held in almost every country to plan united efforts.[57]

Attempts at Protestant cooperation were, therefore, not uncommon in the 19th century. The Evangelical Alliance, organized in London in 1846, addressed, among other matters, the issue of global missions. Later conferences devoted to missions convened to confront common problems on the foreign fields and to discuss strategy. These gatherings promoted cooperation and mutual understanding. The best known conferences took place at Liverpool (1860), London (1885), and New York City (1900).

A growing need among North American missions societies for consultation led to the formation of the Foreign Missions Conference of North America in 1893. The records indicate that the meetings were primarily devoted to business, rather than preaching and oratory. As a result, "every conceivable practical problem of mission work was treated in a paper or discussion at one point or another, but corporate statements or declarations were made hesitantly, if at all, during the early decades."[58]

These missions conferences and cooperative ventures prepared the way for the great World Missionary Conference held at Edinburgh, Scotland, in 1910. The significance of this gathering surpassed all others because of its meticulous planning, opportunities for serious consideration of pressing issues instead of focusing on just edification and enthusiasm for the work, and the concrete steps it took to permanent cooperation in the years ahead.[59]

Edinburgh 1910 proved to be a watershed in modern church history. In relation to Christian missions, it strongly endorsed the creating of indigenous churches on the foreign fields. Because of cooperation and unity, the creation of the permanent Continuation Committee led to the establishment of the International Missionary Council in 1921. Thus the foundation was laid at Edinburgh for the ecumenical movement and the establishment of the World Council of Churches in 1948.

Two recent perspectives on the Edinburgh conference, however, illustrate the divisions that have developed among Protestant church historians and theologians over its significance. W. Richie Hogg, an eminent historian of the ecumenical movement, writes: "From Edinburgh sprang a new willingness to respect and recognize wide differences and at the same time to work together as Christians. Here was born the kind of international and interdenominational Christian cooperation that has increasingly characterized the twentieth century."[60] Fundamentalists, on the other hand, became increasingly wary of the inroads of liberal theology with its limited view of Biblical authority and changing attitudes about the meaning of Christian missions and, hence, increasingly opposed ecumenical endeavors. Arthur P. Johnston, former chairman of the Division of World Mission and Evangelism at Trinity Evangelical Divinity School, concludes that "Edinburgh 1910 hoped to harness the global forces of Christianity, to complete world evangelization, and to introduce the coming Kingdom of God upon the earth. It served rather to hinder evangelism by what it did *not* say concerning the authority of Scripture, and what it did say through the agencies which grew out of it."[61] To Johnston, the years following the Edinburgh gathering point to a steady decline in evangelistic zeal among many of the missions agencies represented there.

John L. Nevius (1829–1893), a Presbyterian missionary to China, became well-known for his indigenous church principles. His approach to building the indigenous church overseas has often been referred to as the Nevius method.

The revival campaigns of Evangelist Dwight L. Moody (1837–1899) strongly influenced the developing American missionary movement in the latter half of the 19th century.

John R. Mott (1865–1955) served as general secretary of the YMCA and chairman of the Student Volunteer Movement for Foreign Missions. He later became chairman of the International Missionary Council.

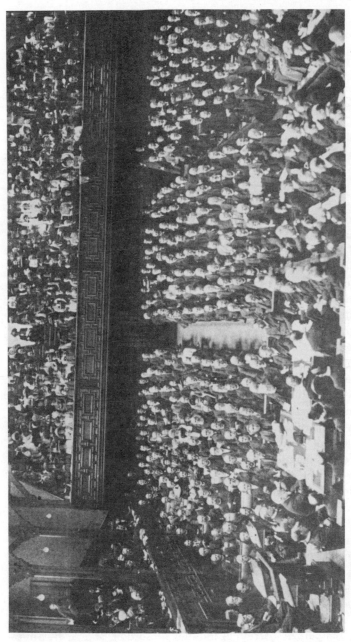

The World Missionary Conference convened at Edinburgh, Scotland, in 1910. This conference made a major impact on the course of 20th-century Christian missions.

2

The Pentecostal Revival Begins

The Roots of the Pentecostal Movement

The turn of the 20th century witnessed the beginning of what has been called "the Third Force" in Christendom, namely the Pentecostal movement and its most prominent denominational expression, the General Council of the Assemblies of God.[1] Arising during a time of worldwide revival, Pentecostalism stressed that the gifts of the Holy Spirit mentioned in Acts 2 and 1 Corinthians 12 and 14 were intended to characterize the life of the contemporary church.[2] The most prominent and controversial of these gifts was speaking in tongues. This emphasis marked the organized Pentecostal churches and denominations that grew out of the revival. Never an exclusively American phenomenon, Pentecostal revivals took place in India, China, Africa, Europe, and Latin America. More recently, they have occurred in charismatic segments of older Protestant denominations and the Roman Catholic Church.

Throughout church history, various groups have claimed to experience the manifestations of the Spirit referred to in the New Testament.[3] The most immediate heritage of modern Pentecostalism can be found in the late 19th-century quest for holiness among some groups of American evangelicals.[4] Tracing its roots to John Wesley, the Methodist-oriented holiness movement emphasized that an experience after salvation brought about an overcoming Christian life by cleansing, or eradicating, the believer's sinful nature, what adherents called entire sanctification.

A Reformed point of view emphasizing a deeper life experience developed late in the 19th century through the preaching and writing of several prominent American preachers, notably Dwight L. Moody, Reuben A. Torrey, Adoniram J. Gordon, and A. B. Simpson. The same emphasis appeared in sermons at the Keswick Conference grounds in Great Britain. According to this Reformed perspective, at conversion the believer is baptized by the Holy Spirit into the body of Christ and this begins a lifelong process of sanctification. After conversion, and closely associated with the process of sanctification, a second baptism should be undergone by the believer. This second experience in the Holy Spirit by Christ produces an "enduement of power" for effective Christian witness.

These preachers and writers also generally stressed the absolute authority of Scripture, divine healing, and the premillennial return of Christ—doctrines that eventually shaped much of the theology of the Assemblies of God.[5] These people were also leading advocates of Christian missions; in the Bible institutes they started, they prepared young men and women for overseas ministry.

Historians usually associate the origin of modern Pentecostalism with a revival in Topeka, Kansas, that began on January 1, 1901; participants identified speaking in tongues as the evidence of the baptism in the Holy Spirit. Representing greater and more international significance, however, was the Azusa Street Revival of 1906–1907 in Los Angeles, California. Leaders of these revivals proclaimed the need of a salvation experience, faith healing, a life of holiness, the baptism in the Holy Spirit for power in Christian witness, the premillennial return of Christ, and the absolute necessity to evangelize the world through missionary endeavors.

The Topeka Revival

The 1900–1901 revival in Topeka, Kansas, stemmed from the work of Charles F. Parham, a holiness preacher born in Muscatine, Iowa. At the time of his conversion in the Congregational Church, Parham felt a distinct call to serve as a missionary in Africa. Although he never fulfilled this call, he did serve for a time as a Methodist pastor, but he ultimately renounced denominationalism in all its forms. Theologically, Parham identified with the holiness movement of his day, preached faith healing, and believed in the imminent premillennial return of Christ.

Parham moved to Topeka in 1898, where he opened the Bethel Healing Home. During his extensive travels over the next 2 years, he visited Zion, Illinois, to see the work of John Alexander Dowie and Nyack, New York, to see the work of A. B. Simpson. In 1900 he opened the Bethel Bible School in Topeka "to fit men and women to go to the ends of the earth to preach, 'This Gospel of the Kingdom'. . . as a witness to all the world before the end of the age."[6]

During his travels, Parham became convinced that after salvation and sanctification, the believer could receive another supernatural experience: baptism in the Holy Spirit. Opinions, however, varied about the evidence for such an experience. Leaving for a series of meetings in Kansas City before the Christmas holidays in 1900, Parham assigned his students the responsibility of studying the baptism in the Holy Spirit and determining its Biblical evidence. When he returned, he found that the students had concluded that speaking in tongues was the evidence of this Baptism.

Beginning with a New Year's Eve service on December 31, 1900, the revival began to take shape as the students sought this experience. On January 1, the first one to receive the Baptism was Agnes Ozman. Like Parham, she had visited other centers where the doctrines of faith healing, sanctification, and the baptism in the Holy Spirit had produced much interest. For a time she had studied at Simpson's Bible school in Nyack. When Parham laid his hands on her to receive the baptism in the Holy Spirit, she recounted, "I began to speak in tongues, glorifying God. I talked several languages. It was as though rivers of living water were proceeding from my innermost being."[7] For several days she spoke only in tongues.

Before long the newspapers publicized this unusual happening and visitors flocked to the school to investigate. Parham said that "one government interpreter claimed to have heard twenty Chinese dialects distinctly spoken in one night" and further asserted that "the students of the college were speaking the languages of the world."[8]

Parham recognized the revolutionary significance of the identification of the baptism in the Holy Spirit with speaking in tongues. It also confirmed what he had believed for some time, that missionaries going to foreign lands should preach in the native languages. He stated that "if Balaam's mule could stop in the middle of the road and give the first preacher that went out for money a 'bawling out' in Arabic that [sic] anybody today ought to be able to preach in any language of the world if they had horse sense enough to let God use their tongue and throat."[9] Parham never changed his view on the missionary purpose of tongues, though most Pentecostals eventually rejected it.

The recipients of this new experience showed a sense of urgency. To them, the Old Testament prophecy of Joel (2:28,29) as recounted in Acts 2 ("In the last days . . . I will pour out my Spirit upon all flesh") meant that the end times had come. Accordingly, "they felt constrained to preach the gospel to every creature. The Lord was at hand, the day was far spent, night was near. That which ought to be done for God must be done quickly."[10] Parham and his band of followers began to proclaim the new message in eastern Kansas, Missouri, and eventually as far south as Houston, Texas, where they opened a short-term Bible school. About the Houston meetings, the *Galveston News* reported:

> One of the principle [*sic*] passages of the Bible quoted by those who hold to this belief is the injunction as set forth in Mark 16:15-18, "Go ye into all the world and preach the gospel to every creature. He that believeth and is baptized shall be saved, but he that believeth not shall be damned. And these signs shall follow them that believe: In my name shall they cast out devils; they shall speak with new tongues; they shall take up serpents, and if they drink any deadly thing it shall not hurt them; they shall lay hands on the sick and they shall recover."[11]

Thus, those who believed that these events were the fulfillment of Joel's prophecy also called for world evangelization.

The Azusa Street Revival

During the days of the Bible school in Houston, William J. Seymour, a black holiness preacher, listened to the class lectures that were given. Responding to an invitation from a Nazarene visitor, Seymour traveled to Los Angeles in 1906 to hold a meeting in a holiness church. When he arrived and began preaching, the church rejected his teaching about tongues as the evidence for the baptism in the Holy Spirit.

Undaunted, Seymour accepted an invitation to preach his Pentecostal message in a home. Shortly afterward a former African Methodist Episcopal church on Azusa Street was secured to hold the crowds.[12] Under his leadership and that of others, unusual religious services took place. Sinners repented, believers were sanctified, prayer was offered for the sick (with reports of numerous spectacular healings), and many received visions. Spontaneous singing, the manifestation of the gifts of the Holy Spirit, praises shouted to the Lord, zeal to spread the gospel around the world, spontaneous missionary offerings, and an awareness of the soon return of Christ marked the meetings in this modest two-storied frame building. Many interested individuals from different parts of the country heard about the Azusa Street Revival, as it came to be known, and went to see it for themselves. Some traveled from other countries to attend. One missionary, Bernt Bernsten, traveled all the way from China to investigate the happenings.[13] Other missionaries who were in the country at the time also visited the meetings and received the baptism in the Holy Spirit with speaking in tongues.

An extremely important aspect of this revival is that many who received the Pentecostal baptism also felt a heightened concern for world evangelization. The Azusa Street participants, in the pattern of Parham and his students, believed that they were living in the last days and anticipated the premillennial return of Christ. To them, the fulfillment of Joel's prophecy gave global evangelism an additional thrust. For example, publishing the news of the revival from Los Angeles and the opinions of its leaders, *The Apostolic Faith* reported:

> Pentecost has surely come and with it the Bible evidences are following, many being converted and sanctified and filled with the Holy Ghost, speaking in tongues as they did on the day of Pentecost. . . . the real revival is only started, as God has been working with His children mostly, getting them through to Pentecost, and laying the foundation for a mighty wave of salvation among the unconverted.[14]

Seymour and his associates believed with Parham that the languages spoken by the power of the Holy Spirit were meant to be used in missions. Distinct foreign languages were reported to have been spoken in the services. Early participants stated:

> The gift of languages is given with the commission, "Go ye into all the world and preach the Gospel to every creature." The Lord has given languages to the unlearned, Greek, Latin, Hebrew, French, German, Italian, Chinese, Japanese, Zulu and the languages of Africa, Hindu and Bengali and dialects of

India, Chippewa and other languages of the Indians, Esqui-
maux, the deaf mute language and, in fact the Holy Ghost
speaks all the languages of the world through His children.[15]

Many are the prophesies spoken in unknown tongues and
many the visions that God is giving concerning His soon coming. The heathen must first receive the gospel. One prophecy
given in an unknown tongue was interpreted, "The time is
short, and I am going to send out a large number in the Spirit
of God to preach the full gospel in the power of the Spirit."[16]

God is solving the missionary problem, sending out new-
tongued missionaries . . . without purse or scrib [sic], and the
Lord is going before them preparing the way.[17]

This Gospel, the full Gospel of Jesus must be preached in
all the earth for a witness then shall the end come.[18]

Thus, many believed that speaking in tongues was a language gift
to be used in overseas ministry. Those missionaries who held this
position found only disillusionment on the foreign fields. Evidence
of any early Pentecostal missionary ever receiving a new language
in this manner does not exist.[19] However, numerous Pentecostals
through the years, including missionaries, have claimed to speak at
some specific time in a known language in the proclamation of the
gospel to someone who knew that language. In these instances,
however, the Pentecostals did not know what they were saying and
found this to be only a brief phenomenon.[20]

Viewing tongues from a different perspective than the Azusa Street
participants, J. Roswell Flower, a Midwestern Pentecostal editor/
publisher, wrote an early significant description of the meaning of
speaking in tongues and its relevance for Christian missions. In 1908,
he editorialized:

The baptism of the Holy Ghost does not consist in simply
speaking in tongues. No. It has a much more grand and deeper
meaning than that. It fills our souls with the love of God for
lost humanity, and makes us much more willing to leave home,
friends, and all to work in His vineyard, even if it be far away
among the heathen. . . .

"Go ye into all the world and preach the gospel to every
creature." This command of Jesus can only be properly fulfilled
when we have obeyed that other command, "Tarry ye in the
City of Jerusalem till ye be endued with power from on high."

> When we have tarried and received that power, then, and then
> only are we fit to carry the gospel. When the Holy Spirit comes
> into our hearts, the missionary spirit comes in with it; they are
> inseparable, as the missionary spirit is but one of the fruits of
> the Holy Spirit. Carrying the gospel to hungry souls in this
> and other lands is but a natural result of receiving the baptism
> of the Holy Ghost.[21]

Most Pentecostal converts came to view tongues as a divine em-
powerment.

Several other items also indicate the importance of the concepts
of ministry and missionary evangelism that radiated from the Azusa
Street Revival: the prominent role of women in ministry, the unique
sense of being led by the Spirit, and the concept of living by faith,
that is, believing that God would miraculously provide all of one's
needs.

The willingness of participants to accept female leadership represents one characteristic of the revival. From the start, several
notable women, such as Florence L. Crawford, took an active role.
Frank Bartleman, a participant, reported that services did not de-
pend on any one individual, but those in attendance prayed that
God would speak through the person of His choice. After a period
of waiting, "someone would finally get up anointed for the message. . . . It might be a child, a woman, or a man. . . . It made no
difference. We rejoiced that God was working."[22]

Since anyone could be chosen by the Spirit for a particular ministry, it is not surprising that *The Apostolic Faith* reported numerous
women who felt called to overseas missionary work: among others,
Louise Condit and Lucy M. Leatherman to Jerusalem; Lizzie Frazer
to India; Mrs. J. W. Hutchins, who "received the baptism with the
Holy Ghost and the gift of the Uganda language," to Africa;[23] Mrs.
A. G. Garr, who "improves every day in her Tibetan and Chinese"
to China;[24] and Lucy Farrow to Africa. This ministry role for women
became a characteristic of early Pentecostalism and its missionary
enterprises.[25]

A second characteristic of the revival was the unique sense of
being "led" by the Spirit to go overseas in ministry. Representative
of this belief is the following news item carried by *The Apostolic
Faith:* "A brother recently received the gift of the French language.
He waited on God to know his call, and while laid out under the

power, was given a vision of Paris and called there. He saw Paris upheaved as it were by a great destruction. The Lord told him to go and preach the Gospel to them."[26]

The same periodical recorded numerous other individuals and groups who sailed overseas to continue or begin missionary work. The Samuel J. Meads had sailed to Africa in 1885 as Methodist missionaries under the leadership of Bishop William Taylor: "God called Bro. Mead and wife from the Central part of Africa to Los Angeles to get their Pentecost. They recognize some of the languages spoken as being dialects of Africa. When God has fully equipped them they will return. "[27]

Others who went out included Thomas P. Mahler to Africa, Andrew Johnson to Jerusalem, and the A. G. Garrs to India (and eventually to China), the A. H. Posts to Egypt, and the G. W. Batmans to Liberia, West Africa. *The Apostolic Faith* published news of other Pentecostal believers who went overseas but were not directly related to the Azusa Street Revival. In one item, the publication reported that a group of 14 new missionaries from Spokane, Washington, traveled to Japan and China and found themselves able "to talk to the Chinese and Japanese at the dock and on the ship in their native language."[28]

A third characteristic of the revival was the faith element. Most of these people went on missionary journeys by using their own financial means, for they believed that since God had called them, He would supply whatever they needed. Occasionally, mention is made of contributions being spontaneously given to help them on their way. No formal missionary organization existed, however, to provide these missionaries with assistance or direction.

Apart from testimonials about conversions, healings, and persons receiving the baptism in the Holy Spirit, these people wrote little about the long-term effect or permanence of their work. The focus of their activity appears to have been on proclaiming the gospel and the Pentecostal baptism in the final days before the Second Advent. Perhaps this explains the lack of any concrete missionary strategy such as the establishment of indigenous churches or Bible institutes for training national clergy. These concerns would have to be addressed by others as the Movement matured.

Participants in the Azusa Street Revival became instrumental in the rise of Pentecostalism in many parts of the United States and

Canada. *The Apostolic Faith* abounds with reports of events similar to those at Azusa Street in such places as San Diego, Indianapolis, Dayton, New Orleans, San Antonio, and Toronto.

Reports of revivals from overseas mission fields also illustrate the impact of events in Los Angeles. One issue of *The Apostolic Faith* reported, "Missionaries write that they are hungry for this out-pouring of the Spirit which they believe to be the real Pentecost."[29] Numerous missionaries overseas reported receiving the Pentecostal baptism and a new power from God. For example, Susan C. Easton, the director of the American Women's Board of Missions in India, received this experience. Easton had attended the Ecumenical Mis-sionary Conference at New York City in 1900 and later played a role in the early missions program of the Assemblies of God.[30]

Not everyone rejoiced about such news from the mission fields, however. Arthur T. Pierson, editor of *The Missionary Review of the World* and a watchdog for missions interest, received many inquiries about the legitimacy of speaking in tongues. Pierson as-sociated the recent events with the Irvingite Revival, a revival in mid 19th-century England where some reported speaking in tongues and other gifts of the Holy Spirit. He editorialized in July 1907 that it was a distortion of Paul's teaching in 1 Corinthians, subject to all sorts of bizarre excesses, divisive in the churches, and probably an instrument of Satan. He did note, however, that "there is a spirit of *propaganda*—a determination to go to China, Japan, etc."[31] Two months later, Pierson concluded that "the psychical and pneumatical realms lie close together, and we may unconsciously pass from one to the other, mistaking fleshly enthusiasm and emotional excitement for spiritual ardor and fervor—and hysterical mania for supernatural exaltation to some third heaven."[32]

The impact of the Azusa Street Revival extended far beyond the North American scene and the traditional sites of missionary en-deavor to the historic countries of the Protestant Reformation: En-gland, Scandinavia, Germany, and the Netherlands. For example, Thomas B. Barratt of Norway traveled to America seeking a deeper work of the Spirit in his life. After spending a long time at A. B. Simpson's Missionary Home in New York City, he got word about the Azusa Street Revival. Although he never visited Los Angeles, through correspondence he remained in touch with happenings there.

On November 16, 1906, Barratt received the Pentecostal baptism when other believers laid hands on him with prayer:

> It is affirmed that a supernatural light was seen like a cloven tongue over his head. . . . "I was filled," says Barratt, "with light and such a power that I began to shout as loud as I could in a foreign language. I must have spoken seven or eight languages, to judge from the various sounds and forms of speech used. I stood erect at times, preaching in one foreign tongue after another, and I know from the strength of my voice that 10,000 might easily have heard all I said. . . . At times I had seasons of prayer in the Spirit when all New York, the United States, Norway, Scandinavia and Europe, my loved ones and friends, lay like an intense burden on my soul. Oh, what power was given in prayer! My whole being was at times as if it were on fire inside, and then I would quiet down into sweet songs in a foreign language. Oh, what praises to God arose from my soul for His mercy! I felt as strong as a lion, and know now from whence David and Samson got their strength."[33]

Just like that of other early Pentecostals, Barratt's testimony reflects the close correlation between the baptism in the Holy Spirit and the concern for evangelism. He returned to Norway and became the Pentecostal "Apostle to Scandinavia," his influence extending into Sweden, Finland, Denmark, Switzerland, and Germany.[34]

Charles F. Parham established the Bethel Bible School in Topeka, Kansas, where a great Pentecostal revival began on January 1, 1901.

One of the earliest participants in the Azusa Street Revival to head for overseas ministry was A. G. Garr. He and his wife ministered in India and Hong Kong.

The first Pentecostal missionaries from the West Coast to the Orient (1907) are pictured above. Children seated in the front row (left to right): Leonard Colyar, Maynard Colyar, Paul Ryan, Lester Ryan, Harland Lawler, Beatrice Lawler. Center row (adults): Mrs. Will Colyar, Mrs. M. L. Ryan, M. L. Ryan, Mr. Lawler, Mrs. Emma B. Lawler. Back row (standing): Will Colyar, Rosa Downing, Mrs. Cora Fritsch Faulkner, Rev. Edward Reilly, Mrs. May Law Michael, Lillian Callahan, Bertha Milligan, Mrs. Vinnie McDonald, Archie McDonald.

Early leaders of the Azusa Street Revival. Seated (left to right): Sister Evans (?), Hiram Smith, William J. Seymour, Clara Lum. Standing (left to right): unidentified woman, Brother Evans (?), Jennie Moore (Mrs. W. J. Seymour), Glen A. Cook, Florence Crawford, unidentified man, Sister Prince (?). Florence Crawford's daughter is seated in front of Hiram Smith.

3

Revivals in the East

Many present-day Pentecostal groups recognize their roots in the revivals of Topeka, Kansas, and Azusa Street. Several revivals that followed, however, had a more immediate influence on the future Assemblies of God foreign missions program, notably those that occurred in Rochester, New York; North Bergen, New Jersey; and the one that swept the Christian and Missionary Alliance founded by A. B. Simpson. As has been noted, overseas evangelism was a concern of all the early participants of these revivals, but only the Christian and Missionary Alliance had an articulate and tested missiology.

The Rochester Revival

The events in Rochester, New York, originated with the ministry of the five daughters of James Duncan, a veteran Methodist pastor. The eldest, Elizabeth V. Baker, led in the establishment of the Elim Faith Home in 1895. Having reported a miraculous physical healing, Baker later recounted that the Spirit directed them to open a home where seekers could come for faith healing and "be surrounded with an atmosphere of faith, where tired missionaries and Christian workers could for a time find rest for soul and body."[1]

Baker and her husband, a medical doctor, had for a time lived in Boston, where she was influenced by the teachings of Adoniram J. Gordon, especially his premillennialism. In the beginning years of the work in Rochester, Baker and her sisters (Mary E. Work, Nellie A. Fell, Susan A. Duncan, and Harriet "Hattie" M. Duncan) emphasized divine healing, the premillennial return of Christ, and the necessity of foreign missions. As a result, numerous missionaries traveled to Rochester during their furloughs from the mission fields.

Early in the Elim ministry, Baker reported that the Spirit directed her to visit India.[2] In the fall of 1898, she sailed to India and made contact with the famous Pandita Ramabai, director of the Mukti Mission.[3] Following this voyage, the Rochester work continued to support that effort and had an increased awareness of the value of Christian missions. Thus the Duncan sisters vigorously supported missions a number of years before the Pentecostal revival occurred in Rochester in 1907.

The Elim ministry foreshadowed the role that would be given to women in the Pentecostal movement. Elizabeth Baker had experienced two tragic marriages by the time the Faith Home opened in 1895, yet she directed the ministry throughout her lifetime. In connection with the faith home, she led the sisters in building the Elim Tabernacle Church. They earnestly prayed that God would send the right man as pastor. But when no suitable candidate arrived, they accepted this as a sign from the Holy Spirit that they were to have charge of the work (to that point they had opposed women pastors). While fulfilling the pastoral responsibilities of the church, they nevertheless refused ordination.

Stirred by the reports of the revival in Wales, people attending the June convention at the Elim Tabernacle in 1907 sought God for a revival. Later in the same year, news from Azusa Street reached Rochester. Among the first to receive the Pentecostal baptism was Marguerite Fell, a sister-in-law of Nellie (Duncan) Fell. Baker recounted

> when the Spirit fell upon her she lay helpless under His mighty power. As we listened we could see that the Spirit was showing her the needs and awful darkness of the heathen fields, and a real soul travail came upon her for the perishing souls in darkness. She cried out agonizingly in English for God to send help, then as the Spirit pointed her to the cross she broke out in joyful praise for the victory of Calvary, and immediately broke out in fluent Chinese, not a word of which did she know.[4]

Typical of individuals in other Pentecostal revivals, those who took part in the Rochester revival quickly associated the purpose of the baptism in the Holy Spirit with Christ's command to evangelize the world before He returned.

In October 1906, the sisters established the Rochester Bible

Training School "for the training of those who felt His call to some special work, but lacked the educational fitness." The curriculum of the school included courses on the doctrines of the Christian faith, Biblical studies, personal evangelistic work, homiletics, dispensationalism, typology, and missionary studies.[5] Carl Brumback, a noted authority on the history of the Assemblies of God, contends that this was the first permanent Pentecostal school to genuinely influence the Movement.[6] Although the sisters and the school never formally affiliated with the Assemblies of God, many of the alumni from this institution distinguished themselves in the Assemblies of God foreign missions program: Alfred Blakeney (India), Joseph Blakeney (Africa), Eric Booth–Clibburn (Africa), John Burgess (India), Marguerite Flint (India), Jennie Kirkland (India), Evelyn Lewis (India), Jacob J. Mueller (India), Charles Personeus (Alaska), Ralph Riggs (Africa; General Superintendent of the Assemblies of God: 1953–1959), Gustave H. Schmidt (Eastern Europe), Grace Walther (India), and Anna Ziese (China). The Rochester Bible Training School operated until 1924, when the remaining sisters were too old to continue their ministry.

The Revival in North Bergen, New Jersey

Another important Pentecostal revival in the East resulted in the establishment of two institutions in North Bergen, New Jersey: Beulah Heights Assembly and the Beulah Heights Bible and Missionary Training School. These initiatives were outgrowths of the work of Virginia E. Moss.

Although in generally poor health for most of her life, "Mother" Moss, as she was known, reported numerous miraculous healings of different ailments from which she suffered. Beginning in 1902, she suffered a form of crippling paralysis. Two years later, promising God she would become a preacher, she reported an instantaneous healing.[7]

Desiring to tell others about faith healing, Moss took her new message to the Methodist church she attended; it gave her a chilly reception. This prompted her to begin teaching small groups of interested people in private homes. Withdrawing from the church, she founded the Door of Hope Mission in February 1906; this later became the Beulah Heights Assembly.

During the following year, Moss was stirred by reports in *The*

Triumphs of Faith, a West Coast publication, that the "latter rain" (predicted by the prophet Joel) was falling. In the summer of 1907 when a Pentecostal revival occurred at A. B. Simpson's Missionary Training Institute in Nyack, New York, Moss and several of her followers attended the meetings. After one of them received the Pentecostal baptism, the others returned home and "began tarrying more earnestly than ever, and one after another received their baptisms and many more came from other towns and were baptized in the Spirit and spoke in tongues."[8] This type of activity continued to attract more people to her services at Beulah Heights Assembly.

From her early years, Moss was acquainted with the missionary call to India her mother professed to have received from God. However, due to several circumstances, her mother had been unable to fulfill it. This call and the guilt the mother felt for not obeying it made a lasting impression on the daughter.

Virginia Moss never claimed to have received a missionary call. However, she did say that God had commanded her to open the Beulah Heights Bible and Missionary Training School, which she did in 1912. Realizing that most Pentecostal missionaries might reject academic preparation, being inclined to travel immediately to the mission fields after receiving their calls, she nevertheless pursued the venture. *The Latter Rain Evangel,* an early Pentecostal publication, applauded the initiative and recommended the school because "its objective will be to give a thorough knowledge of the English Bible and practical methods of missionary work; at the same time students will be encouraged to seek personal experiences of God's grace and power to meet the needs and conditions on the home and foreign fields."[9] Seventeen students enrolled in the fall of 1912. Moss directed the school until her death in 1919.

The school became noted in early Pentecostal circles for the missionaries it produced. Of the students who attended it between 1912 and 1919, thirty-one became missionaries. Those who served as Assemblies of God missionaries included Jennie Carlson (Africa), Edgar Barrick (India), Frank Finkenbinder (Puerto Rico), Mr. and Mrs. John Juergensen (Japan), Henry Garlock (Africa; Field Secretary for Africa: 1943–1954), Mr. and Mrs. Frank Nicodem (India), Edgar Personeus (Africa), and Blanche Garlock Trotter (Africa).[10] Maynard L. Ketcham, a missionary to India and later Field Secretary for Southern Asia (1951–1955) and eventually for the Far East (1955–

1970), graduated from the school a few years later. Thus, numerous missionaries and two later field secretaries came from this school to make a long-range effect on Assemblies of God foreign missions.

The Revival in the Christian and Missionary Alliance

Another significant Pentecostal revival in the East took place within the ranks of the Christian and Missionary Alliance.[11] This organization later played a key role in the development of the Assemblies of God.

A. B. Simpson, a Presbyterian minister from Canada, wanted to organize evangelistic and missionary activities that would go beyond denominational barriers. To that end, he set up two societies in 1887: the Christian Alliance for American and Canadian activities and the Evangelical Missionary Alliance for foreign missions. In 1897 they merged, forming the Christian and Missionary Alliance. Allowing laity, both men and women, a major role in the organization, it reflected the two great passions of Simpson's ministry: revivalism and foreign missions.

Simpson's theology centered around his "four-fold" gospel: salvation, sanctification, faith healing, and the second coming of Christ. His doctrine of sanctification largely followed the Reformed Evangelical, or Keswick, pattern of Dwight L. Moody and Adoniram J. Gordon, featuring its progressive emphasis and the belief that the baptism in the Holy Spirit is a separate experience, which follows regeneration and is intended to empower the believer for Christian witness.

Simpson's belief in faith healing for the physical needs of the believer became pronounced in his theology and ministry following a miraculous healing he reported to receive in his own body. As a result, he preached that "the death of Christ destroys sin—the root of sickness. But it is the life of Jesus which supplies the source of health and life for our redeemed bodies."[12] He carried this view on healing into his foreign missions program. The following statement by Simpson in 1881 illustrates the identification of his theology with that of the New Testament Church:

> We know something of the value of medical missions in commending Christianity to the heathen. But if we may go to the world and the early teachers of Christianity and offer men

> complete redemption for body and soul, and receive the public
> seal of their divine commissions in the healing of diseases and
> the manifestations of divine power before the eyes of men,
> then Christian missions will stand henceforth on a new basis,
> and men will begin to pray for faith in God as the real secret
> of the world's evangelization. [13]

While Simpson found his mixture of healing and foreign missions
to be controversial in his own lifetime, it reappeared in Pentecostal
missions. [14]

The last tenet of Simpson's fourfold gospel pointed to the second
coming of Christ. Simpson, an ardent premillennialist, initially believed that this event would occur by 1900. [15] When it did not, his
belief that Christ's coming would be soon never faltered. In the
Annual Report to the Alliance convention in 1900, he wrote:

> We believe God wants us to deeply realize our special calling
> as a distinct spiritual and missionary agency in these last days . . .
> to feed the hungry hearts that are starving for the living
> bread . . . to move back to the spirit of Pentecost, to move
> forward to the coming of the Lord . . . to give the whole gospel
> to the whole world. This is an object sufficient to rouse us from
> indifference, selfishness and discouragement, to draw from us
> the most intense and earnest aspirations of our being and to
> incite us to the noblest of possibilities of consecrated life on
> the solemn threshold of the closing and the coming century,
> may the Holy Spirit help us to behold the vision, to receive
> anew the great commission, and then go forth in the power of
> a new baptism of the Holy Ghost to make it real. [16]

To Simpson, "the best way to be filled with the Spirit is to be true
to the great trust for which He was given—the evangelization of the
world."[17] This enduement with power, coupled with the zeal for
world evangelism, characterized his theology. His missionary hymns,
such as "To the Regions Beyond I Must Go" and "A Hundred
Thousand Souls Are Passing One by One Away," reflect this thinking. The missions program of the Alliance evolved from this burden
to evangelize the world.

Patterning his organization after the China Inland Mission of J.
Hudson Taylor, Simpson appealed widely for missionary candidates
who would meet a list of 10 qualifications (qualifications that did not
include education). Daryl Westwood Cartmel, professor at Fort

Wayne Bible College, writes that the Alliance examiners looked for candidates whose religious experience included "a thorough conversion, evidence of sanctification, a love for souls, a distinct call to missionary service and a record of the candidate's ability to convert other people."[18] These missionaries, not representing the ranks of the professional clergy or specific denominations, were to fulfill a Bible text that carried great meaning for Simpson: "This gospel of the kingdom shall be preached in all the world for a witness unto all nations; and then shall the end come" (Matthew 24:14).

Influenced by William Taylor, the Methodist Episcopal Bishop for Africa, Simpson strongly supported the principle of self-governing, indigenous churches on the foreign fields.[19] The constitution of the organization stated, "The Alliance proposes to encourage and foster the principle of self-support, in whole or in part, wherever practicable in the foreign field."[20] To achieve that goal, he founded the Missionary Training Institute in 1882 "to teach the whole Word of God, to present Christ as sufficient for the whole man, and to send the good tidings to the whole world."[21] Thus, the first Bible institute in America came into being, predating Moody's school in Chicago by several years. At the Nyack, New York, campus the students studied the teachings of John Nevius and S. J. Burton on the indigenous church and the famous three selfs: self-support, self-government, self-propagation.

The Alliance missionaries traveled overseas trusting God to supply their needs. Simpson and his associates appealed to the American members of his organization for financial help, but the missionaries received no fixed salaries. At the end of each month, the monies that came in were sent overseas and divided proportionally among the missionaries. This procedure enabled Simpson to avoid both the expense of the denominational missionary boards and the frugal approach of William Taylor.[22] Consequently, the missionaries lived a simple life-style near the level of the people.[23]

One of the chief means of support for the missions program proved to be Simpson's conventions, which he began in 1884 in New York City and eventually held with great success across the country. A. E. Thompson, Simpson's foremost biographer, recorded that

> the object was "to gather Christians of common faith and spirit for fellowship; to study the word of God; to promote a

deeper spiritual life among Christians; to seek a better understanding of the teachings of the Scriptures respecting our physical life in Christ; to wait upon the Lord for a special baptism
of the Holy Spirit for life and service; to encourage each other's
hearts in the prospect of the glorious appearing of the Lord;
and to promote the work of evangelization at home and missions
abroad."[24]

As reports of the revival at Azusa Street circulated, a number of
Christian and Missionary Alliance churches and foreign missionaries
began to seek the Pentecostal baptism. Many in the Alliance, at
home and abroad, were prepared for just such a revival. The Committee on Foreign Work, chaired by William Cramer, reported to
the Alliance convention in 1906 that missionaries from every field
were requesting prayer that God would send a mighty outpouring
of His Spirit, baptizing them and their national workers. In their
view, besides enhancing holy living, "the thorough and speedy evangelization of the dark lands of heathenism depends largely upon a
Spirit-filled native ministry and church."[25]

The revival in the Christian and Missionary Alliance apparently
began in late 1906, the same year the revival began at the Azusa
Street Mission. Although it soon received internal opposition, the
revival continued in some areas for much more than a decade. To
the May 1907 convention, George N. Eldridge, a superintendent
and chairman of the Committee on Home Work, reported: "There
is bursting out in many centers a revival which is surely a visitation
of God upon the earth and which may be the beginning of the final
outpouring of the Holy Ghost which is to immediately precede the
coming of the Lord."[26] On a more cautious note, J. H. Stumpf,
chairman of the Prayer Committee, urged that members of the
Alliance "tread softly in the presence of God . . . that we may act
with wisdom and discernment according to the will of God and the
mind of the Spirit."[27]

During 1907, more and more Alliance members reported receiving the Pentecostal baptism as evidenced by speaking in tongues.
Reports came from Akron and Cleveland, Ohio; Homestead, New-
castle, Pittsburgh, and Rocky Springs Park, Pennsylvania; Indianapolis, Indiana; Portland, Oregon; and Toronto, Canada. Finally the
Missionary Training Institute at Nyack felt the impact of the new
movement. When a letter describing the recent happenings at Azusa

Street arrived in late 1906, the school underwent a great spiritual awakening.[28] W. C. Stevens, the principal of the school, reported to the May 1907 convention of the Alliance about "the most signal and sacred feature of this year's history, namely, the visitation of God's Spirit last November and December."[29] While it had been a remarkable revival, it fell short in his estimation of the great enduement of power that many had anticipated.

The May convention, which coincided with the closing of the school year, witnessed a revival with some speaking in tongues. Not knowing how to handle such a situation, the leadership appealed to several men who had spoken in tongues, including William Cramer and John Coxe. This only "seemed to heighten the already supercharged atmosphere."[30]

Simpson and many of his associates, while open to such activity, could not accept the teaching that speaking in tongues was the determining evidence for the baptism in the Holy Spirit. Among the errors in the new movement, reported Simpson, "one of the greatest . . . is a disposition to make special manifestations an evidence of the baptism of the Holy Ghost, giving to them the name of Pentecost as though none had received the spirit of Pentecost but those who had the power to speak in tongues."[31]

Nevertheless, Pentecostalism spread in the ranks of the Alliance, reaching into their overseas work. As early as November 1906, *The Apostolic Faith* from Azusa Street reported:

> News comes from India that the baptism with the Holy Ghost and the gift of tongues is being received there by natives who are simply taught of God. The India Alliance says: "Some of the gifts which have been scarcely heard of in the church for many centuries, are now being given by the Holy Ghost to simple, unlearned members of the body of Christ, and communities are being stirred and transformed by the wonderful grace of God. Healing, the gift of tongues, visions, and dreams, discernment of spirits, the power to prophecy [sic] and to pray the prayer of faith, all have a place in the present revival."[32]

By the time the Alliance convention met in 1908, missionaries and Chinese Christians at Wuchow in South China reported similar phenomena. At the reopening service for the mission schools in September 1907 "a heavenly baptism fell upon them and many began to speak with tongues and magnify God. . . . All the workers have had a distinct quickening of their spiritual life, and a new enduement for service."[33]

Eventually many who had experienced the Pentecostal baptism with speaking in tongues left the Alliance when opposition arose. Some of them joined the Assemblies of God, which had organized in 1914, and became leaders in the new organization. Of those who left the Alliance and later served in Assemblies of God foreign missions, many had studied at Nyack. This list shows the large number of missionaries and later missionary personnel trained by the Alliance. Through the early 1920s, the largest number of alumni from any one school serving as missionaries for the Assemblies of God came from the Missionary Training Institute at Nyack.[34]

Missionary	Foreign Field
Grace Agar*	China
Myrtle Bailey*	China
Agnes N. T. Beckdahl*	India
Gottfried Bender*	Venezuela
Myrtle Kievell Blakeney*	India
Ada Buchwalter Bolton*	China
George Bowie	Africa
A. Elizabeth Brown	Palestine
Bernice Andrews Burgess*	India
Barbara Cox*	India
Herbert H. Cox	India
Sarah Coxe*	India
Clara M. Cragin	Latin America
H. W. Cragin	Latin America
Margaret Felch*	India
Marguerite Flint	India
Edna Francisco*	China
Laura Gardner*	India
Anna Helmbrecht	India
Etta M. Hinckley*	China
Frances Kauffman*	China
Ivan S. Kauffman*	China
Mary E. Lewer**	China
Lillian Merian	India
Jacob J. Mueller*	India (Assistant Foreign Missions Secretary of the Assemblies of God: 1939–1959)
Harold K. Needham*	(Overseas representative for the General Council of the Assemblies of God: 1920–1921)

Missionary	Foreign Field
Nettie D. Nichols*	China
Noel Perkin	Argentina (Foreign Missions Director of the Assemblies of God: 1927–1959)
Victor Plymire*	Tibet, China
Edith Priest*	Egypt
Christian Schoonmaker*	India
Clara W. Siemens*	West Indies (later joined the Pentecostal Assemblies of Canada)
William W. Simpson*	Tibet, China
Mary O. Smith*	Africa
Wycliffe M. Smith*	Africa
Marie Stephany*	Mongolia
Allan Swift*	China
John Wilbur Taylor*	Africa
Harry T. Waggoner*	India
John G. Warton*	Persia
Adah Winger Wegner	Latin America
Alice C. Wood*	Latin America

*studied at Nyack
**studied at Wilson Memorial Academy (high school) at Nyack

The separation caused difficulties for those Alliance missionaries who left because of their new Pentecostal baptism. Carl Brumback observes that "it . . . was hard on missionaries who lost their appointments, and were forced to raise their support all over again."[35]

At the same time, the Alliance organization itself suffered from the loss of such members as Minnie T. Draper, George N. Eldridge, Daniel W. Kerr, David Wesley Myland, and John W. Welch. In an oblique reference to the division in the Alliance, Kenneth Mackenzie, an associate of Simpson, wrote in a memorial to him: "I cannot refrain from recording the agony through which he passed when so many of his most trusted and valued friends and workers withdrew from him because he did not go with them to the limit which was their ideal. He could not say of them, as did St. John, 'They went out from us, but they were not of us,' for they were. Their presence and prayers, their sympathy and service had been a bulwark to him in times of stress and strain."[36] Unwittingly, Simpson had trained a portion of the early leadership of the Assemblies of God.

The influence of the Christian and Missionary Alliance on the

General Council of the Assemblies of God extended into many areas. The doctrines of the new organization, minus the unique requirement for the baptism in the Holy Spirit, reflected Alliance beliefs. The hymns and books of Simpson enjoyed popularity among Assemblies of God members for many years. There were also distinct organizational similarities.[37]

Simpson and the Alliance also played a significant role in the development of Assemblies of God missions. Besides training people who later filled major roles in the new organization, Simpson's missionary vision combined with his premillennial eschatology to stir his followers to action in the last days.

Alice Reynolds Flower, wife of a founding father of the Assemblies of God and an influential writer herself, recalls: "Once a year, Dr. Simpson came to Indianapolis for a stirring missionary convention. A large auditorium . . . was secured for the meetings and the missionary fervor encouraged through the year arose to fever height as we listened to Dr. Simpson's searching missionary message, delivered quietly but most impressively. . . . That missionary emphasis did something to me as a child which has been intensified through the years."[38]

Christine Kerr Pierce, reflecting on her father Daniel W. Kerr and the members of his former Alliance church in Cleveland, states: "The missionary vision inculcated in their hearts through association with Dr. Simpson and the Christian and Missionary Alliance permeated this church and the burden and vision of missions never dimmed through all of Father and Mother Kerr's ministry."[39] When the Assemblies of God started Central Bible Institute in 1922 for training ministers and missionaries, Kerr received appointment as its first president. He also played key roles in the establishment of two other early Assemblies of God Bible institutes: Glad Tidings Bible Institute (later Bethany Bible College) and Southern California Bible School (later Southern California College).

The fusing of Alliance theology and Pentecostalism took early form in the writings of David Wesley Myland, one of the founding members of the Alliance. After he left the Alliance, Myland wrote that the *early* rain of Joel's prophecy received fulfillment on the Day of Pentecost in Acts 2. The *latter* rain described the contemporary revival. One was for the beginning of the dispensation and the other for its consummation.[40] Because of the urgency of the hour to reach the lost, he stated that he "would rather see one person baptized in the Holy Ghost and fire, dead in love with God's Word, reading it day and night and praying the heathen through to salvation than to see a score of missionaries go out with only intellectual equipment."[41] This position and Myland's advice to missionaries to trust God for their physical well-being reflected important concepts held by Simpson.

Another Alliance influence on the Assemblies of God was the plan to set up indigenous churches on foreign mission fields, a plan that met with unquestioned acceptance in the new Assemblies of God. The ninth General Council of the Assemblies of God, meeting in St. Louis in 1921, placed itself on record "as being ready to follow the New Testament methods in the conduct of its work in foreign lands, and . . . to seek to establish self-supporting, self-propagating and self-governing native churches."[42] Although the Council's decision cannot be entirely attributed to the influence of Alliance missiology—indigenous church principles were widely discussed in missions circles at the time—Simpson's concern for New Testament principles and methods of evangelism undoubtedly placed a permanent imprint on Assemblies of God missiology. As the early Pentecostals studied the outpouring of the Spirit on the Day of Pentecost, followed by the evangelization of Jews and Gentiles and accompanied by "signs and wonders," they observed the development of indigenous local churches. It was this pattern, echoed by Simpson, that they sought to follow.

One other influence of the Alliance on the Assemblies of God was the development of a missionary agency and two institutions patterned after the Nyack school and staffed by former members of the Alliance: Bethel Bible Training School in Newark, New Jersey, and Central Bible Institute, Springfield, Missouri.

The Bethel Pentecostal Assembly of Newark, New Jersey, was founded in 1907 through the efforts of Emily Tompkins, pastor of the Christian and Missionary Alliance church in Ossining, New York; Minnie T. Draper, an associate of A. B. Simpson and member of the governing board of the Alliance until 1912; and Mrs. Lewis B. Heath, wife of a wealthy New York lumber merchant.[43] Allan Swift, a recent graduate of Nyack, became the first full-time pastor in 1911. A writer in *The Pentecostal Evangel* later described it as one of the most influential Pentecostal missionary centers in the country, noting particularly its generous financial contributions.[44] This farsighted congregation sponsored two significant agencies to expand its influence: the South and Central African Pentecostal Mission (1910) and, closely associated with it, the Bethel Bible Training School (1916).

In 1910, the fledgling congregation in Newark incorporated under the name "Executive Council of the Bethel Pentecostal Assembly" with the express desire "to maintain and conduct a general evangelistic work in the State of New Jersey, in all other States of the United States and any and all foreign countries."[45] It was one of the earliest Pentecostal missionary agencies organized in the United States.[46] It became known as the South and Central African Pentecostal Mission. The organization published the *South and Central African Pentecostal Herald* (later known as the *Full Gospel Missionary Herald*) to promote its overseas effort. In policy matters, it retained strict control over the activities of its missionaries (which often caused unrest on the mission fields).

For many years Minnie T. Draper served as the president of the council and was assisted by Joseph R. Potter, Mr. and Mrs. Lewis B. Heath, Mary S. Stone, Mrs. William R. Schoenborn, and Christian J. Lucas, among others. Several members were quite wealthy and donated monies to a trust fund for the maintenance of the organization.[47] By 1925, the council's budget reached $30,150 and supported missionaries in Liberia, the Union of South Africa, Swaziland, and Portuguese East Africa; two mission works were also sponsored in Mexico and Venezuela.[48] With the collapse of the stock market in 1929, the trust fund suffered a major setback and missionary endeavors were seriously curtailed. During that year, a proposed union with the Assemblies of God mission program was considered, but nothing came of it.[49]

Bethel Bible Training School was set up in 1916 through the efforts of Allan Swift, Pastor Christian Lucas of Ossining, and Minnie T. Draper. Draper's presence at the school was particularly significant in view of her longtime acquaintance with the ministry and objectives of the Alliance. William W. Simpson (no relation to A. B. Simpson), a pioneer missionary of the Alliance in Tibet since 1892, served as the first dean. Dismissed from the Alliance in 1916 for refusing to change his teaching that speaking in tongues was a determining evidence for the Pentecostal baptism, he took up the new ministry at Bethel until he returned to China in 1918 as an Assemblies of God missionary. Simpson represented another articulate voice of Alliance theology. In addition, he had attended the significant Ecumenical Missionary Conference at New York City in 1900.[50] Other prominent faculty members included Frank M. Boyd, a 1911 graduate of Nyack and later an influential theologian in the Assemblies of God, and William I. Evans, a 1910 Nyack graduate and later dean of Bethel itself and then Central Bible Institute.

Many graduates of the Bethel Bible Training School later served in the Assemblies of God as ministers and missionaries. Several missionaries, unhappy with rigid policies, left the South and Central African Pentecostal Mission to enlist as Assemblies of God missionaries. These enterprises at Newark, New Jersey, made significant contributions to the Assemblies of God through the efforts of various individuals, notably John Burgess (India), Edith Dutton (India), Margaret Felch (India), Reginald Jamieson (China), Fred and Lillian Merian (India), Nicholas and Martha Nikoloff (Eastern Europe), Howard C. Osgood (China; field secretary for China and the Far East: 1945–1955), Edgar and Mabel Pettenger (Africa), Ralph and Lillian Riggs (Africa; general superintendent of the Assemblies of God: 1953–1959)[51] and Anna Richards Scoble.[52]

Central Bible Institute, established by the General Council of the Assemblies of God in 1922 for the training of ministers and missionaries, has continued to emphasize the training of missionaries. Besides being patterned somewhat after Nyack with its missionary prayer groups and special missions emphases, the school has also felt the effect of former Alliance people through some of its teachers and administrators: Daniel W. Kerr (former Alliance pastor, president 1922–1923), John W. Welch (former Alliance pastor, president 1931–1939), Frank M. Boyd (Nyack graduate and dean 1923–1929), William I. Evans (Nyack graduate, former Alliance pastor, dean 1929–1954), and Donald F. Johns (Nyack graduate of 1949, instructor from 1954 and dean 1965–1973).[53]

The five daughters of Methodist pastor James Duncan established the Rochester (N.Y.) Bible Training School in 1906. The eldest, Elizabeth V. Baker, pictured left, directed the school in its earlier years.

Virginia E. "Mother" Moss founded the Beulah Heights Bible and Missionary Training School in North Bergen, New Jersey, in 1912. This school became well known in Pentecostal circles for the missionaries it produced.

Above: In the foreground is the Rochester (N.Y.) Bible Training School. The Elim Tabernacle is to the right.

Pictured above are the 1927 graduates of the Beulah Heights Bible and Missionary Training School of North Bergen, New Jersey. Seated (left to right): Lillian Martin Woolever, Sarah Burman, unidentified woman, Virginia Hill, Bertha Meyers, Mary Waters. Standing (left to right): Charles Woolever, Willie Stewart, Mary Lindberg, unidentified woman, unidentified woman, George Wood, Sydney Bryant.

The Missionary Training Institute at Nyack, New York, as it appeared in the earlier part of this century. The institute was founded by A. B. Simpson.

Albert B. Simpson founded the Christian and Missionary Alliance in 1887. Many of the early members and leaders of the Assemblies of God had been affiliated with his organization.

David Wesley Myland, pictured above with his wife, was an early and prominent leader in the Christian and Missionary Alliance. Later he identified with Pentecostalism and influenced a number of early Assemblies of God members even though he never joined their organization.

This photograph taken at the 1906 Old Orchard Convention in Maine reflects the early link between the Christian and Missionary Alliance and the emergence of Pentecostalism. (1) Henry Wilson, who investigated and opposed the movement within the Alliance; (2) Mrs. A. B. Simpson; (3) Rev. A. B. Simpson; (4) W. C. Stevens, principal of the Missionary Training Institute; and (5) Minnie T. Draper, prominent Alliance official and speaker who later helped in the founding of the Bethel Pentecostal Assembly, Newark, New Jersey, and the agencies associated with that church.

William W. Simpson was a pioneer missionary to China and Tibet for the Christian and Missionary Alliance beginning in 1892. Later joining the Assemblies of God, he continued his ministry there. In the above picture, he is teaching at the Truth Bible Institute in Beijing, China.

Christian Schoonmaker was a pioneer missionary to India for the Christian and Missionary Alliance. After he received the baptism in the Holy Spirit, he was instrumental in leading other Alliance missionaries into this experience. Later joining the Assemblies of God, he had a marked influence on its missions program and Noel Perkin, foreign missions secretary from 1927 to 1959.

Minnie T. Draper served for many years as an associate to A. B. Simpson and was a member of the Executive Board of the Christian and Missionary Alliance until 1912. She was a founder of the Bethel Pentecostal Assembly, the Bethel Bible Training School, and the South and Central African Pentecostal Mission.

The influence of the Bethel Pentecostal Assembly, Newark, New Jersey, on the Assemblies of God is reflected in this picture taken in 1918. (Left to right) Ernest S. Williams, pastor, Frank M. Boyd, dean of the Bethel Bible Training School, and William I. Evans, instructor. Williams later served as general superintendent of the Assemblies of God (1929–1949) and Boyd and Evans became prominent educators.

An important early center of Pentecostal ministry in the eastern part of the United States was in Newark, New Jersey. The church at the right was the Bethel Pentecostal Assembly, the four-story building in the center was the Bethel Bible Training School, and the building at the left served as the men's dormitory (ca. 1928).

4

The Formation of the General Council

Farsighted leaders among independent Pentecostals recognized the need to organize to assist the missionary activities they supported. Lack of legal recognition, inconsistent financial support, questionable practices overseas by some missionaries, as well as other difficulties, caused the editors of several Pentecostal publications to address the need for cooperation. Many saw the formation of the General Council of the Assemblies of God in 1914 as a remedy to the ills of the missions enterprise.

The Demand for Organization

As the Pentecostal movement grew, more and more of its followers found themselves ostracized from the traditional Protestant denominations. Such painful experiences created a deep antagonism toward anything that resembled a formal organization. In addition, many missionaries who became Pentecostal were dismissed by their boards.

In the years following the Azusa Street Revival, a number of Pentecostal leaders recognized the necessity of some form of organization to eliminate occasional abuses in local churches, deal with doctrinal problems, gain legal recognition for local churches, and help missionaries on the foreign fields. Independent Pentecostal missionaries in some countries found it impossible to purchase property because they lacked legal recognition. At times they purchased property and built structures in their own names or those of established missions agencies, such as the Presbyterian Board. Arrangements such as these jeopardized the long-term investments of the home supporters as well as the longevity of the work.

Several writers have discussed the general movement toward the organization of the General Council of the Assemblies of God. The present work, however, focuses attention on the role missions occupied in that organizing process.[1]

The need for organization to preserve the Pentecostal missions effort became obvious by 1912. The revival had renewed emphasis on the divine call as the chief criterion for missionary work at the expense of other qualifications. Those who went overseas often had no conception of the new culture or language that would confront them, no clear strategy for their efforts, and they were sometimes in poor health and too old to meet the rigors awaiting them. An editorial in *The Latter Rain Evangel,* a significant early publication in the development of the Assemblies of God, was representative: "No board would ever have accepted our dear Sister Murray, who is blind and far beyond the age that new recruits are sent out, but God distinctly called her to India and verified it through others."[2]

Optimism about such missionary candidates soon dimmed as victories overseas were tempered by tragedies. Although Holiness–Pentecostal denominations in the South organized missionary efforts early in the century and Pentecostals in Great Britain had established the Pentecostal Missionary Union in 1909, attempts at the same type of organization among independent Pentecostal groups in the United States often ended in failure due to the fear of organizational tyranny.[3] When a group of Ohio ministers tried to form such a union, *The Gospel Witness,* an early Pentecostal publication edited by Harry Van Loon and published in Los Angeles, chastised them for being blinded by the devil and implored "these self-constituted Popes and Archbishops, who would 'lord it over God's heritage' under the guise of protection, to vacate the offices which they have assumed and to lay aside the authority which they have arrogated to themselves."[4]

In the steps leading to the formation of the General Council, three publications played a particularly significant role: *The Christian Evangel,* published by J. Roswell Flower, *The Latter Rain Evangel,* published by William H. Piper, and *Word and Witness,* published by E. N. Bell. Through their news of events at home and abroad, testimonials, and Bible teachings, these periodicals served to unify the many independent congregations. They also served as agencies for the collection and distribution of missionary offerings.

Eventually these publications would carry urgent pleas for organization of the overseas missions effort.

The Christian Evangel owed its origin in 1913 to the ministry of J. Roswell and Alice Reynolds Flower. Having been members of the Christian and Missionary Alliance church in Indianapolis, Indiana, the Flowers came under the influence of A. B. Simpson, George N. Eldridge, and David Wesley Myland. J. Roswell Flower received ordination through Myland's World Faith Missionary Association and began pastoring in the area, ultimately joining Myland in opening the Gibeah Bible School in Plainfield, Indiana. About their pastoral ministry, Alice Reynolds Flower recalls:

> We wanted our people to "feel missions" from the start. So, the first weekly offering of each month went to specified missionaries. . . . We trusted God for our support that week. We never lacked, praise God, and some of His promises were providential supplies which brought spiritual uplift to our souls. For us, the truth was established for all our lives—be faithful and systematic in missionary giving, and God will never fail to supply your own needs.[5]

A practical man, Flower soon recognized the need for more cooperation among pastors and churches to achieve a more effective overseas missions program. In the first issue of *The Christian Evangel,* July 19, 1913, Flower reported about the recent camp meeting at the Gibeah Bible School and the establishment of The Association of Christian Assemblies for interested Pentecostal churches in Indiana and the surrounding states. The purpose "shall be to represent and propagate a full Pentecostal Gospel according to the Apostolic Faith and practice in the unity of the Spirit and the bond of peace, for the deepest and most progressive Christian experience and fellowship, and aggressive evangelistic and missionary work in home and foreign fields."[6] Myland received nomination as general superintendent and Flower as general secretary. This organization foreshadowed the General Council of the Assemblies of God a year later and illustrated the concerns of the latter body.

Beginning publication in 1908, *The Latter Rain Evangel* was edited by William H. Piper, pastor of the Stone Church in Chicago. Like Flower and Bell, Piper distributed funds for specific missionaries and sent the undesignated monies to whoever needed them the most. None of these men, however, exercised control over the missionaries they supported.

By 1913, Anna C. Reiff, Piper's successor, began to address the missionary problem in the publication. There were many aspects to it. First, the editor did not want to continue supporting missionaries who had defected theologically or morally from the Pentecostal cause and she wanted to be informed of any such developments.

Second, the frequent travels of some missionaries to and from the United States had generated "a great deal of dissatisfaction among people in the homeland who have the evangelization of the heathen on their hearts."[7] Evidently some missionaries never stayed on the field long enough to begin a lasting work. Clearly the concern for preaching the gospel in the last days had not been dropped—testimonies abounded about conversions, miraculous healings, and Pentecostal baptisms—but the sober realities of ministering in other cultures appeared ominously on the horizon.

Third, it gradually became apparent that some process of missionary selection needed consideration. The publication charged that "while we are strong in our conviction that everyone on the field who has a real call from God should be supported, we do feel that some have been sent out who should never have gone."[8] Pastors were urged to discourage unlikely candidates, in an attitude of love and concern for their best interests.

Fourth, the disbursement of funds proved to be the thorniest difficulty of all. By recent standards, the sums sent out by all three publications were not large. In one six-month period, for example, the total distributed by Piper came to $3,337.78. Nevertheless, a keen sense of using every penny carefully for God's work shows in all three of the publications.

The financial problem related to the accountability by the recipient and to the equity of distribution. Some missionaries used funds for purposes other than for which they were designated. For example, one missionary kept the funds that were intended for national workers and then exhorted them to live by faith. Some missionaries received far more funds than others because they often returned to the United States and presented the needs of their fields with emotional appeals and graphic portrayals. Other missionaries, unable to return home as frequently or to write stirring appeals, received far less financial assistance even though they may have been equally successful in establishing lasting works.[9]

The Latter Rain Evangel also addressed the concept of going to the field only on faith. It charged that everyone does not receive a "George Mueller call" and therefore needs assistance from the saints at home.[10] The death of one early missionary, Nellie Clark Bettex, from exhaustion and starvation—traceable "not to the Chinese mob . . . but to the callousness of the home saints"—showed the need for dependable, regular support for the overseas missionaries.[11] Nor was living by faith the only concern expressed by the periodical. If a missionary received just enough money to stay alive, how could he open new works on the foreign field?

An editorial expressed the distress of some early Pentecostals in trying to find a balance between the extremes of the organizational restrictions of the contemporary missions boards and the total independence of the Pentecostal missionaries. The writer said:

> Is there no middle ground where the missionary will have full liberty to work as God leads, and an exercise for his faith, without being compelled to take a stand beyond that to which God has called him?
>
> Let us earnestly pray that in some way God will enable us more effectively to help our brothers and sisters who are toiling in the darkness of heathenism. We feel the leaders of the Pentecostal Movement should realize the need of an effective systematic arrangement so that faithful, tried missionaries will not suffer for the common necessities of life.[12]

Reiff and her staff shared these concerns with other discerning Pentecostal leaders.

One such leader was E. N. Bell, a pastor in Malvern, Arkansas, who studied at the Southern Baptist Theological Seminary and the University of Chicago, and served as editor of the *Word and Witness.* Bell's editorials on the problems of missionary support closely aligned with Reiff's concerns. He wrote in 1912 that "our people are tired, sick, and ashamed of traveling, sight-seeing, experimenting missionaries, who expect to make a trip around the world and come home. . . . We want missionaries who go out to live and die on foreign fields."[13] In the same issue, he listed the damage done to the entire effort by these itinerant missionaries.

More assertive than Reiff on financial matters, Bell began to require a quarterly report from the missionaries who received money from him, listing their receipts and expenditures, the size of their families, the number of national workers under their supervision, and names of other missionaries living with them. For the more than 80 missionaries who received support through the auspices of this publication, this became a new condition for their assistance continuing.

Two other items stand out in Bell's policy on missions. First, he strongly urged missionaries to learn the language of the people to whom they planned to minister. He wrote that "if missionaries expect to receive the constant help of sensible saints in the homeland, they must go to fight the good fight of faith, to learn the languages, to train the native workers in their own tongue."[14]

The second item would prove to be a harbinger of problems in the implementation of the indigenous church on some mission fields. Following the practice of many missions agencies at the time, he issued an appeal for the financial support of national workers in China. For $250 a year, he asserted, a Chinese preacher could be supported, including the rent for the hall in which he preached and lived. Because of their familiarity with language and culture, national workers supported in this manner, according to Bell, could do far more effective work than the missionary.[15]

Bell's common sense advice on missionary procedures reflected his intense desire to bring a sense of order to the enterprise.[16] This concern figured strongly in the December 20, 1913, issue of the *Word and Witness*, calling, as it did, for a "General Convention of Pentecostal Saints and Churches of God in Christ" to convene the following April. Of the five subjects listed for discussion at the conference, the third addressed the problems of the missionary effort.

The First General Council

When the first General Council convened in Hot Springs, Arkansas, April 2–12, 1914, the Assemblies of God came into being. The chief instrument that brought the organization into being was the "Preamble and Resolution on Constitution." Since a formal constitution did not come into existence until 1927, the Preamble provided the basis of fellowship and cooperation among ministers and churches for many years. Although not a formal declaration of faith, this document expressed the unanimity felt on several important theological topics: the work of the Father, Son, and Holy Spirit in the plan of redemption; the authority of the Scriptures; and the importance of the unity of the body of Christ, the Church. The sovereignty of the local church received high priority, for the delegates did not wish to form a new sect within Christendom and thus contribute further to the already existing division. Thus the members of the first General Council viewed themselves as a fellowship of

> Pentecostal (Spirit Baptized) saints from local Churches of God in Christ, Assemblies of God and various Apostolic Faith Missions and Churches, and Full Gospel Pentecostal Missions, and Assemblies of like faith in the United States of America, Canada, and Foreign Lands, whose purpose is . . . to recognize Scriptural methods and order for worship, unity, fellowship, work and business for God, and to disapprove of all unscriptural methods, doctrine and conduct, and approve all Scriptural truth and conduct, endeavoring to keep the unity of the Spirit in the bonds of peace, until we all come into the unity of the faith, and of the knowledge of the Son of God, unto a perfect man, unto the measure of the stature of the fulness of Christ.[17]

As a cooperative fellowship of churches, the delegates took the name Assemblies of God, thus providing them with a basis for transacting business, purchasing property, and conducting missionary activities overseas.

In the first issue of the *Word and Witness* following the Hot Springs convention, Bell editorialized: "We are standing for the truth of God and for divine order among His people and in His church. . . . some few say Jesus is coming too soon to waste any time on divine order; but if Jesus comes tomorrow, I had rather be found in divine order than out of it."[18] As he applied this to missions, it meant that the long-standing problems could now be effectively addressed.

Conclusion

In the history of modern Christian missions, 1914 signaled the close of an era. The Protestant missions movement had stood on a peak of worldwide success and unity, looking optimistically toward the gradual establishment of the kingdom of God on earth. But the growing inroads of liberal theology, the decline of Biblical authority and the growing uncertainty about the finality of the Christian message, the coming of the fundamentalist/modernist controversy, and the advent of World War I dispelled that vision for many.

From the time of the Topeka revival to the call to Hot Springs, Arkansas, the Pentecostals, like many evangelicals of the day, viewed themselves as living "in the last days" with a commission to evangelize the heathen, since the end of history was approaching and the Lord would soon return. They differed from others in their belief that the Pentecostal baptism with speaking in tongues provided them a divine enduement of power to carry out that responsibility. It was also fervently believed that the "signs and wonders" that followed the preaching of the apostles in the Book of Acts had been restored with the outpouring of the Spirit.

Several prominent revivals, particularly the one within the Christian and Missionary Alliance, helped to provide missionaries and mold the future missiology of the Assemblies of God. The role of notable women in the eastern revivals, such as Elizabeth V. Baker, Minnie T. Draper, and Virginia E. Moss, and the Bible institutes they founded for the preparation of ministers and missionaries made long-lasting contributions to the Assemblies of God.

The realities confronting missionaries on the foreign fields, including their lack of legal recognition and the difficulties in the distribution of funds, prompted a large group of Pentecostals to organize in 1914 at Hot Springs to more effectively achieve their objectives. John W. Welch, an early leader and general superintendent, later stated: "The General Council of the Assemblies of God was never meant to be an institution; it is just a missionary agency."[19]

Thus in 1914, the last year of the Great Century, the Assemblies of God foreign missions program—shaped as it was by its historical context—came into existence, representing (with other Pentecostal missions societies) a vigorous new thrust in the Christian world mission.

Eudorus N. Bell served as the first general chairman of the General Council of the Assemblies of God. Through his editorial work in the *Word and Witness* and as an executive officer, he exerted considerable influence on the development of Assemblies of God foreign missions in the early years.

Early Pentecostal publications that had a marked influence on the growth and development of the Assemblies of God and its missions program were *The Christian Evangel* (after 1919 known as *The Pentecostal Evangel), The Latter Rain Evangel,* and the *Word and Witness.*

Part Two

The Early Years
(1914–1926)

5

Missionaries and Missiology

In the months that followed the adjournment of the first General Council in April 1914, several hundred ministers joined its ranks. About 27 of them were missionaries.[1] The number of missionaries and records of its meetings illustrate that from the beginning foreign missions commanded the Council's attention. Some missions agencies at the time, such as the China Inland Mission founded by J. Hudson Taylor, were strongly identified with well-known personalities; the foreign missions program of the newly formed General Council of the Assemblies of God, however, had no single figure to direct its overseas enterprise and marshal support from the member churches in the United States.

The early leaders faced both strong antiorganizational sentiments at home and the often desperate needs of a mushrooming missionary force abroad. Years of instability followed the Hot Springs meeting and earnest efforts were made to bring order out of chaos.

In spite of these obstacles, a strong ideal of establishing indigenous churches overseas, based on a New Testament pattern, persisted from the earliest years. While not shared by everyone and only occasionally realized, this ideal would, nevertheless, eventually dominate the enterprise.

The period from 1914 to 1926 represents the most unstable years in the history of the Assemblies of God missions program. To understand this era, it is necessary to study the missionaries, their theology, the slow development of a few organizational structures, and General Council policies.[2]

The Missionaries

The enthusiasm of the earliest General Council missionaries for world evangelization before the return of Christ took them largely to the traditional sites of Protestant missionary endeavor: China, India, and Africa. Others were scattered from the Fiji Islands to Mexico.[3] Many reported that distinct calls from God to specific geographical regions propelled them overseas. Blanche Trotter, an early missionary to Liberia, West Africa, reported that she saw the word *Africa* spelled out in letters of fire during a time of prayer.[4]

At least four groups can be distinguished in the early missionary lists of the General Council. The first group consisted of those who felt the urgency of the hour but were not prepared for the actual requirements of the foreign fields: language and cultural studies, dependable financial support from the home churches to meet expenses and expand activities, and a long-term strategy. Many of these individuals failed overseas and returned home when their zeal faded.

A second group was made up of those who lacked any formal theological and missiological training but persevered in their ministries. These men and women recognized the need to study the language and culture of their fields and learned as they continued their efforts. One outstanding representative of this group was Henry C. Ball of Kingsville, Texas. Converted in a Methodist church and later receiving the Pentecostal baptism, Ball spearheaded missionary endeavors among Hispanics in the United States and Latin America for many years.

A third group represented a considerable number of veterans from other missionary agencies who had received the baptism in the Holy Spirit and then joined the ranks of the Assemblies of God. Many of these veterans provided stability in the early days: Gottfried Bender (Venezuela), Laura Gardner (India), Christian Schoonmaker (India), and Alice M. Wood (Argentina) came from the Christian and Missionary Alliance; J. M. Perkins (Liberia) from the Methodist Episcopal Church; and Susan C. Easton from the American Women's Board of Missions in India.

Unlike many in the early part of this century, the Pentecostal missionaries, including those of the Assemblies of God, had rarely received training in universities and Christian colleges. Shorter than the traditional program of ministerial preparation, the new Bible institute approach to theological education quickly gained favor. The Bible institute offered the student an intense training in Biblical studies, a dynamic spiritual atmosphere through daily chapel services and prayer meetings, and, of course, a speedier entry into the ministry. These institutions produced a fourth group of missionaries: those who received Bible institute education.

Missionary Training

Several Bible institutes supplied missionary candidates for the Assemblies of God in the early years: Berean Bible Institute, founded in 1923 (San Diego, California); Bethel Bible Training School, 1916 (Newark, New Jersey; independent, but closely associated with the Assemblies of God until its merger with Central Bible Institute in 1929); Beulah Heights Bible and Missionary Training School, 1911 (North Bergen, New Jersey); Glad Tidings Bible Institute, 1919 (San Francisco, California); Rochester Bible Training School, 1906 (Rochester, New York; independent, but also closely related with the Assemblies of God); Southern California Bible School, 1921 (Highland Park, California; founded by Harold K. Needham, an Assemblies of God pastor and 1909 graduate of Nyack, Daniel W. Kerr, and Willard C. Pierce); and Central Bible Institute, 1922 (Springfield, Missouri).

For decades Central Bible Institute stood as the most significant missionary training school in the Assemblies of God.[5] Modeled extensively after A. B. Simpson's Missionary Training Institute at Nyack by its early, former Alliance faculty members, Central Bible Institute strongly promoted the cause of overseas missions. The faculty desired a distinctively Pentecostal atmosphere. Frank M. Boyd, principal (dean) at the school from 1923–1929, believed that

> the purpose of the Bible school was not to turn out a lot of dried up students; . . . that he expected all the students to be more filled with fire and love and zeal and more filled with the Spirit when they left than when they came. He said that when men had the Word without the Spirit they were often dead and dull and dry; and when men had the Spirit without the

Word there is always a tendency towards fanaticism. But where men had the Word and the Spirit, they would be equipped as the Master wants His ministers equipped.[6]

Student life at the school largely revolved around its missionary activities. The following news item from *The Pentecostal Evangel* (formerly *The Christian Evangel*) described daily life at the school:

> The students organized into a missionary society and the following were elected officers: Mr. Arthur Wilson, president; Mr. Meyer [sic] Pearlman, vice-president; Miss Nina Mayfield, treasurer; Mr. Finis Dake, gentleman curator [i.e., noon prayer leader]; and Mrs. J. Arthur Wilson, lady curator. Then began daily noon intercession for missionaries and mission fields at 12 to 12:30. On Monday, the field for prayer is China; on Tuesday, India, Persia, Arabia; on Wednesday, Africa; on Thursday, Europe; on Friday, South America; and on Saturday, the Jews. The names of 21 students were placed on the board at the missionary meeting as having received a definite call from God for a special field and 34 gave their names as being particularly interested in some special field. In solemn meetings such as these it is certain that God is speaking to hearts and that consecrations to God's service are being made.[7]

Unfortunately, Central Bible Institute and the other schools listed above provided little actual academic preparation for missionaries. The 1922–1923 school catalog, for example, listed only one missions course: "Missions and Missionaries." The course description read: "In this course is covered the history of Christian Missions up to and including the present efforts being made under the various Boards and by independent missionaries on the world-wide field. The Home Missionary work necessary in our own land is also given due prominence."[8] More extensive preparation for missionary candidates would not be seriously undertaken until near the close of World War II.

Missionary Turnover

The years from 1914 to 1919 represent the period of greatest instability among the missionaries. The following chart illustrates the rapid turnover with three different groups of missionary personnel:

Missionary Turnover in the General Council

Group 1	In 1914 27 new missionaries were added	By 1918 13 of them remained 14 had withdrawn
Group 2	In 1915 43 new missionaries were added	By 1919 20 of them remained 23 had withdrawn
Group 3	In 1918 56 new missionaries were added	By 1921 39 of them remained 17 had withdrawn

The rapid turnover would decline sharply after 1919, the year in which the General Council set up its Foreign Missions Department. However, many factors account for the personnel changes before that year. First, some of the individuals may have died from old age since several who joined the new organization were veteran missionaries. Second, many early missionaries died from tropical fevers and diseases contracted while on the field. Henry B. Garlock, an early Assemblies of God missionary to West Africa, for example, recalled that "during the first 25 years of the Pentecostal work in Liberia, no less than a missionary a year died of malaria or some tropical disease. And many others were sent home because of serious illness."[9] Third, occasionally missionaries married or remarried on the field, thus leading to changes on the missionary rosters.

Fourth, the eruption of the New Issue from 1913 to 1916 caused a small number of missionaries to leave the Council. Beginning with a camp meeting at Arroyo Seco, California, a number of Assemblies of God believers accepted a Oneness, or Modal Monarchian, view of the Trinity and consequently began to baptize or rebaptize believers in the name of Jesus to the exclusion of the Trinitarian formula of Matthew 28:19.[10] After the issue caused considerable confusion and debate, the General Council meeting at St. Louis in 1916 condemned the view and adopted an official list of doctrines, including a lengthy Trinitarian position. Although the new doctrine spread to some foreign fields, notably China, perhaps as few as two missionaries left the Council because of this matter.[11]

Fifth, furloughed missionaries traveling or living in the United States may not have been placed on the active missionary list. Sixth, many of these individuals who went overseas were not adequately trained and may have had only a naive view of what to expect. Disillusioned by harsh realities, they soon returned home. Such conditions undoubtedly discouraged others from remaining overseas.

Finally, the early missionaries who persevered on the foreign fields were rugged individualists who often remained skeptical of growing organizational structures at home. Some movement from the ranks of the organization may possibly be attributed to an intense desire to be governed exclusively by the Spirit's leading, unhampered by organizational restraints.

Missionary Support

The path to overseas ministry began with the sense of an intense call from God, followed by the pledged support of prayer and money on the part of friends, relatives, and local churches. After this, the prospective missionary then headed for the foreign field with or without the approval of the Foreign Missions Department of the new organization based in Springfield, Missouri. Many missionaries who followed this course enlisted the endorsement and financial support of the General Council after arriving at their field of ministry.

The support from the General Council in these early years was minimal, sometimes $20 or less a month from undesignated funds that had been received.[12] All designated funds were sent overseas to the intended recipients. Many of the early missionaries maintained correspondence with various publications, such as *The Christian Evangel* (later *The Pentecostal Evangel*) and *The Latter Rain Evangel*, to publicize their spiritual and financial needs.[13] Correspondence by Assemblies of God missionaries with non-Council periodicals, such as *The Bridegroom's Messenger* (Atlanta, Georgia), also continued for many years in an era when organizational restrictions remained in an embryonic stage.

Assurances that friends at home were praying for them also played a vital role in the minds of the missionaries. Indeed, some felt spiritual support was more important than financial assistance. William W. Simpson stated:

> Beloved, the Lord's time has come for me to return to China . . . and I want to be sent forth with the hearty cooperation, sympathy and prayers of the Church of God following me. I don't care for a Mission Board to back me up with pledged financial support, but I must have the people of God who are of like precious faith with me, to uphold me with their prayers and fellowship if I am to do the work the Lord expects of me in China.[14]

In spite of hardships, financial needs, and disillusionment and retreat by some, the number of applicants willing to minister on foreign fields mushroomed. From 27 in 1914, the missionary force rose to 206 in 1919 and 250 in 1925.[15]

The missionaries' length of stay overseas was not predetermined. Some missionaries thought Christ's return was so imminent that they never expected to see the United States again once they had left. A few, such as Mabel Dean (Egypt) and Alice M. Wood (Latin America), never took furloughs and spent decades overseas. For most, however, the hardships of the mission fields forced them to return occasionally to the homeland, sometimes having served overseas as long as 9 years or more. Getting money for the return trip, however, was not always easy, so the readerships of the various magazines were appealed to in one way or another. One such appeal represented the plight of Mr. and Mrs. Thomas Hindle, missionaries to Mongolia: "Brother and Sister Hindle are much in need of a furlough. They have been on the field for eight years, and recently passed through the sad experience of losing their little daughter. Pray for them that their return fare may be forth-coming."[16] On their return to the United States, missionaries often took up residence at various missionary homes, provided by the General Council or interested individuals.

Women in Missions

In spite of those hardships, foreign missions in the Assemblies of God afforded women a wide opportunity for ministry. For couples, both the husband and wife were considered missionaries; this usually meant many responsibilities in ministry for the latter. Although the percentage of *single* women missionaries remained about the same from 1914 to 1925 (37 to 38 percent), they played notable roles and increased their number from 10 (of 27) to 95 (of 250) by 1925. The *total* number of women missionaries (single and married) to men increased by 9 percent (to 161) between 1914 and 1925. Twenty-one years later they had gained only 1 percent but they numbered 329 of a missionary force of 503.

Women could not receive ordination as an elder (i.e., pastor) during the early years of the Assemblies of God. In addition, they were not permitted to vote at the General Council meetings; they served instead as advisory members. (The restriction on voting was removed in 1920.) However, besides serving as evangelists, women could also be ordained as missionaries. But when pressed by Hattie Hacker and Jennie Kirkland, former missionaries to India, the Executive Presbytery, the highest administrative board in the General Council, had granted them the privilege of performing "the functions of the Christian ministry, such as baptism, marriage, burial of the dead and the Lord's Supper, when a man is not available for the purpose, and [having] a certificate to that effect . . . attached to the credentials as special privilege in the case of emergency only."[17] The large number of women involved in missionary service and the unusual circumstances of the foreign field evidently overcame any hesitations about ordaining them, at least for this type of service.

Women did not generally serve in decision-making positions. When the Council approved a Foreign Missions Committee in 1917, Susan C. Easton, a missionary to India since 1885, was appointed to serve. She was the last woman to serve as a full-fledged member. Her time on the committee amounted to only one year when its responsibilities were transferred to the Executive Presbytery.[18]

As the missions program developed, numerous articles appeared in *The Pentecostal Evangel* appealing for more men, presumably married, to serve overseas. J. Roswell Flower, the missionary secretary from 1919 to 1923, wrote:

> The crying need on every mission field which has been opened by consecrated Pentecostal missionaries is for MEN. There is not one field but what is suffering for the want of men. Young women have volunteered in far greater numbers than men for pioneering in China, India, and Africa and South America. They have struggled with the building projects, the management of stations, the supervision of native workers, etc., and have been called upon to perform a multitude of tasks which should have been placed upon the stronger shoulders of men.

They are compelled to assume these burdens as there were *no men* to take them. They have struggled and suffered, and many of them have been compelled to come home broken in body and spirit because of the heavy tasks which were laid upon them.[19]

Flower, always practical in his administrative approach, expressed concern for the welfare of the single women missionaries and the future of the enterprise.

The Effect of War on Missionaries

Since the Assemblies of God organized just before World War I, events naturally affected the work of foreign missions. The new organization advocated loyalty to the government, but opposed participation in the war effort "because of the unswerving conviction that this holocaust was the unmistakable prelude to the Second Coming."[20]

Numerous difficulties faced prospective missionaries who attempted to leave the United States for foreign missions service during the war years. Often passports took months to get. Young male missionaries needed draft exemption and clearance from their district boards before leaving the country. Departure times for ships were often changed and guarded with secrecy. (Once a ship left port, many prayed that it would not be torpedoed.) All this red tape led to additional expenses, which had not been anticipated.

Difficulties did not diminish after the war ended. Rising prices, high rents, difficulties in getting homes for missionaries abroad, and new restrictions on independent missionaries in the territories of the British Empire served only to increase the pressures on the infant Assemblies of God Foreign Missions Department. (The restrictions on independent missionaries led several Pentecostal missionaries to seek General Council endorsement to reach India.) By 1920, fifty newly endorsed missionaries waited for sufficient funds to go overseas. Because of the increased financial strain on the organization, further endorsements were withheld until "our offerings measure up with the consecration of the workers."[21]

Missiological Perspectives

Several Scripture verses, frequently cited in early Assemblies of

God publications, reveal the theological motivation that impelled these people to risk the hazards of overseas missionary work:

> [Jesus] said unto them, Go ye into all the world, and preach the gospel to every creature. . . . And these signs shall follow them that believe; In my name shall they cast out devils; they shall speak with new tongues; they shall take up serpents; and if they drink any deadly thing, it shall not hurt them; they shall lay hands on the sick, and they shall recover (Mark 16:15,17,18).

> This gospel of the kingdom shall be preached in all the world for a witness unto all nations; and then shall the end come (Matthew 24:14).

> Ye shall receive power, after that the Holy Ghost is come upon you: and ye shall be witnesses unto me both in Jerusalem, and in all Judea, and in Samaria, and unto the uttermost parts of the earth (Acts 1:8).

These verses, favorites of Assemblies of God and other Pentecostal missionaries because of their appeal to apostolic practices, show the strong link between their view of the baptism in the Holy Spirit as an enduement of power for Christian witness, the expectancy of signs and wonders to follow the proclamation of the gospel to the uninitiated, the imminent premillennial return of Jesus Christ, and their own work. Identification with the beliefs, practices, and successes of the early Christian church shows in Assemblies of God preaching and teaching. Flower reported to the General Council meeting in 1920 that "the vision of our Pentecostal missionaries is becoming more clarified and it is realized we have a distinctive mission in the world, differing from that of all other people. An apostolic ministry in apostolic power and fulness is the aim of our Pentecostal Missionaries and God is signally blessing as they have dared to launch out and trust God."[22]

Many missionaries believed, as had other evangelicals before them, such as A. B. Simpson, that the world would need to be evangelized "to the uttermost parts" before Christ's return. This effectively placed the responsibility for bringing Christ back to earth on the shoulders of His followers. One missionary to West Africa, J. Wilbur Taylor, pleaded with his listeners by stating, "Friends, you cannot keep Jesus waiting any longer; you cannot afford it."[23] Grace Agar, an early Assemblies of God missionary to China and formerly affiliated with the Christian and Missionary Alliance, believed that every Christian had the responsibility to evangelize the heathen. She charged that "our going will hasten the Coming of Christ. He is waiting for a people to be gathered for Himself out of the world. We can help gather them out and thus hasten His Coming. The longer He delays, the more people will be born and they are being born faster than they are being saved."[24] This belief received widespread acceptance in the Assemblies of God and remained popular for many years.

Reports circulated widely through various Pentecostal publications that signs and wonders were indeed following the preaching of the gospel by Spirit-baptized missionaries. Stories recounted scores of miraculous healings and also incidents of people being raised from the dead. Walter Clifford, an early missionary, reported making a divine healing tour through South India and Ceylon and seeing scores of people healed of various ailments.[25] Marie Stephany, a missionary to China after 1916, citing Mark 16:17, wrote:

> Thank God, we have seen signs following the preaching of the gospel in China. The Lord has given the gift of healing to some of the native evangelists and pastors. A native pastor who has charge of one of the outstations has prayed for hopeless cases, one a man who had been an invalid from rheumatism for five years. As he was prayed for he was able to get up and make his own living. . . . Because of these many healings people were attracted to the services and the chapel had to be enlarged.[26]

The numerous conversions that followed the reported healings, deliverances (from opium addiction, etc.), and exorcisms confirmed to the missionaries the validity of their theology.

As early as the third meeting of the General Council, in Chicago, October 1915, the organization went on record as promoting the evangelization of the heathen according to New Testament methods.[27] Not until the 1921 General Council meeting in St. Louis, however, would the methods be more carefully defined. The Council instructed the Foreign Missions Department (the Foreign Missions Committee and the missionary personnel) to be guided by the following New Testament practices:

> First. The missionary work of the Council shall be on the

"Co-operative faith" basis, viz., the missionaries, the Foreign Missions Committee and the home constituency shall look to God together to supply the needs of the work. Publicity will be given to the needs of the field through the printed page and by word of mouth, leaving the results with God. Furthermore, the work at home and abroad shall be conducted on a cash basis. Debts will not be incurred and the work shall be undertaken only as funds are available.

Second. The Pauline example will be followed so far as possible, by seeking out neglected regions where the gospel has not yet been preached, lest we build upon another's foundation (Rom. 15:20).

Third. It shall be our purpose to seek to establish self-supporting, self-propagating and self-governing native churches.

Fourth. The system of supporting missions and missionaries shall be based on the principle outlined in Acts 4:34,35, which principle found favor by the apostles and was put into operation by the early church in caring for its poor. This system is based on the principle of a common fund, placed in the hands of a committee for distribution among those who are eligible, according to the needs. . . .

Fifth. If funds are needed for the support of native workers . . . [n]o offerings for the native workers shall be sent direct to the natives, but to the missionaries in charge of the station. The native workers should receive a call from God for the work, just as do the missionaries who go from the home base. When necessary, the training of these native workers should include industrial or agricultural work so that they will not look to the missionaries for their support, nor be actuated by the love of money in their choice of Christian service. All native workers should be moved alone by a direct call from God and a burning desire to bring Christ to their own people.

Sixth. The Foreign Missions Committee shall define proper standards for training and testing of candidates about their call and qualifications for foreign service, as the needs of the work shall require.

Whereas, The above policy will of necessity require some adjustment of existing conditions in order to bring it into operation, it is understood that in the carrying out of the above policy, it shall be considered by the Foreign Missions Committee as the ideal toward which we are working.[28]

This ideal toward which the missions program would strive reflects the practical concerns of the leadership, observations about apostolic and ecclesiastical practices in New Testament times, and the widespread impact of writers, such as Nevius and Allen, supporting the establishment of indigenous churches on the mission fields. As stated in chapter 3, the influence of A. B. Simpson also shaped this ideal.

Building Indigenous Churches

The clearest dependence on the writings of Roland Allen, author of *Missionary Methods: St. Paul's or Ours?* (1912), can be seen in a three-part article written for *The Pentecostal Evangel* entitled "Paul's Missionary Methods" by Alice E. Luce, a former missionary to India and currently ministering to Hispanics in the United States. Citing her dependence on Allen, Luce strongly advocated the development of self-supporting, self-governing, and self-propagating churches on the foreign fields.[29]

Another early practitioner of the indigenous church principles as described by the "Three Selfs" was Henry C. Ball, a missionary to Hispanics in Texas. Ball's commonsense approach to missions and long-time association with Alice E. Luce prompted him constantly to seek new ways to evangelize the Latin American people. Annual conventions were held among the converts to provide fellowship and instruction. Ball began publishing *La Luz Apostolica* ("The Apostolic Light") in 1916 to propagate the gospel among the Hispanics. When political turmoil in Mexico closed the door to American missionaries he founded the Latin American Bible Institute in San Antonio, Texas, (1926) to prepare Hispanics for the ministry. Its graduates carried the message to various parts of the United States, Mexico, Spain, Nicaragua, Puerto Rico, and Cuba. James E. Richardson, a former Assemblies of God missionary to Central America, states that "this decision by Ball displays a characteristic which has become the hallmark of all missionary work of the Assemblies of God, namely adaptability or flexibility."[30] As the years passed, Ball proved to be one of the most farsighted and creative missionary strategists in the Assemblies of God.[31]

Every mission field did not move so swiftly toward the ideal of the indigenous church. Finding the opposition to Christianity especially intense in North India, many Pentecostal missionaries followed the mission-station pattern of the earlier established Protestant missions. This approach focused on setting up a mission station with a church, school, and missionary residence, and gathering a

Christian community around it. Unfortunately, with the passage of time it became a place of shelter and the nationals became absorbed in following the life-style of the missionary. The late Benjamin P. Shinde, an Indian Assemblies of God missiologist and author, concedes that this practice may have been necessary in the face of Hindu opposition, but it seriously retarded the development of a strong indigenous church leadership. In marked contrast, the work in South India, facing less opposition, attained more success in the development of an indigenous church. Founded by John H. Burgess in 1927 at Mavelikara, the Bethel Bible Institute immediately began training national clergy.[32]

The early concern for the fulfillment of Christ's Commission to evangelize the world and the accompanying desire to establish indigenous churches overseas on New Testament principles caused the missionaries to set up Bible institutes for training national clergy. As early as 1922, a Bible institute, accommodating from 50 to 60 students, was started in North China. It may have been the earliest long-term school established overseas. The school founded by John H. Burgess is the longest continuing foreign Bible institute in the Assemblies of God. Within three decades of setting up these schools, the Assemblies of God would be the leader among Protestant missions societies in the establishment and maintenance of overseas theological institutions.

Relieving the Suffering

Preaching the gospel and expecting signs and wonders to follow may have been the paramount concern, but before long some of the missionaries directed their efforts toward relieving the suffering of those around them. James and Esther Harvey, early missionaries to India, had their ministry altered by the effects of a devastating famine and the appeals of naked and starving people. Esther Harvey recalls:

> Could we preach the love of Christ to these and turn them away naked and hungry to die along the roadside? We could not. The Lord gave us Isa. 58:4–14. "Is not this the fast that I have chosen? To loose the bands of wickedness, to undo the heavy burdens, and to let the oppressed go free, and that ye break every yoke? Is it not to deal thy bread to the hungry,

and that thou bring the poor that are cast out to thy house?"
As the people came we took in those who cared to stay and
provided for them. This meant breaking their caste. To an
Indian that is a terrible thing, for they become an outcast. Most
of them would rather die than break caste. However, some
with little children preferred to stay in the Mission. We had
to build quarters for the widows' Home and houses were added
to it as our family grew. It became a home, not only for widows,
but fallen girls and wives who had been cast off. Numbers of
young women in trouble were taken in and cared for and seeing
the love of Christ manifested to them they surrendered to
Christ. Some we were able to get married to good husbands,
some dedicated their lives to God for His service and we were
able to find employment for some in Christian hospitals, etc.[33]

Better known than the work of the Harveys was the orphanage
started in Assiout, Egypt, by Lillian Trasher. Hundreds of Egyptian
youngsters found food, shelter, and instruction over the years. International acclaim eventually surrounded the institution.[34]

In these early years, the missionaries, largely unsupervised, followed what they believed to be the leading of the Holy Spirit. Thus,
when charitable institutions were begun, their continuance depended on the missionary's certainty that he had been directed by
the Holy Spirit to enter this kind of activity; financial support was
often uncertain. Following World War II, the missions department,
by then able to assert more of a leadership role, strongly pushed
for the implementation of indigenous churches in accord with the
original ideal of missions activity, although not to the exclusion of
institutional work.

Faith Healing

The early missionaries, reflecting the theology of A. B. Simpson,
David Wesley Myland, and other early Pentecostal advocates of
faith healing for physical ailments, often rejected any use of drugs,
serums, or medical treatment. Grace Agar recalled:

Knowing that I was going to the border of Tibet and not
expecting to have any doctors in case of sickness, I definitely
took the Lord as my Physician. He has kept me in health and
strength for the past 38 years. He has protected me from all
harm, from accidents on ice, slippery roads, from robbers, wild

beasts and from epidemics so common in China. I have proved
it true that the "Angel of the Lord encampeth round about
them that fear Him and delivereth them." Ps.34:7.[35]

Others did not fare so well. Christian Schoonmaker, a former Alliance missionary to India and later serving there with the Assemblies of God, died of smallpox in 1919. He refused vaccination because of his strong convictions on faith healing.[36]

Eventually, moderating voices prevailed and missionaries often
submitted to vaccinations and medical treatment. When Flower was
serving as missionary secretary (1919–1923), a party of six missionaries traveled from Leopoldville to Stanleyville, in the Belgian Congo.
The Belgian authorities refused to allow them to travel farther because they didn't have an adequate supply of quinine. They wrote
to Flower to explain their dilemma and affirm their belief in faith
healing. The letter took three months to reach Springfield, Missouri.
Flower responded: "Trust in God, praying with all your might, and
go ahead and take the quinine."[37] By 1925, passing a physical examination became a requirement for overseas ministry.

The Role of the Local Church

During these early years the missionaries were closely attached
to the local church or churches that had promised them support.
Since few Council policies existed which governed overseas ministry, the missionaries and their supporting congregations enjoyed
considerable freedom in the directing of their endeavors. Loyalty
and submission to the policies of the Foreign Missions Department
did not supersede the bond of the missionary to the local church
for some time.

Not surprisingly, Council members linked the success of the missionaries with the faith and support of the home churches. Numerous
writers and speakers stressed the necessity of supporting the missionary enterprise. Spiritual stagnation in local churches allegedly
resulted from their failure to properly perceive their responsibility
for assisting the evangelization of the heathen, according to Christian
Schoonmaker. In contrast to this condition, churches could be assured of spiritual vitality and growth when actively supporting missions.[38]

The Carl and John Juergensen families arrived for ministry in Japan before the General Council of the Assemblies of God organized. Later affiliating with the Council, they served in Japan for many years. In the above photograph, they are conducting street evangelism. The man in the back row at the far right is Carl F. Juergensen. In front of him stand his two daughters, Marie (left) and Agnes (right). Also in the front row, second from left, is his son, John. Beside John is his wife, Esther (Kelchner), and his baby daughter, Grace Marie.

Lillian Trasher traveled to Egypt as a missionary and opened the Assiout Orphanage in 1911 for homeless children and widows. The above photograph was taken during the earlier years of her work.

A pioneer missionary to South Africa, Mrs. Anna Richards-Scoble is pictured teaching an open-air class of women in 1923.

At his desk as the first field secretary for Latin America and the West Indies, Henry C. Ball was an early missionary to the Hispanics of Texas.

Alice E. Luce (pictured ca. 1940), formerly a missionary to India with the Church Missionary Society, joined the General Council in 1915. She had a marked influence on the development of an indigenous work among Hispanics in North America.

Edgar Pettenger was an early Assemblies of God missionary to the blacks in the Republic of South Africa. Here he is pictured with African leaders in the East Rand in 1947.

Assemblies of God missionaries opened the country of Upper Volta (now Burkina Faso) to Protestant mission work in 1924 and translated the Bible into the language of the Mossi tribe. Seated at the table (left to right), missionaries Florence Smith, Cuba Hall, and Jenny and Arthur E. Wilson, in their translation work, consult with Mossi tribesmen.

6

Administrative and Structural Developments

The administrative and structural development of the foreign missions program of the Assemblies of God from 1914 to 1926 can be divided into three periods: (1) supervision by the Executive Presbytery, the highest administrative board in the Council: 1914–1919; (2) establishment of a separate department under the direction of J. Roswell Flower: 1919–1923; and (3) the administration of William M. Faux: 1923–1926.

Supervision by the Executive Presbytery: 1914–1919

From the first two meetings of the General Council in April and November 1914, the Executive Presbytery administered the foreign missions program. The chairman of the Council apparently served as director of the program by virtue of his office, although Flower, the secretary, served in this capacity by 1919.[1] The responsibilities of the Presbytery up to 1917 largely consisted of publicizing the needs of missionaries through the pages of *The Pentecostal Evangel* and distributing the funds to the designated recipients. E. N. Bell, editor of *The Christian Evangel* (later *The Pentecostal Evangel*) and first chairman of the General Council, wrote that all monies forwarded to his office for missionaries would be sent "without charging a cent for postage, cost of drafts, or time consumed in taking care of this phase of the work."[2] This established a long-term policy of forwarding 100 percent of all missionary offerings to the missionaries.

Financial integrity with missionary funds remained a high priority because of the sacred imperative for which they were given. Members of local churches were urged to give sacrificially and consistently to missions. The missionary treasurer, Stanley H. Frodsham, accepted Liberty Bonds and jewelry, which were converted into legal tender and forwarded to the missionaries. Numerous stories, exhibiting sacrificial giving, appeared on the pages of *The Pentecostal Evangel*. One woman, for example, wrote: "Please send this, the Lord's money, to the most needy missionary you know of. How I wish it were more, but it comes from a cheerful heart. I did want to give something to these dear ones so badly. I just asked Father to make my hens lay so I could give money to the missionaries. I told Him I would give all of it, so here it is."[3] Sunday school children in Frostburg, Maryland, gave up their Christmas festivities to send $20 for missions.[4] The Council needed roughly $3,000 every month to meet the missionary budget.

Before long, however, Bell reported to the organization that untrustworthy persons, at home and abroad, were soliciting local churches and receiving offerings from them. At the same time, he attested that the financial integrity of the General Council could be trusted since the missionary treasurer was responsible to the Executive Presbytery and every dollar contributed received public notice in the *Evangel*, ensuring that the entire offering reached the intended recipient. Bell could boast, "Everything is open and above board. Nothing is done in a corner. No secrets about what was received or what has gone with it."[5] Financial integrity resulted in the increased confidence of the local churches in the Council office. Even offerings to non-Council missionaries were dutifully sent out.[6]

The 1915 session of the General Council proposed three policies for achieving New Testament principles in their overseas evangelism. First, approval for overseas ministry would require an examination of the candidate by the Council leaders. Evidence of a "full" New Testament salvation (presumably including the Pentecostal baptism), a definite call to the mission field, and overall fitness (physical, mental, and spiritual) would have to be supplied. The earliest application form contained just 18 questions. Besides requiring routine information and questions about one's Pentecostal baptism, doctrinal views, and present ministry, it asked: "Do you trust God for your support?"[7] The second policy adopted by the Council made the missionaries responsible to their local churches and in turn held that they should receive faithful contributions. This policy reflects the largely congregational form of church government evident in the early years of the Council. The third policy stated that local assemblies should continue their support of a missionary while he was on furlough and the missionary should be encouraged to visit them to present the needs of his field.[8]

To better understand the needs of the missionaries, the hope was that Executive Presbyters would travel widely at home and abroad. Although some presbyters may have surveyed the churches at home, there is no record of any of them traveling overseas. Council funds were not sufficient for travel abroad.

Through 1915 and 1916, the Council reeled from the growing schism over the New Issue (Oneness doctrine). At the 1916 meeting of the Council, a Statement of Fundamental Truths proposed to settle the matter won approval. Article 9 of the Statement, "The Ministry and Evangelism," declared: "A divinely called and a scripturally ordained ministry for the evangelization of the world, is the command of the Lord, and the chief concern of the Church."[9] The following year, the Council ruled that all missionary candidates would have to agree with Statement of Fundamental Truths, presumably because the New Issue had stirred controversy on some mission fields, notably China. In addition, every outgoing missionary would need endorsement and a certificate of appointment. Prospective missionaries often ignored endorsement and certification as they ventured overseas, since the Council had promised to forward all designated offerings anyway.

Many realized in 1917 that the efficient administration of the foreign missions program required serious attention. There was urgent need of a corresponding secretary, a supervising committee, and a policy for handling the distribution of undesignated funds. The General Council recognized this need by approving the appointment of a study committee to suggest proposals.

The committee responded with several recommendations that won approval on the Council floor. First, missionaries overseas could set up their own overseas district councils and elect general presbyters to represent their interests to the Council.[10] Second, a foreign missions committee could serve the missions program more efficiently than the contemporary operation. Third, the post of corresponding secretary was suggested.

A missionary nominating committee then presented seven nominees who were subsequently approved to serve on this new committee: John W. Welch, Arch P. Collins, E. N. Bell, Stanley H.

Frodsham, George N. Eldridge, William W. Simpson, and Susan C. Easton. Two were missionaries (Simpson and Easton) and three had formerly been affiliated with the Christian and Missionary Alliance (Welch, Eldridge, and Simpson), again reflecting the continuing influence of that body on the Council.

Another adopted proposal stipulated that undesignated funds should be sent to approved and successful missionaries. Those who could not sign the Statement of Fundamental Truths or were "inefficient" in their labors forfeited any assistance from this fund.

The Council also adopted guidelines for the conduct of missionary work. Prospective missionaries needed to have a certificate of fellowship with the Council, agree with its doctrinal tenets, file a full report of their work, and submit quarterly reports to the Foreign Missions Committee to ensure the equitable distribution of undesignated funds. Missionaries abroad could elect advisory committees of three to determine and report to the Foreign Missions Committee what constituted an adequate term of service. When on furlough, missionaries would be expected to consult with the committee about their itinerary in order to avoid overlapping with their fellow missionaries and to reach as many local churches as possible. The committee was also concerned about consulting with them about financial arrangements.[11]

With its establishment that year, the Foreign Missions Committee received authority (1) to require that overseas properties, purchased with missions funds, be transferred to the General Council; (2) to instruct prospective missionaries to take two years of language study and additional courses of study; and (3) to appoint a visiting representative to survey the work for its increased coordination and effectiveness.[12] Years would pass before the committee and the later department could enforce many of these regulations. However, these proposals reflected the leadership's attempts to bring order to the program; they recognized the need for stability. As one writer observed:

> What we have to lament these days is the unpreparedness of candidates for the fields, and the imperfect criterion of what that preparedness demands. . . . Looseness and irresponsibility is dangerous and usually results in disaster on the mission field where the missionary forces are militant forces, and can only be successfully directed in the campaign in these vast

fields of foe when there is a disposition to form a rank and file
and conform to divinely appointed plans and directorship. [13]

The 1918 meeting of the General Council in Springfield, Missouri,
witnessed few important policy changes and recommendations in
the area of foreign missions. Two of the resolutions from the Foreign
Missions Committee's recommendations (quarterly reports and
transfer of missionary property) received slight modifications. A major change took place with the resolution that the Executive Presbytery constitute the Foreign Missions Committee. Apparently the
seven-member committee appointed by the previous Council had
proved unworkable. The geographical distance between the various
members of the group may have been a factor in making regular
meetings impossible. [14]

Before adjournment, the Council recommended that a series of
Bible and missionary conferences be held in various locations
throughout the country under the direction of the Council chairman.
Finally, to heed the Great Commission, the Council stated that
every assembly should take up a monthly offering for the support
of the Council's missionaries.

The Council session at Chicago the next year marked a milestone
in the history of the missions program: the establishment of a distinct
missionary department under the supervision of the Executive Presbytery. With this move, the Council put in place the first department in its organizational structure. The department's support was
to come from offerings taken by the churches to assist with its
expenses. Although the new department was to be responsible for
pioneer church evangelism, or home missions, in the United States,
it would focus its attention primarily on foreign missions. J. Roswell
Flower was elected to serve as the first missionary secretary-
treasurer (i.e., head of the department).

The Council also authorized the establishment of a Missionary
Rest Home in Evanston, Illinois; reaffirmed the policy of sending
100 percent of all designated and undesignated funds to the missionaries; and encouraged missionaries to settle down overseas in
permanent locations and learn the national language. In addition,
the Council approved rules for the travel and beginning ministry of
women missionaries and set up a special fund to support Hispanic
missions.

The Council moreover encouraged "the establishment of schools for the education of duly accredited native workers, in the various fields where practicable, also schools for the education of the young children of missionaries where possible."[15] In response to pressure from the missionaries for a missionary representative to survey the work overseas, as the Foreign Missions Committee had originally stipulated, the Council authorized the General Presbytery to make such arrangements.[16]

The Administration of J. Roswell Flower: 1919–1923

When J. Roswell Flower took office as missionary secretary-treasurer in the fall of 1919, he faced the unenviable task of coordinating the activities of 206 independently oriented missionaries, sending monies overseas that had reached $63,548.59 (up from $4,879.50 in 1916), endorsing an ever-growing number of prospective missionaries, and taking care of various lesser administrative responsibilities—all this with the assistance of one secretary and an uncertain budget. John W. Welch, the chairman at the 1920 meeting of the Council, reported that the missionary enterprise appeared to be unbalanced, "there being more missionaries on the field, and ready to go, than the present development of the home fields would seem to warrant sending out, which condition is sufficient reason for giving special attention to the consideration of the Missionary policy and plans of the Council."[17] Concerned for the welfare of the missionaries and the progress of the program, Flower proved to be a wise choice for the post.

As he began his tenure of office, Flower faced the topsy-turvy arrangement of financial support for the missions department that the Council had adopted. Pledge cards had been introduced at the 1918 Council to encourage members to give regularly to missions, and contributions steadily increased. Between 1919 and 1920, giving increased by 43 percent, to $90,812.40. Nevertheless, the operation of the department itself depended on contributions specifically designated for that purpose. Apparently most people, inspired by specific missionary speakers, were more inclined to support individual missionaries than to send money to the headquarters of the organization to cover the problem of administrative expenses. Because of the Council's policy of sending 100 percent of all designated and undesignated missionary offerings overseas, the financial expenses of administration would plague the Council for many years.

As an immediate solution, the Council subsidized the Foreign Missions Department with earnings from Gospel Publishing House. The sale of subscriptions to *The Pentecostal Evangel* also assisted the department. Flower wrote that "in the old days it was a small matter for the publishing house to carry this missionary feature of the work. A few missionary offerings were received each day and were acknowledged by card. At the end of the month a part of the day was set apart for forwarding these funds to the field. . . . This work was not considered a great burden."[18] However, the coming of World War I and the growing size of the missionary force brought greater demands for personnel and finances in the Foreign Missions Department. This strained the budget of the publishing house. Chairman Welch wrote that the burden had become so great that the local churches needed to send in designated offerings for the support of the missions department.[19]

Seeing the need for change, Flower soon proposed to the Council, meeting in 1920, a major overhaul of the financial structure of the missions program. Previously, every missionary, claiming to be called of God, assumed almost the entire responsibility for raising the necessary financial support of his own work. If approved by the department, the missionary's endorsement followed and he headed overseas. This arrangement required minimum departmental work, since the department simply forwarded the designated offerings. Remaining alert to what other agencies for the distribution of missionary funds (e.g., the office of *The Latter Rain Evangel*) were sending the missionaries, the missionary secretary-treasurer would divide the undesignated funds as equitably as possible every month. A missionary could expect to receive an average of $20 to $25 a month from this source. Thus, "the foreign missionary has no interference in his faith life. If the offerings from the Treasurer are not adequate for his needs, he can pray through and trust the Lord to meet his need from other quarters."[20]

Flower soon identified major weaknesses with the policy of distributing funds. First, offerings varied from month to month, creating hardships for the recipients. Second, this system left no reserve fund for emergencies (e.g., bringing home the infirm, helping prospective missionaries to get overseas, building mission stations, costs for the education of missionary children, expenses for providing rest periods overseas). Third, because many churches and individuals sent funds directly overseas, the missionary secretary-treasurer had no way of knowing how much money a missionary received. The secretary-treasurer's careful attempts to equitably distribute funds could easily be thwarted.

The new policy he proposed stressed supporting missions rather than missionaries. Accordingly, "it will mean concentration of forces, only sending to the field those missionaries that we can be assured of safely supporting, building mission stations, etc."[21] After considerable discussion at the 1920 General Council session in Springfield, the missionaries and delegates in attendance rejected Flower's proposal in favor of the current policy.

Despite questions over the financial policy, missionary contributions steadily climbed during 1920 and reached a total of $107,953.55 on September 1, 1921, even though the country suffered from a business depression and widespread unemployment. At the same time, monthly giving was erratic. The offerings in April 1921 reached a peak of $12,341.29, but in May plummeted to a low of $6,653.44

Missionary support dipped 3.5 percent by 1922. However, by 1923, giving had skyrocketed 37.33 percent, passing $140,000. The outlook for the equitable distribution of funds looked better as well and the new goal of $40 per month for each missionary, and $15 for every child, and meeting various other missions expenses seemed promising. Besides travel funds for each missionary (estimated to be $500 whether traveling to or from a field) and the expenses of each mission station, Flower figured that a budget of $233,800 needed to be raised annually. It would take nearly 10 years to reach this goal.[22]

In spite of the increased giving, Flower informed the Council in 1923 that offerings for the expenses of the department had reached only $4,405.88, an increase of only $379 over the previous year. The giving for the department represented only 3 percent of all the money given to missions. At least 6 to 8 percent was necessary for the efficient operation of the national office. Flower reported that

> when the magnitude of the work is considered, the large number of fields we are developing, the large number of mission-

aries who must be provided for, the purchase of goods to be shipped to missionaries, arrangement for passage to and from the fields, editorial work on the *Evangel,* etc., the marvel is that the work has been carried on as well as it has been. Few have considered the fact that we have developed the equivalent of a $150,000 a year business with three hundred agencies located on forty different fields. Such a business cannot be efficiently managed with the [present] small office force. . . .[23]

Recognizing the increased workload of the department, J. Narver Gortner, chairman of the committee on nominations, recommended that the office of missionary secretary-treasurer be divided into two offices, and the new missionary secretary direct the program. This met with approval and the Council elected William M. Faux, principal of the Beulah Heights Bible and Missionary Training School in North Bergen, New Jersey, as secretary and Flower as treasurer. To support the enlarged staff, appeals continued to be made for the churches to designate special offerings for departmental expenses.

The years from 1919 to 1923 witnessed other significant developments in the missions enterprise. Following the directive of a previous Council meeting, the substance of which had been recommended by the Foreign Missions Committee, the Executive Presbyters authorized Harold K. Needham, a well-known minister in the organization, to make a tour of the mission fields and report his findings to the leadership. It had been hoped that the Council could provide for the expenses of Needham and his wife, but funds were not any more available than they had been for the executive presbyters; the Needhams had to raise their own support. The journey took over a year (1920–1921); Needham visited the missionaries in Japan, China, India, Egypt, and Palestine. Mrs. (Huldah) Needham died while they were in India.

Needham's report proved to be less than complimentary about some missions activities. He lamented that contention and individualism had brought havoc to some mission fields. Rather than finding the missionaries united spiritually and working together, in some places he discovered "duplications of work, missionaries bumping elbows with each other, chaffing [sic] under the circumstances and bringing friction between the native constituencies. At the same time wide expanses of territory in surrounding districts were wholly unevangelized and untouched."[24] However, the greater importance of the trip lay in the fact that for the first time the Council had sent a representative to survey and evaluate the progress of its missions enterprise.

At the 1921 General Council meeting, Needham urged Council ministers to take more time with prospective candidates to determine their fitness for missionary service before recommending them as missionaries. He also urged that every candidate should acquire Bible institute training, both for the value of the instruction and the lessons of living and working with others. It was Needham's observation that better preparation or first proving oneself in successful ministry at home would eliminate the waste of funds used to send a missionary out only to have him return home. Needham further felt that the adoption of his proposals would inspire a spirit of confidence in the missions work of the Council.[25]

New policy guidelines, previously discussed, received adoption at the Council meeting. These new policies pointed out the necessity of following the Pauline example of evangelism and for establishing indigenous churches overseas. They empowered the Foreign Missions Committee to set standards for the training and screening of prospective missionaries. They also placed more responsibility on the shoulders of the local churches for the care of the missionaries. Designated as a "Co-operative faith" basis, "the missionaries, the Foreign Missions Committee and the home constituency shall look to God together to supply the needs of the work."[26]

In February 1923, Flower announced that since the current Foreign Missions Committee had never personally met most of the missionary candidates, everyone seeking endorsement by the Council would be required to visit with the Committee at its headquarters in Springfield, Missouri. This guaranteed that the candidate would become acquainted with the Foreign Missions Committee and Council procedures; he also recommended that those considering missions work attend the newly established Central Bible Institute. Flower urged furloughed missionaries to visit the headquarters to improve communication and clear up any misunderstandings and difficulties that correspondence could not resolve.

Later in the year, Flower reported that the new Council missions policies had greatly improved the whole missions program. An increasing number of better trained, more cooperative, and more responsible missionaries served overseas. The Foreign Missions Department was also encouraging the evangelization of several new fields as a priority.

Not every missionary, however, had cheerfully accepted the new policies. Several withdrew to continue their work in an independent fashion, unhampered by the new guidelines. Flower attributed their departure to the disruption of the old ways and methods by newer and more efficient ones. In his words, "there can be no backward move in our missionary policy. We must continue to go right straight ahead. Our vision must comprehend more than a personal interest in a few missionaries of our acquaintance. We must get the vision of the millions who are lost. . . ."[27]

Individualism slowly began to decline as cooperative activities increased. The new policies clearly indicated the department's ideals of, and urgency for, missionary evangelism. Flower articulated this view of the distinctive nature of Pentecostal missions by writing:

> Pentecostal missionaries have a holy calling. They cannot follow the methods of non-Pentecostals who have gone before. Neither can they bend their efforts in building up charitable institutions, hospitals, and schools. Pentecostal missionaries have a Pentecostal commission—to be witnesses in Jerusalem, in Judea, and to the uttermost parts of the earth. Witnesses![28]

This concern for evangelism motivated missionaries to begin establishing Bible institutes overseas to train leaders for indigenous churches. By the mid-1920s, missionaries had set up Bible institutes in each region of major endeavor: China, India, Japan, Egypt, and Liberia.

Each of these regions was organized into a district council during Flower's administration, a major development in Assemblies of God foreign missions. At this time, the councils represented only missionary personnel and not the national ministers of the respective fields. Later, indigenous councils of national ministers replaced these organizations. Missionaries serving in these areas were subject to the supervision of their respective councils.[29] These organizational structures, together with stricter policies, provided for better regulation of missionary activities.[30]

The Administration of William M. Faux: 1923–1926

Upon dividing departmental responsibilities between a missionary secretary (director) and treasurer, the Council turned to William Faux, principal of the Beulah Heights Bible and Missionary Training School in North Bergen, New Jersey, one of the leading missionary training centers of the organization. Faux's credentials included membership in the Council since 1914 (previously he had been a Baptist pastor), college and seminary education and, more recently, leadership at Beulah Heights. Highly regarded by his students at the school, he nevertheless accepted the call to move to Springfield and head the Foreign Missions Department. Faux's tenure in this office, however, proved to be stormy.

Faux followed through with the recently adopted Council mission policies. He pushed ardently for cooperative efforts on the mission fields and condemned the activities of independent missionaries by arguing that this approach was "unscriptural, inefficient, rank self-ishness, and criminal."[31] He was concerned about the establishment of Bible institutes overseas for building the national churches; therefore, he commissioned John H. Burgess in 1925 to start such a school in South India. The Bethel Bible Institute that Burgess founded is the oldest existing theological institution of the Assemblies of God abroad.

More than many others, Faux recognized the necessity of his office having firsthand knowledge of the foreign fields and promoting missionary needs at home. At the request of missionaries in India, Faux traveled to that country, as well as Egypt, Palestine, and Syria, taking the latter part of 1924 and a portion of the next year. Faux anticipated that the trip would take 6 months and he ardently hoped that funds would become available to take his wife along. The proposal met with criticism because of the perennially strained finances of the department. He finally made the trip alone. As a result of visiting the missionaries and seeing their work, he found that some of his convictions about the missions enterprise deepened and others radically changed.

To the 1925 General Council session, Faux reported his observations about the difficulties missionaries faced and praised them for their dedication and loyalty. He also strongly condemned independent missionary efforts and encouraged cooperative efforts with other Pentecostal workers, notably in India.[32] In a later article in the *Evangel,* Faux presented other conclusions he had drawn: the need for wise supervision on the mission fields and the importance of training indigenous national clergy. Thus, "with a Bible training school in North India, South India, and Egypt, turning out Bible trained native workers, thousands of souls could be won for Christ. The need is imperative for such institutions. . . ."[33]

The missionary treasurer, J. Roswell Flower, also informed the 1925 Council that missions giving had increased; he felt this reflected the increased confidence that the constituency had in the department. The actual funding of the department's expenses continued to be a problem, especially with the addition of a new officer. Without a grant of $300 from the Executive Presbytery in 1924, the department would have ended the year with a deficit. At this Council, Flower's tenure as missionary treasurer came to an end. These duties were then assumed by the general treasurer of the Council.

After his return from the mission fields, Faux continued to travel for the department. He visited mission stations in Mexico and attended the Latin American Convention in Laredo, Texas, in 1925. He also urged starting a Bible institute in San Antonio or another suitable location for training Hispanic pastors. It was with his blessing that Henry C. Ball took up this task and started the Latin American Bible Institute in San Antonio a year later. Characteristic of his approach to promotion, Faux took advantage of a new medium—the slide projector—to enhance his presentations of missionary information in his travels.

Another innovation by Faux to promote foreign missions was his encouragement of missions conventions in local churches. When missionary George M. Kelly returned from China, Faux asked him to conduct conventions in Alabama, Georgia, Mississippi, and Florida. After a year of this the value of such missionary itineraries for the promotion of the work became obvious. Consequently, similar plans were made for other furloughed missionaries.

Faux's plans came to a stop in December 1926. The other executive officers of the General Council charged him with misappropriation of funds for personal use. Although faced with incriminating evidence, Faux denied any complicity. He was discharged from office and removed as a Council minister. In spite of the severity of their action, the leaders of the Council, the records indicate, exhibited a genuine pastoral concern for Faux and his future.

The Executive Presbytery made a temporary appointment to fill the remainder of Faux's term: that of a recently hired bookkeeper in the missions department, Noel Perkin.[34]

J. Roswell Flower, a prominent leader in the Assemblies of God for many years, received appointment as the first missionary secretary-treasurer in 1919.

7

Cooperation and Popular Support

In the early years of the Assemblies of God, the independent Missionary Conference, a loose-knit association of Pentecostal missionaries, became closely linked with the General Council. This reflected the fraternal bond the Council shared with many independent missionaries. On an organizational level, the close relationship between the General Council of the Assemblies of God and the Pentecostal Assemblies of Canada with their missions program dates from this period. Overseas, Pentecostal missionaries often banded together for fellowship and ministry.

The enthusiasm on the home front for the missions program was fired by prophetic preaching and concern for the lost. Concerned to help the missionaries and the needy, Etta Calhoun began to organize Assemblies of God women for prayer and practical assistance in 1925.

The Missionary Conference

During the infant years of the foreign missions program, a little-known agency assisted in representing missionary interests. Not actually affiliated with the General Council, the Missionary Conference represented itself as "the general missionary body working in the interest of all Pentecostal missionaries everywhere."[1]

The First Missionary Conference convened in St. Louis in 1917 at the close of the General Council meeting. In fact, the chairman of the Council urged that the business matters end as soon as possible so the auditorium would be available for the missionaries. The conference came into existence because many Council and non-Council missionaries and ministers recognized "that a closer bond of fellowship, and a better understanding of the great problems which confront us along missionary lines, could be had if we could get together for a heart to heart talk concerning these matters."[2] The first gathering received such a positive response that Chairman S. A. Jamieson and Secretary Anna Reiff, who served as the editor of *The Latter Rain Evangel,* urged another such meeting. Willa B. Lowther, a missionary to China in attendance, wrote:

> I am sure you cannot realize what a blessing the steps taken by the recent meetings at St. Louis is going to be to the foreign missionaries. I am sure there is no body of people [that] suffers so much from disorganization and splits and issues as the missionaries. I believe that every missionary can say "Amen" to every one of the Resolutions passed. We are looking forward to the time when every missionary sent out to the field will come well recommended and tried at home first. Sometimes new inexperienced ones go to the field and do such unwise things before the heathen that apparently they hinder the gospel more than promote it. . . .[3]

The Second Missionary Conference occurred in May 1918 at the Stone Church in Chicago. Because many who attended were affiliated with the Assemblies of God, the Council officers who were present listened attentively. Stanley H. Frodsham, an early leader and editor of the *Evangel,* reported that Council chairman John W. Welch attended the sessions, answering questions and allaying suspicions that some held about the Council's purposes and plans; fears of organizational tyranny were widespread.[4] Daniel W. Kerr, pastor of The Pentecostal Church of Cleveland, Ohio, was elected chairman; Zella Reynolds, sister of Alice Reynolds Flower, was elected secretary. The Second Conference recommended that Pentecostal Sunday schools should be urged to collect missionary offerings through distributing little wooden barrels into which children could put their money. Gospel Publishing House promptly advertised the sale of such barrels.[5]

Many church leaders began to recognize the value of such missionary conventions. They provided opportunities for missionaries to present their needs and recount their triumphs. Laymen and pastors kept in touch with overseas developments, received inspiration to continue their support, and had a forum for proposing recommendations. However, the proposals were not binding on any organization; the delegates could only hope that their united voices would be heard.

The Third Missionary Conference convened at Kerr's church in Cleveland and approved several practical resolutions to assist the missionary effort.[6] One of them resulted in the publication of a missionary prayer calendar booklet by Gospel Publishing House prepared by Kerr. Prayer was considered of utmost importance for the missionary enterprise and the booklet would assist the missions supporters in their intercessory prayers.

As with the original conference, later conferences were usually held after the meetings of the General Council. Nevertheless, they retained their undenominational character. Many missionaries later joined the Assemblies of God because of the positive relationships they had formed with the organization during the conferences.[7] More independent missionaries joined as the foreign missions program developed, and as this occurred, the conferences outlived their usefulness. The last of at least six was held in 1921.

Cooperative Relationships

The interdenominational contact maintained by the Assemblies of God with the Foreign Missions Conference of North America provided numerous helpful services. The conference, organized in 1893, eventually included many North American missions societies. Annual meetings focused on study, discussion, and cooperative planning. In 1921, the Conference joined the newly organized International Missionary Council.[8]

In the absence of missionary secretary William M. Faux, John W. Welch, the chairman of the General Council, attended the International Missionary Council meeting in Washington, D.C., in 1925. Reflecting the conservative evangelical moorings of the Pentecostal movement and shocked by what he heard at the meeting, Welch reported to the Foreign Missions Committee in Springfield that "the church has abandoned its program of evangelism and has turned to Christian education or community salvation."[9] In the *Evangel,* Welch wrote:

> I did not imagine that the whole situation had practically turned from the idea of individual salvation into talking now about salvation as a community matter. They have not only lost the vision of individual salvation, but have gone so far from the vision of the gospel that they are actually talking boastfully

about saving the world through the great brotherhood of man. God help them![10]

Regardless of these sensitivities to the changing theological landscape among Protestants, the General Council's association with the Foreign Missions Conference continued to provide needed services for many years. This relationship did not require any doctrinal changes by the Council.

The elected leaders of the Council and many of its members had positive attitudes toward cooperative endeavors with fellow Pentecostals. Indeed, most viewed the General Council primarily as a service agency and not in any way as a denominational structure. Hence, contacts with non-Council Pentecostals were common, as the Council's contact with the Missionary Conferences illustrates. Looking at the broad range of Pentecostalism, the General Council authorized in 1921 a committee on worldwide cooperation chaired by F. A. Hale. It was appointed "with a view to calling a conference of brethren of these various branches, with the hope of reaching an agreement on a method of cooperation, and of promoting a closer bond of fellowship, and also arranging the calling of a conference for the formation of an ecumenical union of Pentecostal believers for the more perfect and rapid evangelization of the world. . . ."[11] Hale reported at the convening of the 1923 Council that due to the difficulties of meeting together personally, the committee had been able only to correspond. As a result, no meetings to form a union of Pentecostal believers were planned and the effort collapsed.[12]

The relationship with Canadian Pentecostals proved to be more productive. When the General Council began in 1914, many Canadian Pentecostals joined. For several years the Council's missionary rosters included those from Canada. However, because of legal requirements in the purchasing of overseas properties as well as other problems, the Canadians eventually organized their own missions agency.[13] With the increase in the number of Canadian congregations and the growth of their missionary efforts, the organizational relationship with the Assemblies of God in the United States came to an end in 1922. The Pentecostal Assemblies of Canada resulted from this new arrangement. Because of this change, missionary efforts were divided: the Canadian missionaries assuming primary responsibility for directing the work in the West Indies.[14]

A strong fraternal bond remained and consultation in missionary endeavors has continued through the years.

Overseas, Assemblies of God missionaries often tried to unite their efforts to increase efficiency and strengthen their work. Christian Schoonmaker, a missionary to India, dreamed of a united Pentecostal fellowship of missionaries in that country. Schoonmaker proceeded to organize such a union since "the Lord Jesus Christ wants [us] to present ourselves to the people of this land as a united company of anointed men and women, called to preach the Gospel."[15] The response proved to be positive because the missionaries could keep their ties with their sponsoring agencies while they controlled and conducted the work in India as they saw fit. But with the untimely death of Schoonmaker in 1919, the effort failed.

The missionaries' attempts at unity in Liberia, West Africa, were more successful and persevering. When Council missionary William H. Johnson arrived in 1919, he called a meeting of Pentecostal missionaries to bring about "a closer cooperation for the advancement of the work. It was the unanimous conviction that something should be done to this end."[16] Because of this conference, the Pentecostal missionaries organized as The Interior Mission of Liberia to join their efforts in evangelizing the neglected regions of the country. Even though the first elected officials held General Council membership, each member retained ties to his or her sponsoring missions agency or group of supporters.

Popular Support

To the members of the General Council, the missions program of the Assemblies of God represented much more than policies or headquarters personnel. It represented the vision of world evangelism. The real heroes and heroines were the missionaries themselves who traveled the length of the country on their furloughs, presenting their needs and relating the signs and wonders that had followed their gospel messages.

From the tiny local churches meeting in storefronts to the large missionary conferences, missionary speakers confirmed that indeed the apostolic ministry of the New Testament church had been restored in Pentecostal power. In particular, the proceedings of the General Council sessions reflected the urgency of world evangelization that underlay the whole missions enterprise. During a panel discussion at the 1916 Council, the speakers, Arch P. Collins, E. N. Richey, and T. K. Leonard, focused their addresses on the subject of evangelism. They concluded that "when we today get the burden of going into all the world as the disciples did . . . we also will be brought into great unity in the work of soul winning and God will pour out His Spirit upon us in Pentecostal fullness."[17] The Pentecostal movement as a whole reflected such evangelistic and missionary thinking.

At the 1918 Council gathering in Springfield, Missouri, the audiences heard J. R. Buckley, missionary to British East Africa, and Ada Buchwalter, missionary to China, describe their ministries. Arch P. Collins, a prominent preacher in the Council, followed their presentations by preaching on the second coming of Christ. During his sermon, he was repeatedly "stopped by the unbounded enthusiasm of his audience, and again and again the whole company of saints arose, and with holy hands upraised, worshipped and praised the Lord."[18] For the missionary offering, pledge cards were distributed; on them a member could list the amount he proposed to contribute, "by the help of the Lord, to the cause of the evangelization of the world during the coming Council year."[19]

When the Council convened in 1925, Frank M. Boyd, the principal at Central Bible Institute and a well-known Bible teacher, moved that since the Assemblies of God primarily functioned as a missionary body the evening services at the Council should begin 15 minutes earlier and the preliminaries be shortened to allow the missionaries 30 to 40 minutes with the delegates before the start of the evening evangelistic services. The delegates approved the motion.[20]

On the local level, a major development occurred during the same year with the work of Etta Calhoun in Houston, Texas. With the approval of her pastor, she organized a group of women called to meet for intercessory prayer on behalf of the missionaries. Soon they expanded their activities to include practical assistance. The first project undertaken by these women provided clothes for 300 children at Lillian Trasher's orphanage at Assiout, Egypt.[21]

By August 1925, Calhoun's venture had met with such success that the Texico (Texas and New Mexico) District Council voted to invite her to organize the Women's Missionary Council to assist it "in the great missionary enterprises of the church as well as carrying forward our own work among the prisons, the sick, and the poor of our own land." Calhoun was then asked to be president of the new district agency (she had already proven her leadership capabilities in the Women's Christian Temperance Union).

The Women's Missionary Council proved so successful at the district level that in the 1925 meeting at Eureka Springs, Arkansas, the General Council gave it national recognition.[22] In 1951, the General Council authorized the establishment of the national department of the Women's Missionary Council since by that time 27 other chapters had been organized at the district level. Edith Whipple became the first national secretary of this department.[23]

Over the years the Women's Missionary Council (more recently known as the Women's Ministries Department) gave valuable assistance to the foreign missions program. In addition to sending funds to the foreign fields, the department, through its district and local chapters, provided clothing, Christmas packages, quilts, household furnishings, and other essential items for the missionaries. National ministers, orphans, and lepers have also benefited from their generosity.

Conclusion

During the first 12 years of the General Council, the foreign missions program slowly organized the independent efforts of numerous missionaries abroad into a more cooperative approach.

The ideal of establishing indigenous Pentecostal churches overseas had existed from the beginning of the Council, but it was not until 1921 that this goal was stated more clearly. Its application overseas, however, met with opposition from the missionaries on some occasions. In spite of the hardships, more and more missionary candidates applied for ministry abroad to bring the ideal to fruition.

Widespread recognition of the distinctiveness of Pentecostal missions prevailed among the members of the Council. The gospel, they believed, would be followed by "signs and wonders" in demonstration of Pentecostal power. In their view, the apostolic church had been restored in "the last days."

Funding for the program skyrocketed during these early years as popular support grew. But the problem of financing the administrative expenses of the department at home continued to vex the leadership of the Council.

At first the administrative responsibility of the program rested with the Executive Presbytery. But as its workload grew and the missions program expanded, the Presbytery created the Foreign Missions Department to handle the increasing responsibilities. This move initiated an important transitional period in the development of the whole missions program. J. Roswell Flower headed the new department from 1919 to 1923. During his administration, the Council more precisely defined its goals of world evangelization and the ideal of the indigenous church.

The missions department's initial responsibility was to disburse funds that it received, but gradually it came to provide some leadership and direction to the enterprise. William M. Faux, successor to Flower from 1923 to 1926, established the precedent of traveling abroad to secure firsthand information about conditions on the mission fields and aggressively promoting the work at home. Faux's administration was brief, but he started several important developments. With the coming of Noel Perkin in December 1926, a steady hand had arrived at the helm. A long, stable period of growth would follow.

In 1926 Maynard Ketcham began a long and distinguished ministry as a missionary to India and the Far East. He served as field secretary for the Far East from 1955 to 1969. Here he is on a motor launch (ca. 1959) purchased with funds contributed by church members in America.

Etta Calhoun organized the first local chapter of the Women's Missionary Council in 1925 in Houston, Texas. This photograph (the only known picture of her in existence) was taken 10 years later, when she was 65.

Part Three

The Maturing Years
(1927–1942)

8

Noel Perkin and Departmental Changes

The Foreign Missions Department entered a long era of stability and growth in 1927. To some extent, this condition resulted from the wise and farsighted leadership of Noel Perkin, who had received permanent appointment as missionary secretary. With administrative and numerical growth in the missions program came increasing financial stability, the inauguration of new policies, better organization on the foreign fields, and broader promotion of the whole enterprise.

The Role and Significance of Noel Perkin

When Noel Perkin received appointment as missionary secretary in 1927, the missions department was experiencing unprecedented growth. Giving between 1925 and 1927 jumped 28 percent as total missionary offerings reached $300,000 in fiscal 1927. During the same period the number of overseas personnel increased 18 percent. By 1927, there were 277 missionaries serving in China, India, Japan, Africa, Latin America, Palestine, Latvia, Bulgaria, Hungary, Greece, Poland, Russia, the Fiji Islands, Syria, Hawaii, Persia, and the Philippine Islands.[1] The assistant superintendent of the Council, David H. McDowell, reported to the Council in 1927: "God has raised us up as a missionary people and this feature of the work is essentially connected with the truth of the second coming of the Lord. Therefore we have felt impelled to impress upon the hearers the importance of insisting on world-wide missions."[2] In this arena of increasing missionary enthusiasm within the General Council, Noel Perkin assumed the leadership of a department struggling with financial problems and recent controversy.

Born in London, England, into a moderately well-to-do family in

1893, Perkin grew up in the Wesleyan Methodist Church. His parents sent him to a boarding school at Cambridge sponsored by his denomination and directed by a former missionary to China, who made a deep impression on him. During these years, however, he rebelled against the faith of his parents.

Perkin's hope of studying for a career in dentistry faded when he failed his Latin examination. After turning his attention to banking, he received a position with the Bank of Montreal in Canada. Following his move to Montreal, he settled at the branch office in Toronto, where he served as head of the savings department. He remained in Toronto for 7 ½ years.

During these years, Perkin developed tuberculosis. At this time, he moved into a boarding house operated by a woman who had been a missionary to South America. Under the spiritual influence of his new environment, Perkin was converted, witnessed to being healed of tuberculosis, and began to attend services at the Christian and Missionary Alliance Church in Toronto, where he ardently studied the teachings of A. B. Simpson. During an Alliance missionary convention, he made his first pledge of financial support. Years later he recalled, "My foundation teaching . . . was what I received in the C. and M.A. which finally led to my entering into the Pentecostal experience."[3]

He came into contact with a group of Pentecostal believers who were formerly associated with the Alliance. Christian Schoonmaker, a former student at Nyack and missionary for the Alliance in India, led the group, and Perkin came under his spiritual tutelage. He soon received the Pentecostal baptism and began to engage in evangelistic projects. During this time he became acquainted with others—J. R. Evans, C. A. McKinney, Willard Pierce, and Daniel W. Kerr—who had left the Alliance and eventually joined the Assemblies of God.

In 1918 Perkin became acquainted with Harry L. Turner, a former student at Nyack and an Alliance missionary to Argentina who had apparently received the Pentecostal baptism with speaking in tongues. Turner invited Perkin to Argentina for missionary work; Perkin accepted the invitation and remained in Argentina until 1921. (Turner had resigned from the Alliance in 1918 but later returned to that body and served as its vice president from 1950–1954 and president from 1954–1960.[4]) Through his acquaintance with Turner,

Perkin became much better acquainted with the theological and missiological principles of the Alliance.

Perkin returned to Canada and then entered the United States in 1921. Following a visit to the Rochester Bible Training School in Rochester, New York, he served two pastorates in New York State before he received a call to Springfield to serve as a bookkeeper at Gospel Publishing House and the Foreign Missions Department.

The post of missionary secretary to which the Executive Presbytery temporarily appointed Perkin involved oversight of the entire program, including its finances, personnel, and promotional activities. But Perkin possessed numerous important qualifications that recommended permanent appointment, which he received in 1927.[5] First, he had served as a missionary abroad and understood the hardships and uncertainties of missionary life. Neither Flower nor Faux had this background, although the latter had traveled extensively to survey the work. Perkin's views on missions were identical with those of the Council. He firmly believed in the necessity of building self-supporting, self-governing, and self-propagating churches on the mission fields.[6]

Second, Perkin possessed skill in financial matters, including bookkeeping and currency exchange. Perkin recognized the need in 1926 to reorganize the bookkeeping system of the department. The entire amount of designated offerings had been sent to the intended missionaries and small yellow receipts were sent to the donors. Duplicates were kept in alaphabetical order in an envelope box. Records were also kept of all receipts and expenditures. Perkin established a proper bookkeeping system with an account for every missionary.

Third, having served two pastorates, he was acquainted with many of the members of the Council. Fourth, his warm and winning personality aided him in the many administrative tasks of the post. Finally, he also had a capacity to adjust to new situations and move ahead with the times. It is accurate to say that in his 33 years in office, he grew with the program. In 1959, Melvin L. Hodges, a missionary to Latin America and later field secretary (director) for that region, praised Perkin's long tenure in office: "Perhaps Brother Perkin has gained the appreciation of missionaries most because of his ability to give his sympathetic and undivided attention to the needs of the missionaries that came to him for counsel. He has had an almost equal capacity for sharing the burdens of others and putting himself in their place."[7] This statement represented the sentiments of many missionaries who served under Noel Perkin.

Seven years passed before Perkin visited any of the mission fields. This delay in travel may have been due to several factors: the possible dissatisfaction of some over the travel expenses of his predecessor, the tight financial condition of his department, and a personal reluctance to travel because of heavy administrative responsibilities. By 1936, the financial operation of the department had improved and he made his first trip to survey the condition of missionary work endorsed by the Council, traveling to Puerto Rico, Santo Domingo (Dominican Republic), and Cuba with Henry C. Ball.

Later, at a meeting of the Foreign Missions Conference of North America in Toronto, Emory Ross, a leading missionary spokesman and executive affiliated with the Disciples of Christ, urged Perkin to continue the practice of traveling to the mission fields because this was an encouragement to the missionaries and gave him a better understanding of their situations and problems.[8] The next year Perkin and J. Roswell Flower visited Africa and Palestine. By the end of Perkin's tenure, he had "crossed the ocean twenty-six times and went around the world three times, visiting nearly every country in the world."[9]

The Development of the Department

Structure

The 1927 General Council proved to be noteworthy in another regard besides the appointment of Perkin to the post of missionary secretary. At this gathering the Assemblies of God formally adopted a constitution and bylaws.[10] Article VI of this newly adopted constitution focused on missions policies. Nine sections dealt with items ranging from the purpose of the enterprise to missionary furloughs.

According to the constitution, the missionary secretary would be appointed along with four others by the general superintendent (with the approval of the General Presbytery) to form the Foreign Missions Committee; this committee was responsible to the Executive Presbytery. In 1928, the committee appointed by General Superintendent[11] W. T. Gaston included Gaston; J. R. Evans, general secretary; Harold Moss, missionary field secretary; Stanley H.

Frodsham, editor of *The Pentecostal Evangel*; and Noel Perkin.[12] The committee actually outnumbered the office staff of Perkin, Moss, one secretary, and a part-time bookkeeper/corresponding secretary. It should also be noted that while the committee had the responsibility to oversee all missions projects at home or abroad for the Council, it focused primarily on foreign missions. The 1937 session of the General Council would authorize a separate department for home missions.

In a further development, Harold Moss, former principal of Beulah Heights Bible and Missionary Training School and son of its founder, was appointed as missionary field secretary under Perkin. Moss was apparently responsible for promotional work.[13] (The office was dissolved in 1931.)

Financial Support

After the appointment of Perkin, he began supplying detailed financial statements and a general overview of the missions program to the General Council at its biennial meetings.[14] This was in marked contrast to the financial policies of his predecessor.

A significant financial development came with the suggestion of the Busy Bee Plan started by Arthur F. Berg, a former missionary to Africa in the mid-1920s and later a pastor in the United States. Through his difficult missionary experiences, Berg recognized that "to have and maintain a strong 'foreign mission base' simply means that we must have a strong and expanded 'home missions' base."[15] As a result of his efforts and its enthusiastic reception by many in the North Central District (Minnesota, South Dakota, etc.), where he pastored, his Busy Bee Plan became popular.

One writer in the *Evangel* lamented that only 25 percent of the churches made any meaningful contribution to foreign missions. This failure in missionary zeal allegedly resulted from a lack of scriptural training by the leadership and a practical plan for members to use in giving. The Busy Bee Plan included a missionary visit to a local assembly and the dispensing of small wooden beehive banks to every person in attendance. Everyone had an opportunity to "make honey" for God. A slip of paper handed out with the bank read: "I shall honestly endeavor with the help of the Lord to lay aside out of my income regularly as I receive it the sum under which

I have marked X."[16] Every month the money was to be collected and placed in the missionary offering to the General Council. The offerings sent to the Council under this plan were divided according to the following percentages: 25 percent to home missions for the pioneering of new churches and 75 percent to foreign missions. Five percent of each of these percentages, however, was taken out for office expenses.[17]

In a brief period, the results proved to be spectacular. At the 1929 session of the General Council, General Superintendent W. T. Gaston announced that giving had reached the highest point in the history of the organization: $500,652.91 had been contributed since 1927. Noel Perkin reported that as more new churches were established in the homeland, the foreign program could continue to expand. He added that giving had become more consistent and the usual summer fluctuations in offerings had declined. Further, 117 noncontributing assemblies had begun to support the program. Others had doubled or tripled their previous giving.[18] The missions department later adopted the Busy Bee Plan, changing its name to the World Missions Plan.

The coming of the Great Depression in America eventually had an impact on missionary giving. While giving actually increased by 60 percent from 1925 to 1931, it dipped by 11.5 percent during the following biennium.[19] (This trend, however, was significantly reversed after 1933.) Consequently, the department followed a conservative fiscal policy. Although no missionaries were recalled from their fields for financial reasons, the Foreign Missions Committee did restrain some new applicants from going overseas.[20]

Many churches and individuals continued to send funds directly to the missionaries overseas. Since the missions department sought an equitable distribution of monies, it frowned on this practice. The department continued sending missionaries a monthly allowance without knowing how much money they were actually receiving. Perkin calculated in 1929 that "only about two thirds of the money sent to our missionaries passes through the hands of the missionary department."[21]

At the 1933 General Council meeting, the Assemblies of God felt encouraged about its missions program because it continued to advance at a time when others were retreating. The financial plight of the department's operational expenses, however, grew worse.

Gospel Publishing House had contributed $13,596.42 to the foreign missions program in the 2 years since the last meeting of the Council, besides providing free office space, heating, lighting, and printing. Many felt that something needed to be done to remedy the situation, since the publishing house could not continue to subsidize the program.

Gayle F. Lewis, superintendent of the Central District, presented a resolution from the missions committee at the Council meeting which recommended that "each assembly sending in an offering be requested to add a suitable amount to be used in helping defray the expense involved in administering the office."[22] When asked how much the department needed to operate, Perkin said that expenses amounted to 5 percent of the offerings sent to the office. Additional assistance would enable the department to hire needed staff. And an assistant to the missionary secretary would free him for more travel and promotional work.

Much debate followed. General Superintendent Ernest S. Williams, speaking in favor of the resolution, stated forthrightly to the delegates:

> I wish you could get it out of your minds that the Missionary Department is just a place where we receive offerings and send them out. If you go into the Missionary Department any day you will see tremendous files filled with correspondence pertaining to vital matters that have to be dealt with. Were you to sit with us in our Missionary Committee for an hour or two you would be amazed at all the problems that are arising in the thirty-four fields where we are working, and I believe you would be able to grasp in some measure the tremendous problems that are being dealt with by this department in doing its best to supervise the work in these various fields.[23]

The motion passed, but the department's support continued to be based entirely on voluntary offerings. The Council did instruct the missionary secretary to occasionally send information to the pastors about the needs of the department and the necessity of their support.

Two years later, Perkin announced to the Council that the 1933 resolution and increased promotional publications had greatly increased designated offerings for the department. Jacob J. Mueller, a graduate of Nyack and the Rochester Bible Training School and former missionary to India, became the assistant missionary secretary in 1934 (continuing in this post until his retirement in 1959). The department also hired three clerical and stenographic secretaries, plus several other part-time helpers. The subsidy of office space and utilities from Gospel Publishing House continued. The problem of administrative expenses, though temporarily alleviated, returned to plague the department.

Policy Changes

The publication in 1931 of the *Missionary Manual* (probably edited or written by Noel Perkin) marked another milestone in the development of the Foreign Missions Department and the entire Assemblies of God missionary enterprise. Although only 28 pages long, it represented the most significant publication of the department since its beginning. The manual included the reason for being, a brief history of the Pentecostal movement, and a lengthy treatment of departmental policies. All General Council policies affecting foreign missions that had been instituted before 1931 were included. The General Council Constitutional Declaration, or Preamble, adopted by the Hot Springs gathering in 1914 was listed first. This statement reflected the purposes for the formation of the Council and emphasized its evangelistic and missionary concerns.

A brief history followed the Declaration. According to the writer, "The Lord's Pentecostal Missionary Fellowship and Movement began on the day of Pentecost nearly two thousand years ago."[24] The Holy Spirit descended at Pentecost to endow the disciples with power for the task of worldwide evangelization Christ had commissioned. The Holy Spirit then directed the missionary expansion of the New Testament church until the Dark Ages brought it to a close. The Reformation, though achieving notable success in the restoration of the gospel and the church, did not fully restore the work of the Spirit. The 20th-century denominations had grown up on the ruins of the early Christian church and were now largely in a state of apostasy. With the coming of the Pentecostal movement at the beginning of the 20th century, God's missionary movement had resumed. Hundreds of overseas Pentecostal missionaries testified to that renewal. God had used the apostles to direct the expansion of the church in the first century; now He was allowing the General Council of the Assemblies of God to administer the affairs of a large part of this revived endeavor. The Foreign Missions Department, therefore, served as the agency of the Council to fulfill that purpose. Acting for the local churches that made up the organization,

> the Missions Department, assisted by its staff, disseminates missionary information, arranges for missionary meetings and conferences, examines and endorses candidates, aids the missionaries—duly appointed—in reaching their fields of labor, receives and disburses mission funds, acquires and holds property at home and abroad, and so on.[25]

This limited and inaccurate view of the history of Christianity probably reflects the understanding of many Pentecostals at the time. Nevertheless, the belief that God had raised up the Council as a missionary movement was the guiding purpose of the organization.

The description of departmental responsibilities in the manual accurately described the department's development through 1931. It primarily served as a distribution center for funds and information, as a vehicle to promote missionary interests in the local churches, and as an agency for examining missionary candidates and offering them assistance in various legal procedures, such as the purchase of properties abroad. These responsibilities marked a substantial increase in authority since the department's beginning in 1919.

In spite of the department's existence, however, the missionaries continued to exercise considerable liberty in their own work on the foreign fields. Accordingly, the manual stated that "it has not been the policy of the General Council to limit the activities of the missionaries, but rather to allow each individual to follow what he feels to be the direction of the Lord in the carrying on of his work."[26] Not until the middle of World War II did the department begin to more directly supervise missionary activities overseas. Before that, strategic planning was done by individual missionaries or the overseas district councils.

The manual stated the program's goals of reaching the unevangelized areas of the world with the gospel and establishing indigenous churches. The financial burden of missionary support rested fully on the shoulders of local churches.

An individual's spirituality was also a major concern. The department expected the missionary candidates to be deeply spiritual.

Perkin informed the members of the Council in 1932 that prayer for the ministers and missionaries was the first item of business every day for the whole staff of Gospel Publishing House and the Foreign Missions Department. Such an example set the pace for others.[27] Perkin recommended as early as 1929 that "every minister and missionary of the gospel should have a reputation for holiness. By this we do not mean something that is measured merely by outward acts or experiences, but rather an attitude of heart submission to the will of God."[28]

The missions department looked for candidates who had received definite calls from God, had proven their effectiveness in ministry in the United States, and were acquainted with "scriptural" methods of missionary work. The General Council voted in 1933 to require all prospective missionaries to have proven ministries in their districts before receiving endorsement for overseas ministry. The department believed that although educational preparation afforded definite advantages, it could not substitute for Pentecostal power in one's ministry. Perkin maintained that a barely educated person, preaching under the anointing of the Spirit, could more likely bring a university professor to Christ than could the university graduate without the assistance of God. He stated that "if we have to choose between the two, let us take the Spirit."[29] Perkin strongly recommended that candidates read Roland Allen's *Missionary Methods—St. Paul's or Ours?* and *The Spontaneous Expansion of the Church and the Causes Which Hinder It.*[30]

A prospective missionary needed to be physically, mentally, and spiritually fit for ministry abroad. The manual required a physical examination and recommended three physicians for this purpose.[31] The Council would no longer endorse missionaries who suffered from a severe disability. Some General Council members, however, still believed that consulting a physician was contradictory to a life of faith. When Hilda Wagenknecht, a missionary to India, refused to take a medical examination before returning to her field because she conscientiously objected to it, the Foreign Missions Committee relented and took her word that she enjoyed good health.[32] Candidates who could not pass the examination due to some physical problem were advised "to pray through" until they received divine healing. Approval would then be forthcoming.[33]

The manual reminded the missionary that he needed to exercise faith in God to help supply his finances. As the missionary trusted God, the local churches were responsible to provide consistent, adequate support. The foreign missions program depended on the united support of the local churches, the efforts of the missionaries, and the work of the department. In the department's point of view,

> the General Council is a co-operative body of God's children, and as such each has his own part to play in carrying forward this great work. Missionary contributors should unite with the Missions Department in regarding all our missionaries on the field as one great family for whose needs we all stand together in united faith and effort, treating all alike with the same loving and faithful consideration. No missionary must regard any pledge as a guarantee of support.[34]

The manual spelled out other policies, including the disbursement of undesignated funds, issuance of fellowship certificates, and the acquisition of properties abroad. The manual also described the responsibility of overseas district councils for placing new missionaries because "the Executives of the Field Council [District Council] are in the best position to determine where this place may be."[35] On the fields where such councils had not been organized, the missionaries were directly answerable to the department.[36]

The department urged that national workers be selected with great care. Funds for their support were not to be sent directly but channeled through the missionaries. The support of national preachers had long been a practice in the Council and actually contradicted the principle of building indigenous, self-supporting churches. Some missionaries excused the practice of financing national preachers and "Bible women" because conversion to Christianity had ostracized them socially and economically.[37] The department recognized the inconsistency but allowed it to continue, stating that "we still find it necessary in some fields to provide financial help for the native ministers who have given up all to preach the gospel."[38] This practice often created problems. When it caused dissatisfaction and friction among national pastors in Egypt, the Foreign Missions Committee, on the recommendation of the Egyptian district superintendent, withdrew the monthly support for this purpose and urged that all national assemblies become self-supporting.[39]

The department regarded missionaries home on furlough as on

vacation, but expected their assistance in the interests and promotion of the work. Thus, the furlough often entailed extensive
travel in the United States, visiting supporting churches and enlisting the aid of others. The overseas district councils determined
the length and frequency of the furloughs. Of course, the department hoped that with the help of God the missionary would remain
in this type of service for the rest of his or her life. If circumstances
warranted, a missionary could choose a rest overseas in a place closer
to his field of activity instead of in his homeland. In any event, the
prospective missionary could not be guaranteed a furlough after any
definite period of time.

Other items in the manual discussed the steps in the application
for missionary appointment. The department regarded 25 to 30 years
of age as desirable for candidacy, although exceptions were allowed.
(Some missionaries went to the field without Council endorsement
and then applied for it. However, Council members and other missionaries criticized this practice.) Passports, the costs of oceanic
travel, baggage, departure, marriage on the field, children, reports,
and other details were also discussed in the manual.

Near the end of the document was a "Suggestive Policy for Missionary Work." It contained four parts: the objective, the national
assembly, the missionary, and the Bible institute. The objective
clearly stated that "the winning of souls to Christ and establishing
of assemblies in all places where converts are won, should be regarded as the primary objective of all missions. All other branches
of ministry should be subordinate to this."[40] The key to the fulfillment of this goal was in the hands of the local assembly on the
mission field as the agency through which God the Holy Spirit
matured believers and inspired them to evangelize the surrounding
areas. With Christ as its head, this self-governing church was to be
a training center for Biblical instruction and spiritual ministry. In
such a church, the line between clergy and laity was to remain
minimal since everyone should be concerned with evangelistic outreach. William Menzies writes that Perkin strongly advocated "the
Pentecostal emphasis on each member being a candidate for an
enduement of power."[41] The church's leadership would not necessarily be paid, but the work could support itself.[42]

As an "ambassador for Christ" the missionary fulfilled the role of
a servant to the emerging church on the field. Neither attitudes of

"racial superiority [nor] control of finances entitle him to exercise lordship over the Assemblies. As soon as the native converts manifest spiritual gifts of ministry they should be encouraged to take responsibility."[43] Therefore, the missionary was never to think of his place of ministry as fixed. When the indigenous church was established, he was to set his sights on the unevangelized areas in his region of the world.[44]

The manual also referred to the Bible institute as "necessary" for training an indigenous church leadership. In the institute students were to maintain the standard of living of their own people; this would prevent their being alienated from them when they returned home. Perkin envisioned a Bible institute on every mission field.[45]

The last page of the manual contained an agreement, or pledge, to be signed by the prospective missionary. The missionary pledged to follow wholeheartedly the principles of the Council and the policies contained in the manual, to avoid dissension on the mission field, to be willing to endure hardship for the sake of the gospel, to trust God for his needs, and to be grateful whether those needs were supplied through the missions department or in some other way. Finally, the missionary agreed to go overseas "with one supreme purpose to glorify Christ, to win souls for Him, and to hasten His coming."[46] In spite of all the policies the document set forth, it is pervaded by the spiritual nature of the enterprise. Each missionary solemnly promised to work toward the fulfillment of the spiritual goals of the General Council.

Publications and Promotions

From the beginning of the Pentecostal movement, the missionaries depended on publications such as *The Pentecost, The Bridegroom's Messenger, The Latter Rain Evangel, Word and Witness,* and *The Christian Evangel* (later *The Pentecostal Evangel*) to publicize their ministries and solicit funds. Many wrote monthly to several publications to ensure support. After the General Council organized in 1914, *The Pentecostal Evangel* emerged as the chief avenue of information and promotion. The *Evangel*, as it came to be known, along with these other publications, included missionary news, letters, testimonies of conversions and healings ("signs and wonders"), and sermons.

By the early 1930s, the need for additional promotional materials appeared. The missions department, through cooperation with Gospel Publishing House, issued a series of booklets that described activities on numerous mission fields. They included *Evangelizing West China* (ca. 1931) by William W. Simpson, *A Visit to Mosi Land, French West Africa* (ca. 1932) by Arthur E. Wilson, *Opportunities in South India and Ceylon* (ca. 1934) by John H. Burgess, *With Our Missionaries in North India* (1937) by Jacob J. Mueller, and *God's Faithfulness in Ningpo* (1938) by Nettie D. Nichols and Joshua Bang.[47] Overall, the booklets contained a broader, more in-depth look at missionary work than the periodicals, including *The Pentecostal Evangel.* Illustrated with photographs, they introduced the reader to the geography and customs of the field under study. A description of missionary activities followed as well as testimonials. In a few places, the booklets discussed missions theory and plans for the future.

In 1938, the department published *A Survey of the Assemblies of God in Foreign Lands.* Larger than the other publications, this book introduced the reader to every mission field the organization had entered. The purpose of the missionary enterprise was followed by a brief sketch of the efforts on each field. Pictures of missionaries, converts, and various activities illustrated the book.

Missionaries also began to privately publish accounts of their overseas ministries. Among others, Mollie Baird, a missionary to India, wrote *Of Whom the World Is Not Worthy: Stories of North India's Christians* in 1941 to further publicize the work. Doris Maloney Edwards wrote about her late husband's ministry in India in *Clarence T. Maloney . . . Ready To Go* (1943). Many other privately published books followed.

The missions department published a small book of missionary songs and a monthly prayer pamphlet, which listed various needs and contained a selected missionary letter. Local assemblies requesting copies received them monthly without charge.

These booklets, books, and newsletters reflected the increasing leadership by the department, growing concern to promote the work in the home churches, developing cooperation overseas, and a rising effort to fulfill the long-term goals of the enterprise. The development of these publications supplemented the coverage in *The Pentecostal Evangel* and significantly heightened the profile of the department among Council members. But still more work needed to be done in awakening the local churches to the program. One speaker alerted the 1939 meeting of the Council to the fact that only one third of the 3,500 churches in the Council had contributed anything to world missions.[48]

To encourage the local churches to get involved in supporting the program, the department established a goal of "hav[ing] missionary speakers visit all assemblies with a definite program for home and foreign missions, and to arrange conventions in suitable centers throughout the country."[49] By using the most effective missionary speakers, the department believed the local churches would respond more readily. Missionaries who were less effective speakers (though equally effective missionaries) could return to their fields earlier through fares paid for by the increased revenues.

Featuring missionary speakers in local conventions, increasing promotional literature,[50] and emphasizing the World Missions Plan (formerly the Busy Bee Plan) helped the missions program gain the support of more local churches.

Ora and Noel Perkin pictured shortly after their wedding in 1921.

The Assemblies of God established several missionary "rest homes" to assist missionaries returning to the United States on furlough. The Mizpah Missionary Home (pictured above) was in The Bronx, New York.

In the years following the permanent appointment of Noel Perkin as Foreign Missions Secretary (1927), the Foreign Missions Department began to publicize the overseas enterprise through the use of booklets, which depicted the work in various overseas fields of endeavor.

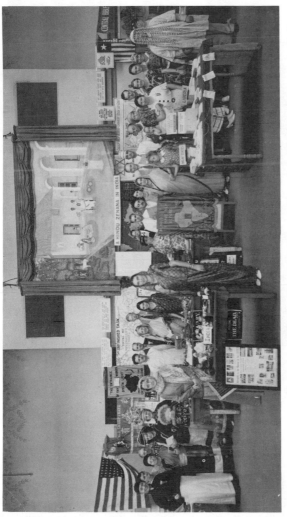

Missionaries, in national costume, attending the 1937 General Council in Memphis, Tennessee. (Left to right) Joshua Bang, Mary Lewer, Jarmila Wagner, Nettie Nichols, Unidentified woman, Blanche Appleby, Trudys Lawrence, Leland Johnson, Gustav Kinderman, Constance Eady, Paul Peterson, Lydia Vaux Bryant, Anne Eberhardt, Kathryn Vogler, Frank Finkenbinder, Herbert Griffin, Jacob Mueller, Esther Griffin, Margaret Felch (holding girl's hand), Noel Perkin, Harold Jones, Emile Chastagner, Margaret Jones (with daughter Virginia), Lois Shelton, Roy Davidson, Pauline Davidson, Beulah Buchwalter, Margaret Shirer, Lloyd Shirer, Julia Richardson (?).

9

Overseas Efforts and World War II

In the years before World War II, most Assemblies of God missionaries worked diligently and successfully toward implementing the long-standing ideal of the indigenous church. The Depression of the 1930s did not diminish enthusiasm within the ranks of the General Council. World War II, however, did traumatize certain regions of missionary endeavor.

Implementing the Ideal Overseas

As early as 1937, Perkin realized that the department needed to exercise more oversight of the work abroad, since "it is obvious to those who know the missionary situation that there are certain fields in which God seems to be moving more definitely than in others, and if we're going to keep step with God we believe it is expedient to try to concentrate more of our workers in the most productive fields."[1] At this time, however, activities overseas depended almost entirely on the individual initiative of the missionary.

During this period, developments abroad confirmed that many of the missionary personnel had indeed taken the initiative to reach unevangelized areas with the gospel and establish indigenous churches. Victor Plymire traveled through Tibet, long a forbidden territory.[2] The Leonard Boltons and Clifford Morrisons contributed to the evangelization of the Lisu people in southwestern China and northern Burma, finding a favorable response. Consequently a strong indigenous church developed among them.[3] The W. L. Shirers from the Gold Coast (Ghana) joined the Everett Phillipses to open the field of Nigeria for Assemblies of God missions. The Assemblies of God in Nigeria became one of the strongest indigenous churches in the foreign missions program.[4]

Such efforts often involved great personal risks. William E. Simpson, a young missionary, died at the hands of bandits in 1932 as he evangelized in western China.[5] Richard Williams, missionary to Peru, died from typhus, contracted while ministering to a dying man in a remote mountain village in 1931.[6]

Nevertheless, the Foreign Missions Department continued to report that remarkable revivals, followed by "signs and wonders," followed the preaching of the gospel. Referring to China, a writer noted that "one singular feature of nearly all these movements of the Spirit has been the accompaniment of the miraculous element. Sick have been healed, demons cast out, and many have spoken in other tongues as the Spirit gives utterance."[7]

As the indigenous national churches organized overseas, democratic or congregational/presbyterial structures developed, patterned after that of the Assemblies of God in America. Such structures received approval from the parent body because "the combined judgment of a large number of Spirit-filled people is more likely to provide an indication of God's will than is the judgment of any individual, no matter how sincere he may be. . . . democracy appears to be the root of our procedures of both discipline and dogma."[8] To the missionaries, this approach represented the New Testament model for church organization.

Ralph D. Williams, missionary to Central America, played a key role in the development of the indigenous church in Latin America.[9] Recognizing the valuable potential of a national clergy, he established a Bible institute in El Salvador in 1931. This school set a pattern for later Bible institutes.[10] Williams described the school:

> We had no funds to build the proper building, but we put the matter before the brethren and trusted the Lord to see us through. We set the date and told the pastors to send in those who had already proven their call to the ministry, and to follow them up with some food and whatever money they could get together. About eighteen or twenty students came. The first two or three days we spent in collecting packing cases and knocking them to pieces to make desks and seats. Then we had three month's Bible school. We began the day at 6:15 with prayer and the classes were from 8 until noon. The afternoons were given to studying the lessons assigned in the morning and the evenings to evangelistic meetings chiefly.[11]

Many more similarly organized schools followed, providing a leadership for many Latin American indigenous churches.

Williams continued to strive for strengthening the national church. In his ministry the spotlight did not focus on buildings but on training and evangelism. In his view, the national churches should "build according to their capacity from the flimsiest to the permanent and ornate—but the richest gift of all is that which they have contributed of their own initiative."[12] He espoused this view not only because he believed it followed the New Testament pattern, but because his support from the missions department barely met his and his wife's personal needs. They had nothing extra that would have allowed them to develop a mission station approach even if they had wanted.

Indigenous, self-governing churches began to appear as early as 1930. In that year, the believers in El Salvador, with missionary assistance, set up their own national organization. This was one of the earliest fields to take this step. Joined in 1936 by a young missionary from the United States, Melvin L. Hodges, Williams met with Nicaraguan believers and put together another national Assemblies of God organization. Hodges, elected as the general superintendent, moved to Nicaragua in 1937 and began the work of converting the organization to the indigenous church model.[13] Thus, the General Council resolution in 1921 calling for the establishment of indigenous churches overseas was slowly coming to fruition. It was no easy endeavor, however, since many early Pentecostal missionaries had built their efforts on the old mission station, or mission compound, approach, which paid national ministers.[14]

Another significant indigenous church developed through the efforts of missionaries in Mossiland, French West Africa (now Burkina Faso). From the beginning, the missionaries worked toward that ideal. Three problems had to be tackled first: (1) the uniform writing of the national language, (2) the translation of the Bible into that language, and (3) literacy training.[15] Arthur E. Wilson, an early missionary to the region, reported that by 1928, a quarter of the New Testament had been translated and distributed.[16]

Concerned about building on a firm foundation, in 1934 the missionaries formally adopted indigenous church principles, "which we had formerly favored, but did not see our way clear to put into practice."[17] Following this decision, emphasis focused on training national clergy, setting up self-governing churches, and making the converts responsible for building their own churches. Because the national ministers had always been supported by local tithes and offerings, this adjustment did not bring on the conflict that it did in some other fields.

Wilson concluded that "a trained native ministry is the cheapest, the most effective, the quickest, and the only way to thoroughly evangelize any foreign nation."[18] But the missionaries recognized that implementation of this ideal would take time and they paced their efforts accordingly.

Indigenous churches in other fields did not develop easily. In every major region of the world where the Assemblies of God sent missionaries, some works based on the mission station pattern with financial underwriting from America proved to be resistant to the self-support concept. Some works in India and China were especially hesitant to change their procedures. Extenuating circumstances must be taken into account, however. Rather than allow some converts to face starvation because of poverty and ostracism, missionaries would support them. Helen I. Gustavson, a missionary to China, admitted that building an indigenous church could be a slow and discouraging process at times "because of extreme poverty among many of the believers."[19]

Nevertheless, missionaries accepted the ideal as a goal. Nicholas Nikoloff, a missionary to Eastern Europe, directed a Bible institute in Danzig, Poland. From that school, trained young men traveled to Germany, Rumania, Bulgaria, Poland, Yugoslavia, and other countries to preach and start churches.[20] Missionary Maynard L. Ketcham trained students in a primitive Bible institute in Bengal, India. He wrote: "We are not seeking to make polished preachers who will work for a salary. But we are seeking to properly indoctrinate converts who have a call to minister to their fellow men. We want the lay members of all our churches to be in a position to effectually witness—so that each church will be a growing church."[21] The struggles to achieve the ideal often severely taxed the missionaries, but observers noticed the benefits as national, self-supporting churches increased.

Despite the push toward indigenous works, the role of overseas charitable institutions did not diminish during this period. The work of Lillian Trasher's orphanage in Egypt was strongly supported by churches in the U.S. and gained widespread respect in the General Council. National acclaim resulted from an article in *American Magazine* describing the work.[22] Florence Steidel, a nurse and later student at Central Bible Institute and the Southern Baptist Theological Seminary, Louisville, Kentucky, won wide acclaim for her work that led to the founding of a leprosarium in Liberia in 1947, New Hope Town. This community included separate homes for infected children and for those healthy children whose parents required treatment. It also operated schools and a farm. Instruction in trades such as carpentry, bricklaying, and tailoring was also available.[23]

In areas such as North India where opposition to Christianity remained intense and poverty was rampant, large numbers of dependent people lived at some mission stations. The missionaries often tried to provide education and instruction in weaving, carpentry, and other trades to help the people become self-supporting. The missions department considered this a positive approach, since it would reduce the financial burden of the missionaries. The goal remained, however, for the establishment of an indigenous church through evangelism and the training of national workers.[24]

In numerous ways institutions such as orphanages and industrial schools helped the development of indigenous churches. Jacob J. Mueller observed that in North India, "not a few of these orphans, trained and developed in our Pentecostal schools, have become excellent Christian workers."[25] In South India, Ted Vassar encouraged young men in his orphanage who desired to enter the ministry to "learn a trade along with their Bible training. They were admonished not to rely solely on the Western Church for their support. From childhood, the orphans had chores for which they received an allowance and they were taught to tithe."[26] Notable Indian church leaders came from this institution.

Building indigenous churches involved the missionaries in publishing Sunday school materials, training books, songbooks, newsletters, and tracts in the national languages. Henry C. Ball had led the way with the publication of *La Luz Apostolica* ("The Apostolic Light"). By 1935, other periodicals in Spanish followed: *El Evangelista Pentecostal* ("The Pentecostal Evangelist") of Puerto Rico and *Agua de Vida* ("Water of Life") of Peru. *The Morning Star*, printed in Arabic in Cairo, circulated in Egypt and surrounding countries. The South China District Council published the *Spiritual News* in Chinese. English language publications included the *Singapore Messenger* and the *Gold Coast News.*

Adaptability proved to be a hallmark of many Assemblies of God missionaries. Louise Jeter, a young missionary to Peru, realized that her Sunday school children had no literature in Spanish and that other Protestant missions agencies faced the same plight. "If the children . . . were to have literature, someone would have to write it. It would have to be illustrated, printed, financed, and distributed. This would obviously require a team effort, and during the following months I realized that God wanted me to be a part of the team."[27] Jeter began a long and distinguished career in the writing of Christian education materials.

Popular Support

Support for the missions program never waned during these turbulent years. Though finances declined between 1931 and 1933 because of the Great Depression, the trend was reversed in the years that followed. Returning from a trip to Texas in 1933, Perkin noted the large attendance and generous offerings at a series of missionary rallies he had conducted. He concluded that in spite of difficult times the spirit of missions continued.[28]

The continuing rise in support must be credited, at least in part, to the growing promotional work of the department. Over the years, missions conventions addressed by missionary speakers or departmental representatives built a grass roots sense of responsibility for missions. The department encouraged people to support the program not only with financial assistance but also with their prayers. As early as 1920, the Executive Presbytery began to designate 3-day prayer periods for all the constituency "to intercede for the moving of God's Spirit upon the work."[29] Although the intercession upheld the work in general, it focused on the overseas missions program.

Early in the 1930s, the department sponsored the Council Ten Thousand throughout the Assemblies of God: having 10,000 people praying daily for missions. The leadership stressed that the growth of the missions program could continue only as believers prayed for God's blessing on it. Not only would God intervene for the missions enterprise, but the person who faithfully prayed would also benefit. Perkin described such intercessory prayer as a glorious and unselfish ministry that would leave the intercessor with "a smile and a holy shine upon the face. Those who are closely associated with God invariably have a beauty about their countenance which nothing else can supply."[30]

After 3 years of promotion, the department reached its goal of 10,000 prayer supporters. The *Evangel* reported that their prayers had been felt on the foreign fields; numerous prayer requests had been answered in response to their labors.[31]

General Superintendent Ernest S. Williams reported in 1939 to the General Council that in the 25-year history of the organization, the missions program had gained the confidence of the local churches, the missionary personnel, and the youth, who continued to volunteer for foreign service. The Council witnessed a remarkable advance. By 1939, the number of missionaries had reached 380, a gain of 9 percent in 2 years and over 1400 percent since 1914. Mission stations, in 48 countries, circled the globe. Other vital statistics included 1,131 Assemblies of God churches and preaching points overseas, 44 missionary institutions (Bible institutes, orphanages, elementary schools, etc.), and 1,231 national ministers. Offerings had climbed to $811,766, from $672,289 in 1937 (a 21-percent increase over the previous biennium) and from $500,652 in 1929 (a 62-percent increase over the decade).[32]

Cooperative Relationships

The foreign missions program maintained informal and formal associations with other missionary organizations during this period. The department continued its practice of sending designated funds overseas to non-Council missionaries. These individuals received nearly $42,000 in 1939 at no administrative cost to them. The support of non-Council missionaries had never been encouraged and at times had been harshly condemned; nevertheless, cordial relationships often existed on various fields. The North China Bible School, for example, was operated on a cooperative basis by Pentecostal missionaries, including those of the Assemblies of God. A notice in the *Evangel* praised this effort: "We wish to give due credit to our brethren who are not affiliated with the General Council for their part in this worthy enterprise."[33] The work in Venezuela also grew on the foundation of such a cooperative effort.

Without doubt, the formal relationship between the Assemblies of God and the Russian and Eastern European Mission (R.E.E.M.), later known simply as Eastern European Mission, proved to be the most significant. The Pentecostal work in Eastern Europe had developed through the ministries of Gustave H. Schmidt, J. E. Varonaeff, Nicholas Nikoloff, and others. Some of the early leaders had been affiliated with the Russian Missionary Society but withdrew when that agency did not fully endorse their Pentecostal theology.

A new agency was formed when R.E.E.M. organized in Chicago in 1927.[34] Since it enlisted Pentecostal members—for example, Schmidt and Nikoloff—who were closely affiliated with the Assemblies of God, the General Council turned its work over to the new organization in the same year. This appeared to be a practical move, since R.E.E.M. members had ministered in Europe for many years and had a field council operating there to care for the needs of the missionaries.

Originally the work encompassed Russia, Poland, Latvia, Lithuania, Bulgaria, Czechoslovakia, Yugoslavia, and Germany. Later it added Greece, Hungary, Rumania, and Siberia. A Bible institute founded by Schmidt in Danzig, Poland, prepared young missionaries to return with the Pentecostal message to their homelands in eastern Europe. Remarkable growth followed. The agency claimed over 80,000 Pentecostal believers by the beginning of World War II.[35]

The relationship of the Council with R.E.E.M. was stormy at times. Due to the close relationship between the two organizations, difficulties arose when the Council occasionally requested the disciplining of one of its members affiliated with R.E.E.M. The problem of two governing boards created friction over such issues.

Dissatisfaction also mounted over the financial operation of R.E.E.M. In addition, the Council officers felt that the agency had not sufficiently strengthened the ties of fellowship between the foreign work and the Assemblies of God in America. Perkin stated:

> The thought is not so much that an organic union should be effected but that a spiritual fellowship might be developed

> using the same doctrinal stand and as far as is permissible the
> same name for the organization or local churches. In this way
> by developing a world-wide fellowship of the Assemblies of
> God, the whole body is strengthened and helped, particularly
> the weaker branches in that they are associated with the stronger
> body.[36]

With the coming of World War II, most of the General Council
workers in Europe had withdrawn, except one in Germany and two
in Greece. In December 1939, the Executive Presbytery extended
an offer to Paul B. Peterson, the president of R.E.E.M., to amal-
gamate the agency as a department of the Council's missionary work;
Peterson would be secretary on par with Perkin. In addition, members of his staff would be transferred to Springfield and supplied
with office space. Provision would be made for the printing of the
agency's periodical, *The Gospel Call,* at Gospel Publishing House.[37]

The officials of R.E.E.M. rejected the invitation, citing the growing international posture of the agency (member missionaries also
ministered to German and Russian communities outside Europe)
and their desire to maintain its separate identity. An unwillingness
to compromise on certain policies also figured into the decision.

In view of past difficulties with R.E.E.M., its failure to merge
with the Council, the withdrawal of most of its missionaries from
Europe with the start of the war, and recent moves away from a
distinctly and uncompromising Pentecostal theology, the Foreign
Missions Committee severed the relationship in the late summer
of 1940.[38]

The Initial Impact of World War II

Little did anyone realize in 1939 that the coming of the war would
revolutionize the missions enterprise. To many Christians, this turn
in world events looked as though the second coming of Christ would
soon take place. Such expectancy made the continuance of foreign
missions more urgent than ever. Ralph M. Riggs, an influential
writer and later general superintendent (1953–1959), stated: "To the
Church of the last days is given the exalted privilege of gathering
in the balance of the quota to make up the bride of Jesus Christ. . . .
Perhaps it will be some humble soul from the mission field who will
complete the number. Then the trumpet will sound and the Bride

will rise to meet her Bridegroom."[39] This simply expressed the feeling of many Christians that once the gospel was preached to all the nations (Matthew 24:14), the end of the present age would arrive.

In the first months of the war, optimism ran high that missionaries would not need to be withdrawn from belligerent areas and the work would be uninterrupted. Fifty new missionaries prepared for travel to foreign fields.[40] A year later, in spite of increasing difficulties and the isolation of some missionaries, none had been withdrawn. However, some missionaries home on furlough found themselves unable to return to their fields and stayed in the United States for the duration of the war. Nevertheless, Perkin reported to the 1941 General Council meeting in Minneapolis that since the war had begun, 104 missionaries had crossed the oceans, 54 of them being new appointees. Only four had failed to reach their destinations.[41]

The war disrupted communications with the missionaries and they often faced distressing circumstances.[42] *Evangel* readers were encouraged to faithfully support the missionaries even though it might be impossible for some to acknowledge receipt of the contributions. A special Scandinavian Missionary Relief Fund supported over a hundred Norwegian and Swedish Pentecostal missionaries in China, Argentina, and Brazil who had been cut off from usual sources of assistance.[43]

As the war worsened in the Far East in 1940, the missions department, following the consensus of many other missions agencies, allowed mothers and children, the physically infirm, and those shortly due for a furlough to return home. Some, at their own discretion, remained at their work.

The Assemblies of God had made a greater investment in its mission fields in the Far East than in other regions, such as Europe. Thus, when the United States entered the war against Japan, a large portion of its overseas enterprise was jeopardized. Circumstances became especially difficult for missionaries in Japan, China, and the surrounding countries. The Japanese invasion of the Chinese mainland added to the perils of missionary work. In November 1941, the missions department sent a message to the missionaries in North China, offering to pay for their transportation expenses if they decided to return immediately. After the Battle of Pearl Harbor, cables with similar proposals were sent to those in Hong Kong and the

Philippines. Perkin praised those who chose to stay, but did not pressure them to do so.[44]

The Japanese forces advanced rapidly when the war started and Assemblies of God missionaries numbered among their captives: 15 in North China, 6 in Hong Kong, and 8 in the Philippines. Those in Hong Kong and a few in China were shortly released and allowed to return to the United States.[45] Others, not so fortunate, remained as prisoners of war until they were released by Allied and American troops. Many of these individuals suffered intensely as a result of their confinement.[46]

As early as 1941, Perkin and others realized that it would be some time before many missionaries, perhaps none at all, could return to Europe, Africa, India, China, and other outlying places embroiled in war. The attention of the Assemblies of God missions program began to focus on South America, an area safe for travel and with vast regions untouched by Pentecostal missionaries.[47]

Reaching the unevangelized had taken the early missionaries from cold Tibet to the warm climates of Latin America. From Tibetan Buddhists to Roman Catholics, all were candidates for the gospel message. However, because of Catholic opposition in Latin America, many had hesitated to venture there in missionary activity. A writer in *The Pentecostal Evangel* in 1920 had referred to South America as "the Neglected Continent."[48]

Conclusion

The appointment of the farsighted and capable leader Noel Perkin as foreign missions secretary opened a new era for Assemblies of God missions. Perkin's work and the continuing enthusiasm of the local churches led to the formation of the World Missions Plan for increased financial assistance and the Council of Ten Thousand for enlisting prayer support. To a large extent, the promotional work of the department through the pages of the *Evangel* and other new publications, as well as the growing popularity of missionary conventions in local churches, made the Council and local congregations more aware of their responsibilities to the enterprise.

The addition of staff members to the department and a new bookkeeping system enabled it to more efficiently serve the growing missionary force. A new missionary policy manual brought clarity and order to a maturing worldwide network of missionary efforts.

Missionary endeavors toward achieving the ideal of the indigenous church on the foreign fields were generally successful. Resistance came from some quarters primarily because initiative continued to rest with the vision and work of the individual missionary. The Foreign Missions Department had not yet begun to orchestrate a global missions strategy.

World War II brought this period to a close, shattering the efforts on some fields. It forced the departmental leadership and the missionaries to reflect on their efforts, goals, and strategies. A new day dawned with the end of the conflict.

John H. Burgess founded the oldest existing overseas Bible institute in the Assemblies of God. Pictured above is a graduating class of the Bethel Bible Institute in South India. The faculty is seated in the second row: (left to right) C. Kunjummen, and missionaries Burgess, Mildred Ginn, and Lydia Graner.

As a young missionary to Peru, Louise Jeter Walker recognized the need to prepare Sunday school materials in Spanish. This began a long and distinguished ministry in the preparation of Christian education materials.

A graduating class of the Danzig Bible Institute before the outbreak of World War II. Pictured in the second row are Gustave H. Schmidt (third from left), Donald Gee (an annual lecturer from England), Nicholas Nikoloff (director of the school), and Gustav Kinderman. Second from the right (second row) is Martha Nikoloff. The students in the picture include (among others) a German-Pole, a converted Jew, a Russian, a Hungarian, a Yugoslav, and two Bulgarians.

Ralph D. Williams (fifth from left) was a pioneer missionary to Latin America and an advocate of the indigenous church. Here he is pictured with students of El Salvador's Bethel Bible Institute preparing to travel to an outstation for evangelistic ministry.

Melvin and Lois Hodges traveled to Nicaragua in 1937 to assist believers in organizing a self-governing national church.

As foreign missions secretary, Noel Perkin traveled extensively overseas. Here he is pictured addressing African pastors.

Members of a local Women's Missionary Council in Illinois are packing a steel drum with can goods, clothing, and other items to send overseas. Such projects were often pursued to assist missionaries.

Part Four

The Era of Strategic Planning (1943–1959)

10

Strategy, Structure, and Promotions

The foreign missions program of the Assemblies of God underwent rapid and far-reaching changes from 1943 to 1959. The war forced the missions department to look for new fields and prepare for the post-war era. Major structural changes took place as field secretaries (called field directors after 1978) joined Noel Perkin in the administration of the enterprise. Concern about stronger relations with local churches resulted in the organization of a promotions division. The development of other new support agencies testified to the continuing enthusiasm of the Council for its overseas ministries.

By 1959 the Assemblies of God foreign missions program would receive favorable recognition in Protestant missions circles and embark on a new strategy for world evangelization that would lead to greater strides in the decades ahead.

Strategy and the Post-War Era

World War II curtailed some missionary activities, notably those in Europe and the Far East. As a result, the missions department gave more of its attention to regions still available for evangelism. Although travel could be perilous, missionaries opened three new fields in Africa: Nyasaland, Tanganyika, and Basutoland.

Latin America and the West Indies, however, presented the safest and most convenient doors of opportunity. During this period, the Assemblies of God began new works in Costa Rica, Paraguay, Colombia, Jamaica, and the Bahamas.[1] As early as 1941, Perkin wrote that "the vast continent of South America is still open to our activities and as there are over eighty million people there needing the gospel message, we are planning for definite advances into that land which was so long known as 'the neglected continent.' "[2] While over 158 furloughed missionaries (out of 403) remained in the United States during the war because of their inability to return overseas, 28 new missionaries went abroad in 1942. Of these, 24 headed for Latin America and the West Indies.[3]

In spite of intense opposition from Roman Catholic constituents, great advances occurred in the Latin American endeavors.[4] Like their conservative evangelical counterparts, the Assemblies of God missionaries viewed the Roman Catholic Church in Latin America as a distortion of New Testament Christianity in theology and practice. One writer asserted that the Roman Catholic Church in Peru was "no more Christian than counterfeit coin is money."[5] Melvin L. Hodges, a missionary to Central America and later field secretary for the region, stated that "there are no people who walk in deeper darkness than these very ones who seem to proclaim Christ. Here there is not absence of truth, but truth distorted into falsehood, for there is no religion in the world more adept at 'changing the truth of God into a lie' than Romanism."[6] This reflected the attitudes of Assemblies of God members in the United States, a posture that remained largely unchanged until the rise of the Catholic charismatic movement in the 1960s. With that development, many Council members began to review their attitude toward Catholics and make some contacts. Even then, the General Council officially viewed the Roman Catholic Church with cautious suspicion for many years.[7]

To survey the conditions on the mission fields and prepare for the post-war era, the department called for a 3-day conference of missionaries to convene at Central Bible Institute in April 1943. Fifty-eight missionaries from 18 countries attended the sessions and offered their advice. Chairmen or representatives of the various overseas district councils read reports describing the work and needs of their fields.[8]

The missionary conference produced six major goals for the future. First, field secretaries, or regional missionary administrators, would be appointed for all the major areas of activity. Two had already been appointed and others would follow. Second, the department would attempt to recruit 500 new missionaries who had received Bible institute training and practical experience in ministry.[9] Such recruits could evangelize abroad and staff foreign Bible institutes to prepare other young people for service. A third recommendation called for the formation of advisory committees of ministers and missionaries to advise on activities in specific regions, such as Europe.[10]

A fourth major objective called for the provision of additional missionary training "so that those we send out may be better prepared to meet the complex task of presenting the gospel to the peoples of a foreign race and tongue under the adverse conditions of trying climates and sometimes undesirable living conditions."[11]

A special meeting took place at Central Bible Institute before the missionary conference to propose curricular changes in missionary training.[12] Noel Perkin chaired the meeting, which included Ernest S. Williams, president of CBI and general superintendent of the Council; J. Roswell Flower, general secretary of the Council; other Council executive officers; William I. Evans, dean of the school; and various missionaries. The proposal to offer a post-graduate course in missionary training at Central Bible Institute produced considerable discussion.[13] Several missionaries present spoke in favor of the advantages that such training could mean on the field. J. Roswell Flower added his support for the proposal. Others expressed fears that such training might jeopardize the spiritual life of the institution. In this vein, William I. Evans read a portion of 1 Corinthians 1 in which the apostle Paul condemned reliance on worldly wisdom and training. Another speaker suggested that the department should allow the missionaries to receive supplemental instruction at conservative evangelical colleges.

Toward the end of the meeting, Perkin voiced his support and that persuaded the others to accept the idea. Thus, the institute added the classes necessary to establish "a one-year course offering special missionary subjects to college and Bible school graduates, returned missionaries, and missionaries under appointment, who feel their need of special training in preparation for an effective ministry on the mission field."[14]

Robert W. Cummings, a former Presbyterian missionary to India before joining the Assemblies of God and director of a language school in Landour, India, received appointment to this important post of missionary instruction at Central Bible Institute.[15] With an M.A. from the Kennedy School of Missions (Hartford Seminary Foundation) and an M.Th. from the Pittsburgh-Xenia Theological Seminary, Cummings may have been the highest academically trained missionary in the enterprise.[16] Like William I. Evans, Cummings proved to be a dynamic spiritual leader at the institution. This allayed the concern that a post-graduate course of instruction might alter the nature of the school.

The fifth objective called for the organization of regional missions conventions. Veteran missionaries would serve as speakers to inform their audiences about various phases of their activities. Perkin remarked, "Our objective is not only to have every assembly a missionary contributor, but every individual member a missionary enthusiast."[17]

The sixth and final objective of the Missionary Conference focused on raising $5 million to support the program after the war. This fund could speed new missionaries overseas and help with various projects abroad. At first, the department recommended $1 million. However, after listening to the various speakers at the conference, General Superintendent Ernest S. Williams challenged the figure and proposed that the sum of $5 million be substituted as the objective.[18]

Not all the goals were attained. The Foreign Missions Department was not able to realize the immediate goals of 500 new missionaries and $5 million; however, it did appoint field secretaries, recruit young people, plan for advanced missionary training, organize regional missionary conventions, and raise additional funds. The real significance behind these objectives was that for the first time in its history, the Foreign Missions Department, seeking the advice of its overseas personnel, engaged in setting goals for the overall, worldwide advance of the program. The initiative for strategic planning had been grasped by the department. From 1943 on, the missions department served not only as a center for the disbursement of funds and the examination of candidates, but also as the chief architect of the global effort.

Other goals followed. In 1945, Perkin called for doubling the number of national ministers and converts overseas, the formation of supporting prayer groups ("bands") at home, increased gospel literature production in national languages, larger contributions from local churches, and implementation of radio evangelism on the foreign field.[19] Another missionary conference convened in Springfield in 1948 to prepare for the future.[20]

In 1953 the missions leadership presented additional goals. First, the program would place more emphasis on evangelistic efforts in large population centers. Second, aid to the sick, hungry, and homeless needed to be continued as much as resources permitted. Third, ties between Pentecostal churches around the world should be strengthened, "thereby realizing, to a greater extent in actual experience, the real unity of the body of Christ." Fourth, efforts should be stepped up to advance into unevangelized regions.[21] By the close of Perkin's administration in 1959, the department launched Global Conquest, the most strategic advance that had yet been made.

Despite the strategic planning with its accumulation of objectives, the underlying motivation for the enterprise remained the same as it had been from the beginning: the fulfillment of Christ's commission to evangelize the world before His second coming. Ralph M. Riggs stated the opinion of many in the Council:

> The Lord has actually told us that we can hasten His return. In Second Peter 3:12 (margin) we have it clearly said, "Looking for and hastening the coming of the day of God." Jesus said, "This gospel shall be preached in all the world for a witness, and then shall the end come." God is waiting.
>
> The longsuffering of our Lord means salvation for somebody. He is waiting for somebody to be saved. This evangelistic program of ours, this missionary program of ours, this home missionary program of ours, this Sunday school program of ours, is in God's will. He wants us to go full steam ahead into all the world, preaching the gospel, thereby to hasten His return.[22]

Riggs' interpretation of 2 Peter 3:12 and Matthew 24:14 enjoyed widespread popularity among Council members and missionaries, including Noel Perkin. It emphasized man's role in hastening the return of Christ for His church and the establishment of the kingdom of God on earth after a 7-year Tribulation. Stanley M. Horton, a professor in Biblical studies at Central Bible Institute during this period and a leading theologian in the Council, wrote:

> Jesus did not say that the world must be converted or even that the gospel would have great success in every part of the world. But the gospel must be preached. The witness must go to every part of the world. . . . God is not anxious to bring an end. He wants to let all mankind know that salvation through Christ is available. . . . when He sees the gospel witness going into all the world, faithful in spite of increasingly worse conditions, then He will say it is enough and the end will come.[23]

Interestingly enough, Assemblies of God writers focused most of their attention on the words "gospel" and "end" in Matthew 24:14: "This gospel of the kingdom shall be preached in all the world for a witness unto all nations; and then shall the end come." Little emphasis was placed on the role of the kingdom of God in the present age. Significantly, Riggs did not quote the Matthew passage precisely. Instead of "this gospel shall be preached," the statement should be "this gospel *of the kingdom* shall be preached" (emphasis added). Frank M. Boyd, another leading theologian in the Council, believed that the kingdom of God, while presently in the world, remained veiled. It would not achieve its outward form until the millennial reign of Christ had been brought about after His return for the Church.[24] This eschatological perspective strongly reflected the influence of dispensationalism on the leaders and theologians of the Assemblies of God during this period.[25]

Not everyone agreed, however, with the dispensational orientation to the kingdom of God held by Riggs and Boyd. As early as 1924, the Executive Presbytery of the Assemblies of God stopped the advertisement of *The Scofield Reference Bible* (containing the dispensational interpretations of C. I. Scofield in the form of notes) in *The Pentecostal Evangel*. Several objectionable interpretations were cited in addition to "a theory in the notes of the Scofield Bible that the kingdom of heaven is 'postponed,' which we believe is contrary to the teaching of Rom. 14:17; 1 Cor. 4:20; and Col. 4:11."[26] At the urging of William I. Evans and Frank M. Boyd, permission was granted to begin advertising it once again in 1926.[27]

Later, Ernest S. Williams, a leading theologian in the General Council and general superintendent from 1929–1949, denied that the role of the Kingdom was strictly reserved for the millennial period when he stated: "We must conclude that the Church and the spiritual kingdom are one and the same with slightly different connotations."[28]

Stanley M. Horton also focused attention on the role of the Kingdom in the present age. In writing on Luke's portrayal of Christ, he observed:

> For Luke, there is neither Jew nor Gentile, educated or uneducated, slave or free. Through Luke the Holy Spirit presented the gospel to the whole world, with the need of the whole world in view. The interest of the gospel centers in the human race, not just in the Jew. . . . In the Kingdom, con-

verted people will be welcomed regardless of race, color, or place of origin. . . . The poor, the neglected, and the oppressed will have as much or more opportunity to enter than the rich. Jesus is not interested in flattering any group. Like the good shepherd, His great interest centers on "that which is lost." His great heart of love goes out to the whole world. He does not want to see any part of suffering humanity overlooked. We need the same baptism in the same Holy Spirit that He received in order to do this work. We also need a baptism of the same love and compassion.[29]

Undoubtedly, the imperative to evangelize the world before Christ returns to set up his millennial kingdom and the compassionate concern to reach the heathen with the gospel have served as the underlying motives of the Assemblies of God missionary enterprise. At the same time, some missionaries—faced with the overwhelming material need of their fields—founded various charitable institutions (e.g., leprosariums, orphanages, schools). Perhaps such activities have also illustrated, albeit unwittingly, the manifestation of the kingdom of God in this age.

The new objectives of the missions program, the coming of a new generation of missionaries, the growing administrative structure and authority of the department, and the call for advanced training created tension in the Council and its missionary enterprise. Some questioned the need for so much planning and organization overseas. A columnist in *The Missionary Forum,* a publication of the missions department exclusively for missionary personnel, when asked whether the contemporary missionaries rated as highly in effectiveness as the pioneers of the program, answered:

> They are not producing the results in proportion to their advantages. The earlier missionaries did not have education but today they do. There was a much greater reliance on the Holy Spirit rather than looking to one's own ability. Everybody looked to the Lord in those days. Today, everybody plans; no one thinks of giving the Lord a chance to move and work. I think there was a greater spiritual impact—now with all the aids, they may be accomplishing more in volume, but after that, I don't know.[30]

One missionary resigned from the Council, explaining to the field leadership, "We are so highly organised now . . . that if God were to lead an individual to go to a certain place for evangelistic work, he or she would have to first of all consult with three committees. . . . As a missionary of the Lord Jesus, I want to be allowed to be led by His Spirit and do whatever He may want me to do."[31]

Such an uneasiness about the changes in the missions enterprise lingered. For many, however, including the leadership, there could be no return to the days when the program simply followed the inclinations of various individuals on the foreign fields. Lessons from the past had clearly taught the values of cooperative planning and better organization. Many now believed that increased planning, training, and efficiency could still be energized by the power of the Holy Spirit. As long as the goals remained the same, needed changes were allowed to keep pace with the times.

Structural and Financial Developments

Between 1943 and 1945, the Foreign Missions Department appointed 150 missionaries to its list of personnel. The total number of missionaries stood at 538[32] and the administrative responsibilities ballooned. In 1943, the General Presbytery authorized the Foreign Missions Department to appoint supplementary secretaries whenever they believed it was necessary. The field secretaries were to divide their responsibilities somewhat equally between office duties at headquarters and duties abroad. One year at home and one overseas was the recommendation.

The Foreign Missions Department had actually appointed its first field secretary, Henry C. Ball, in 1942. Long involved in Latin American missions, Ball had visited practically every country in Central and South America where Assemblies of God missionaries conducted mission works. He continued to serve in this capacity until 1953 when he became full-time director of the Spanish Publications Division he had founded in 1946 (now known as Life Publishers International). Ball's labors in evangelism, early Bible institute training, Spanish literature production, and missionary administration gained him widespread respect.

Other notable missionaries soon received appointment as field secretaries. Henry B. Garlock, long-time missionary to West Africa, became the first field secretary for Africa in 1943. Garlock made a tour of Africa from 1945 to early 1947 in which he visited 24 African countries and traveled 50,000 miles: "30,000 by car, 15,000 by airplane, and 5,000 by ship, train, motor launch, surf boat, canoe, horseback, hammock and on foot."[33] By 1945 Gustav Kinderman had been appointed field secretary for Europe (1943); Howard C. Osgood for China (1945) and later for the Far East (1949); and Robert W. Cummings for India, Pakistan, and Ceylon (1945). Later field secretaries included Melvin L. Hodges for Latin America and the West Indies (1954); Everett L. Phillips for Africa (1954); Victor G. Greisen for Europe, Southern Asia, and the Near East (1959); and George Carmichael for Europe and the Middle East (1951). Maynard L. Ketcham, appointed field secretary for Southern Asia initially (1951) and later for the Far East (1955), defined the office of field secretary as

> a liaison officer between the missionaries and the national churches on the field on the one hand and the Foreign Missions Department and the churches of America on the other. In my case, I had served for a number of years in the Bengali speaking area of North India as a missionary before being asked to serve as Field Secretary for the area. Field Secretaries frequently visit their fields, survey the needs and present the same to the faithful friends in America who are backing the work. They also have the responsibility for recruiting new missionaries and arranging to send them to the field with the approval of the Foreign Missions Department.[34]

The responsibilities and authority of the office continued to grow as the department expanded and the number of missionary personnel and converts increased overseas. In addition, from 1947 the field secretaries, along with the district superintendents of the overseas councils, represented the missionary personnel on the General Presbytery of the Assemblies of God.[35] In 1955, two additional missionaries from each major area represented by a field secretary were added to the presbytery.[36]

In 16 years—from 1934, when Perkin and one assistant handled all the correspondence, bookkeeping, and other responsibilities for 200 missionaries, to 1950—the department had grown to include 37 staff members and 11 divisions of responsibility. The foreign missions secretary supervised the general operation and direction of the program. The Foreign Missions Committee included the secretary and four others, appointed by the general superintendent in close cooperation with the foreign missions secretary and subject to the ratification of the General Presbytery. The following people served in this capacity at this time: Perkin; Gayle F. Lewis, assistant general superintendent; Henry C. Ball, field secretary for Latin America and the West Indies; Sydney S. Bryant, correspondence secretary for India; and Henry B. Garlock, field secretary for Africa. Jacob J. Mueller, assistant foreign missions secretary since 1934, served as the secretary for the group. This committee exercised top-level authority over missionary appointments, appropriations, approval of projects, field problems, and general policies.[37]

The field secretaries were responsible for field correspondence, overseas development, advisory service, and promotional work. The Relief and Rehabilitation Division, organized in the early 1950s and directed by Gustav Kinderman, provided assistance to refugees and disaster victims through food commodities and clothing.[38] Other divisions included records, bookkeeping, transportation, deputation, correspondence, promotions, Spanish publications, and purchasing.[39]

To expedite missionary travel by steamship in the 1930s, Perkin organized the Noel Perkin Travel Service on a nonprofit basis. Under this arrangement, he served as a subagent for several steamship lines and was able to make travel arrangements for embarking missionaries. With the growth of commercial air travel after the war, the department sponsored the establishment of the Springfield Travel Service, Inc., in 1956, under the management of W. Neil McDaniel. In 1962, the General Council sold this agency to McDaniel.[40]

The General Council meeting in Oklahoma City in 1955 revised the bylaws governing the Foreign Missions Department to enlarge the top echelon of administration. These extensive amendments arose from the Foreign Missions Seminar held in June 1954 in Springfield and they had the approval of the Executive Presbytery. One proposal brought a foreign missions board into existence. The board, appointed by the Executive Presbytery, consisted of the foreign missions secretary, two executive presbyters, two field secretaries, and two others.[41] In 1957, the General Council added six pastors, representing six established geographical areas of the United States, to the Foreign Missions Board to build closer cooperation with the home constituency. An advisory committee to the Foreign

Missions Board, consisting of six laymen from the six geographical regions, also came into existence that year.[42]

Another change placed the administration of the department in the hands of the reorganized Foreign Missions Committee made up of the foreign missions secretary, the field secretaries, and the heads of the major divisions of the operation. The committee oversaw and directed the work of the program in accordance with the policies of the Council and the Foreign Missions Board.[43] In 1958, the department appointed Emil Balliet as administrative assistant to help Noel Perkin shoulder the burdens of the department. This office, however, came to an end with Perkin's retirement in 1959 and Balliet's failure to succeed him.[44]

A change in nomenclature affected the top post in the department shortly thereafter. The 1957 meeting of the Council authorized that the title "foreign missions secretary" be replaced by "executive director of the Foreign Missions Department."[45] In authority and responsibility, the new title brought little change. In 1959, the Council changed the title to "assistant general superintendent" (with the portfolio of foreign missions). This gave the executive director of the missions program the same title designated to other department heads of the Council.[46]

Another important development came with the establishment of the New York City office of the Foreign Missions Department in 1946. Since the majority of missionaries passed through this port on their way to and from their fields, this office greatly facilitated missionary procedures and plans on the east coast. The office assisted in the purchase of equipment and supplies, the procurement of visas, governmental contacts, and travel arrangements. Robert T. McGlasson, the Eastern representative of the department, set up and directed this office. In this capacity, he was assisted by Stephen Walegir, a New York pastor, who succeeded to that position when McGlasson became foreign missions secretary under J. Philip Hogan in 1959. The office also operated the Mizpah Missionary Home in the Bronx, New York, for visiting missionaries. The entire operation was dismantled in 1962 and moved to Springfield, Missouri.[47]

The financial contributions of the Council continued to rise during these years, crossing the $1 million mark at the end of the biennium in 1944 and passing $7 million in the biennium ending March 1959.[48] The lingering problem of finding money to operate the department continued to frustrate the leadership. Although the World Missions Plan provided a 5 percent subsidy for the department, this did not adequately meet the needs of an expanding program.[49] The bylaws of the Council were amended in 1957 to grant 10 percent of undesignated funds for the use of office expenses.[50] Perkin hoped that this would enable the department to operate without the continuing subsidy from Gospel Publishing House.[51] With the decline in undesignated giving and the increase in designated monies in the years following the administration of Perkin, the General Council changed the policy to better provide for the administration of the foreign missions program. Currently 5 percent of all offerings for foreign missions (with the exception of personal/Christmas offerings) is placed in the General Emergency Fund to provide for office administration, field projects, and the emergency needs of missionaries.[52]

Besides the problem of administrative expense, the cost of the overseas missionary effort continued to expand after the war. By 1949 the general reserve (undesignated) fund was nearly depleted.[53] To head off the crisis, the department canceled all missionary furloughs to lessen overseas travel expenses. The funds accumulated before the end of the war had never come close to the announced goal of $5 million. As a result, "the rising cost of living, the greater number of missionaries now on our list, the increased cost of transportation to so many fields, and the tremendous cost of moving large numbers of missionaries out of fields, such as China—either to the homeland or to other fields—has gradually consumed our general reserve funds."[54] Perkin compared the situation to Moses leading the Israelites across the Red Sea. With God as their leader, the missions program would survive the crisis.

The officers of the department began to further educate the Assemblies of God constituency on how the missionary funds were spent, thus clearing up any possible misunderstandings.[55] A question surfaced in one quarter about the reason for the department's continuing appeal for funds when it already had thousands of dollars in the bank. A published response indicated that while other missions societies kept reserve funds for 1 full year in advance, the missions department did not have such a fund. If the local churches discontinued their financial assistance, the entire program would come to a halt after only 1 month.[56] No hoarding had taken place and the undesignated fund had been overdrawn for months. This seemed to answer the question, for the enthusiasm of the local churches did not wane; in fact, they continued to contribute ever larger amounts to the Council's overseas endeavors.

The Promotions Division

Closely associated with the structural development of the department, the inauguration of a promotions effort to build stronger relations with the districts and local churches marked another important step in the history of the program. Although the department began publishing booklets describing missionary activities in various fields as early as the 1930s, it did not form a specific division to handle this responsibility.

Proving to be the forerunner of a promotions division, missionary Glenn Horst joined the department in 1944 to supervise the itineraries of furloughed missionaries among local assemblies.[57] Kenneth Short, a missionary to Borneo on furlough during the war, came to the department in the same year to begin the first major publication of the program, *The Missionary Challenge.* The Foreign Missions Committee minutes report that

> attention was called to the interesting way in which Brother Kenneth Short writes his letters, and also how he presented the needs of his field, his aggressiveness and vision. It was suggested that he might be a good one to bring to the office to assist in [the] getting out of booklets on the various fields, and the publicity matters required to raise the money for extension work after the war.[58]

Short challenged the local churches in his writing to take advantage of the missionary opportunities abroad when the war ended and sacrificially support the program. In his opinion, "It will mean that once for all we forsake the jellyfish attitude that we cannot afford the program of God."[59] Preparing the churches for the expenses of resuming and expanding the work overseas appears to have been the reason for the addition of Horst and Short to the staff.

The actual setting up of the Promotions Division did not come about until 1949. A Promotions Committee was authorized to carry out the responsibilities for this new assignment. The committee included F. Wildon Colbaugh, editor of *The Missionary Challenge,* as promotional director; Glenn Horst; and others. The division had five objectives: (1) to promote the work of the department, (2) to inform, challenge, and inspire the constituency of the Assemblies of God to fulfill the Great Commission of Christ, (3) to assist the missionaries through publicity, etc., (4) to speed the gospel to the heathen, and (5) to bring the districts into a closer working relationship with the department.[60]

By the next year, Glenn Horst succeeded Colbaugh as director, due to the latter's increasing responsibilities. During that time the Foreign Missions Committee suggested that "every missionary on furlough give about 25 percent of his furlough time to the deputational work in outlying, or non-missionary-minded, assemblies."[61] Overseeing the promotional work of furloughed missionaries became more and more a responsibility of the Promotions Division.

Two years later, in 1952, the division expanded to include Horst, Short, Paul Pipkin, and J. Philip Hogan, a returned missionary from China and Taiwan; the last two men served as field representatives to promote the work in local churches through conducting missionary conventions.

By this time the division had also launched several projects. The "1949 Missionary Advance" solicited funds for 10 major field projects. February 20, 1949, was selected as the day for the presentation of this goal to the local churches. The following 10 projects received assistance as a result: Dahomey, French West Africa (later Benin)—three mission stations; Gold Coast, British West Africa (later Ghana)—Bible institutes; Liberia, West Africa—schools; Ceylon—an evangelistic center; India—Bible institutes and an evangelistic center; the Philippines—a Bible institute; Havana, Cuba—an evangelistic center; Buenos Aires, Argentina—an evangelistic center; home missions (U.S.A.)—new fields of endeavor.[62] The challenge for the next year was "Forward in '50—Double in '51"[63]

The most important achievement during these early years, however, was the appointment by various district councils in the Assemblies of God of (district) missionary representatives. As early as 1949, various districts expressed positive responses to the promotional work of the missions department and began to appoint representatives in their areas to assist in this effort.[64] By 1954, every district had such an officer.

The first national conference of district missionary representatives took place in Springfield on March 13–15, 1950. Thirty-five of the forty-one districts in the Council sent representatives to the sessions conducted at Central Assembly of God and the American Legion Hall. Pledging support for the goal of doubling the missionary giving in their districts for the coming year, they hoped to raise $10 million by June 30, 1952. To achieve these ends, the representatives approved four methods: (1) to encourage 12 annual missionary offerings from each church, (2) to urge each local assembly to contribute a minimum of 10 percent of its income to missions, (3) to establish a means to receive special gifts, and (4) to organize more extensive and effective travel and promotional work. The representatives then pledged to meet biennially in the alternate years between General Council meetings.[65] These conferences became significant for the continuing growth of support for the program within the Council.

The district missionary representative soon became known as the district missionary secretary. He served a dual responsibility in that he represented the district to the Foreign Missions Department and vice versa. The department looked on him

> as a member of the Promotions Division, serving on detached assignment in his district. *He is the spokesman of the Department to whom ammunition is supplied in the form of information to be passed on to the District officers and Pastors.* . . . It is the responsibility of the District Missionary Secretary to expose every church in his district to the missionary message.[66]

Hopefully this goal could be achieved, for the district missionary secretary was responsible for helping visiting missionaries set up their schedules for missions conventions in the local churches. A new publication, *Key* (representing the value placed on the district missionary secretary), came into being in 1953 to keep the secretaries informed of goals, vital information, and coming events.[67]

The Promotions Division also took the occasion of the biennial meetings of the General Council to promote the missions program. Sunday, August 30, 1953, was designated as National Missionary Day at the Council session in Atlanta, Georgia. One hundred missionaries, colorfully dressed to represent their fields, marched on Sunday afternoon into the convention hall to the sound of "Onward, Christian Soldiers." When Charles Greenaway, a missionary from

West Africa, completed his appeal for funds, Noel Perkin stood to add his encouragement. Glenn Horst described the response in *Key:*

> Men wrote checks, for the cash they had with them could not meet the challenge which they had heard. Ladies reached into their pocketbooks and gave beyond what they could afford to give. Talented and experienced young people stood before the cross in the hope that some pastor would hear the voice of the Lord to meet their need so that they could go to those who have never heard His Name. It seemed to all of us that the General Council had been called into session just for this moment.[68]

Assistants recorded the pledges on a huge "cash register," the numbers of which changed as the pledges came in from congregations all over the nation by telephone and telegraph. The total reached over $113,000.[69] Horst's description of the missionary service carried the Council members' enthusiasm for the missions enterprise. He later called for another such event at the next Council gathering.

In media presentations, the division put together a slide library of missionary pictures that churches could borrow throughout the year for missions-related activities. Motion pictures on missions were also circulated, though not without controversy. Since many district officers and pastors viewed motion pictures as a worldly evil, the division defended this medium by stating that "as long as we maintain a proper balance, keep pictures in their legitimate place, and follow them with a Spirit-anointed appeal from the Word of God, we should have nothing to fear from their use."[70] Appeals increased for such means of missions education.

A new promotions goal of a missionary speaker for each local assembly once a year met with approval in 1953. J. Philip Hogan pointed out that during that year over 1,400 local churches contributed nothing to foreign missions (i.e., monies channeled through the Foreign Missions Department) and that of the more than 5,000 that gave, only about half gave systematically. Hogan promised to remedy the situation, saying that "here in the Promotions Division we intend to do something about this situation. We may not make every church and every pastor missionary-minded over night, but we do propose to make them uncomfortable in their neglect."[71] The combined efforts of the Promotions Division and the district missionary secretaries prompted more widespread participation in missions support.

In 1952, Hogan became a field representative for the Promotions Division. A 1936 graduate of Central Bible Institute, he had pastored several churches and served for 3 years as a missionary in China and Taiwan.[72] With his appointment as secretary of the division two years later, the program continued to expand its activities and plans. Hogan and his assistants traveled widely to generate support for the missions enterprise. He also wrote extensively in various Assemblies of God periodicals to broadcast the needs and goals of the program. Whether soliciting money for "Uncle Dudley" (as the undesignated fund was called) or announcing W–E Day (World Evangelism Day) to gather funds for a church building loan fund for overseas churches, he continued to push for greater local church involvement in the missions program.

The Promotions Division sponsored eight World Missions Regional Conferences in 1956 "to spread knowledge-vision of Assemblies of God home and foreign missions."[73] At each conference, executive officers from three General Council departments (including Foreign Missions) and home and foreign missionaries spoke at general sessions and conducted 24 workshops for intensive study of the organization's missionary program. Exhibits, literature, and curios (from various mission fields) at each meeting added to the excitement of the occasion. The first conference took place in Fresno, California, followed by similar meetings in Portland, Oregon; Denver, Colorado; St. Paul, Minnesota; Detroit, Michigan; Asbury Park, New Jersey; Atlanta, Georgia; and Fort Worth, Texas.[74]

Departmental publications also played a key role in enlisting the support of various individuals and local churches. No longer content to use the limited space available in *The Pentecostal Evangel,* the department began publishing *The Missionary Challenge* in 1944.[75] The name of this monthly publication was changed to *The World Challenge* in 1956.[76] A new publication, *Global Conquest,* took its place in 1959 with Raymond T. Brock as its first editor.

Another publication, *The Missionary Forum,* began circulation in 1948. This periodical, intended for missionaries only, addressed unique problems of missionary life. It focused on the need "to provide a medium for the exchanging of ideas, the voicing of constructive criticism and for the defining of missionary policy."[77]

The most important fund-raising project and strategic approach to foreign missions arrived with the development of the Global Conquest program in 1957. Prior to this, Assemblies of God missionaries had scattered to the ends of the earth to preach the gospel in fulfillment of Matthew 24:14 and Mark 16:15. Often, however, this resulted in their laboring in remote and rural areas far away from major population centers. The new program focused on evangelizing the large urban areas of the world and concentrating missionary activities in such population centers. To evangelize the nations, their cities could not be ignored; missionaries had to be prepared for urban evangelism. The choice of the word *conquest* reflected the militant theme of the program. However, because of nationalistic sentiments in some countries the name was changed to Good News Crusades in 1967.

The General Council approved the program in 1957, including the following 3-year goals:

> 10 cents more a week a member to be given for missions
> 60 additional missionaries
> 10 new fields
> 6 more Bible institutes
> 60 gospel broadcasts
> 2,000 more national workers
> 600,000 foreign members
> 4 more foreign print shops
> 10 foreign bookstores[78]

Though more cautious in some respects than the 1943 goals, these goals represented the most ambitious project promoted by the Assemblies of God up to that time.

By 1959, the objectives of Global Conquest had been narrowed to three broad categories: literature production, national workers training, and evangelism. Hogan reported, "We know beyond a shadow of a doubt that it is possible, by means of modern communication, mass-literature saturation programs and, above all, the presentation of the gospel of Jesus Christ in miracle-working power, to force an impact on a great city."[79] Cities targeted included Tokyo, Calcutta, Manila, Djakarta, Bombay, Athens, Beirut, Dakar, and Seoul.

Global Conquest was launched on August 30, 1959, at the General

Council meeting in San Antonio, Texas. Contributors were asked not to designate their gift since the missions department wanted to allocate the money into the three categories as it saw fit. By September 20, less than a month later, the Foreign Missions Department had received approximately $50,000 for Global Conquest.[80] The building of an evangelistic center in Seoul, Korea, became the first Global Conquest project. From this work grew the Full Gospel Central Church pastored by Paul Yonggi Cho; eventually it would become the largest congregation in the world.[81]

Hogan was a major driving force behind the Global Conquest program. During his tenure under Noel Perkin, he gained widespread exposure and respect in the Council. When Perkin retired in 1959, the delegates at the San Antonio Council meeting elected Hogan to succeed him in office.[82]

Support Agencies

Beginning in 1943, popular support for the missions program expressed itself in the formation of several important assisting agencies within the General Council. The Women's Missionary Council, previously mentioned (see Chapter 7), grew to the point that it was made a national department in 1951.

Among other significant efforts to assist missionaries was the Speed–the–Light program, supported by the youth (called Christ's Ambassadors) of the local churches. Developed by Ralph W. Harris, national secretary of the Christ's Ambassadors Department, and launched in 1944, this program initially sought funding to expedite missionary travel overseas. A goal of $100,000 was announced.[83]

One of its important early projects, the purchase of a surplus airplane from the Army, enabled missionaries to return quickly to their fields. Before routine means of transportation had been restored following the war, the airplane, the *Ambassador,* began service in 1948. Its service was so effective in transporting missionaries overseas[84] that it was eventually replaced by a converted B–17 with four engines, the *Ambassador II.* This farsighted endeavor gained considerable publicity but the need for the plane ended when commercial aircraft companies improved their service.[85]

Other projects undertaken by Speed–the–Light involved the purchase of jeeps, motorboats, bicycles, cars, motorbikes, and "any other vehicle which will enable our missionaries to reach the greatest number of people in the shortest possible time."[86] The willingness to use technological advances in transportation greatly improved the efficiency of the missionaries in their pursuit of fulfilling the words of Jesus in Matthew 24:14: "This gospel of the kingdom shall be preached in all the world for a witness unto all nations; and then shall the end come."

By 1959, $3 million had been raised and donated by the Christ's Ambassadors of the Assemblies of God through the Speed–the–Light program. Missionaries in 64 countries had received assistance. J. Philip Hogan reported:

> Investments have been made in equipment as follows: radio equipment—$103,388; printing equipment—$101,183; in 1,384 vehicles—$1,766,827. Vehicles include 24 airplanes; 325 bicycles; 30 boats; 24 buses; 348 cars; 65 jeeps; 98 motor-bikes, cycles, or scooters; 283 station wagons; 31 trailers; 105 trucks; and assorted other mules, horses, ox carts, et cetera.[87]

This particular program, with its concern for helping missionaries spread the gospel, reflected the readiness of the Council and the leadership of the missions department to adapt to changes at the close of the war. It was also a practical manifestation of the central theological concern of the enterprise: the rapid evangelization of the world before the return of Christ. Consequently, Assemblies of God missionaries became some of the best equipped missionaries abroad.

On March 6, 1949, the Boys and Girls Missionary Crusade (B.G.M.C.) was introduced during a missions service at the Assemblies of God National Sunday School Convention in Springfield, Missouri. Conceived to provide gospel literature for overseas evangelism, B.G.M.C., just as its name implied, enlisted the Sunday school missionary offerings of young children. The children received small wooden barrels in which to save their coins for the missionary offerings.[88] A surprising amount of funding from this support agency provided missionaries needed assistance. For the fiscal year ending in 1959, B.G.M.C. contributed $96,621.74 to foreign missions.[89]

The use of radio communication for evangelism caught the imagination of many missionary leaders during this period. The Assemblies of God inaugurated *Sermons in Song*, a national broadcast, in 1946. The General Council renamed this program *Revivaltime* in 1950 when the format underwent revision. As this ministry developed, it reached overseas English-speaking audiences for evangelism through transmission over foreign outlets.[90] In 1953, the General Council appointed C. M. Ward, a prominent Assemblies of God pastor, as the speaker on this program. Ward's voice became familiar to many Americans and foreign nationals as more stations, at home and overseas, carried the program. Missionaries also developed radio programs on their own fields in the languages of the nationals. As early as 1945, over 20 broadcasts were made in five Spanish-speaking countries.[91] The trend toward radio evangelism accelerated during this period.

Participants at the Missionary Conference held at Central Bible Institute in April 1943. (Left to right)

Row 1: Fred Vogler, Alice Stewart, Helen Gustafson, Thelma Hildebrandt, Beatrice Hildebrandt, Ada Bolton, Edith Osgood, Grace Nicholson, Ruth Johnson, Mary Martin, Florence Smith, Jennie Wilson, Elise Simmons, Louise Hackert, Elizabeth Maynard, Eunice Princic

Row 2: Noel Perkin, Henrietta Tielman, Lula Belle Hough, Laura Kritz, Sunshine Ball, Alice E. Luce, Marguerite Flint, Marjorie Trulin, Kathryn Long, Martha Kucera, Ellen Esler, Mildred Ginn, Ruth Vassar, Estelle Vassar, Hattie Hacker, Barbara Cox, Nanny Downey

Row 3: Ida Beck, Nettie Juergensen, Eva Bauer, Dorothy Boyse, Hilda Refke, Howard Osgood, Leonard Bolton, Gladys Short, John Franklin (behind Gladys Short), Kenneth Short, Jacob Mueller, John Burgess, Ted Vassar, William Davis, Clarence Maloney

Row 4: Paul Kitch, Vivan Smith, Lloyd Shirer, Norman Barth, Nicholas Nikoloff, William I. Evans, Gustav Kinderman, Joseph Wannenmacher, Arthur Wilson, J. Roswell Flower, Alfred Blakeney, Ernest S. Williams, Harry Downey, Alois Princic, Lawrence McKinney

The life of a field secretary often required difficult travel to distant mission stations. Pictured left is Henry B. Garlock, first field secretary for Africa, eating lunch beside a trail in the Sturi Forest in the Belgian Congo (Zaire) in December 1950.

Edith and Howard Osgood, pictured above between two Malaysian national ministers, served as missionaries to China and Malaysia. Rev. Osgood was appointed as the first field secretary for the Far East.

Melvin L. Hodges, field secretary for Latin America and the West Indies, is pictured above addressing the 1957 graduates of the Cuban Bible Institute.

A major improvement in communications took place in the Department of Foreign Missions following World War II. *Key* informed district missionary secretaries of departmental policies. *The Missionary Forum* served the interest of the missionaries. *The Missionary Challenge, The World Challenge,* and *Global Conquest* promoted the cause of foreign missions to the membership of the General Council.

J. Philip Hogan (second from left) became secretary of promotions for the Department of Foreign Missions in 1954. Left, he is pictured with other ministers at a missionary service in a local Assemblies of God church. Pictured with Hogan (left to right) are: R. J. Bergstrom, Arvid Ohrnell, Frederick D. Eide, and E. S. Cooke.

Participants attending the first national District Missionary Secretaries conference in Springfield, Missouri, March 13–15, 1950. The sessions were conducted at Central Assembly of God (site of picture) and the American Legion Hall.

Standing in front are (left to right) Noel Perkin, Foreign Missions Secretary; Glenn Horst (behind Perkin), Secretary of Promotions; Sydney S. Bryant, Correspondence Secretary for India; G. Raymond Carlson, North Central District Superintendent; Melvin L. Hodges, missionary to Central America; George H. Carmichael, Field Secretary for the Middle East; Donald G. Foote, DMS for the Michigan District; Russell H. Olsen, DMS for the North Central District.

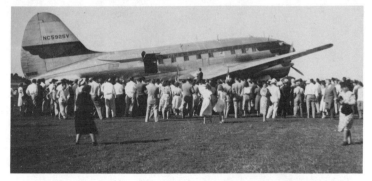

The *Ambassador I* was an airplane purchased in 1948 with Speed–the– Light funds to provide missionary transport overseas following World War II. Assemblies of God church members often gathered at the Springfield, Missouri, airport to say farewell or to meet returning missionaries.

Aboard the *Ambassador I* are missionaries returning to America from Africa.

Speed–the–Light funds provided these Bolivian Bible school students with bicycles to travel to evangelistic services.

Everett L. Phillips at his desk as field secretary for Africa. Before his appointment, he was a pioneer missionary to Nigeria, West Africa.

Robert T. McGlasson served for many years as the eastern representative at the New York City office for the Foreign Missions Department. Later (left) he served as the foreign missions secretary in the administration of J. Philip Hogan.

The Carmichaels served in various capacities in the Department of Foreign Missions. For several years George served as field secretary for Europe and the Middle East and Christine wrote extensively publicizing the missions program.

In 1949 the Boys and Girls Missionary Crusade was introduced to raise funds to pay for gospel literature used in overseas evangelism.

Looking over handcrafts provided by WMC chapters are Edith Whipple, first national WMC secretary (1951–1959), and Mildred Smuland, her successor.

11

Missiology and Cooperation

The changes in departmental structure and strategy following the war were complemented with a clearer and more pronounced articulation of the overseas mission of the Assemblies of God by Melvin L. Hodges. A new generation of missionaries filling the ranks made missionary education a major concern. Problems developed with some missionary-evangelists, which jeopardized the implementation of the indigenous church strategy, but eventually the program weathered the storm. Cooperative relationships with organized Pentecostals and conservative evangelicals became more positive.

Missiological Developments

In the period after 1943, the Foreign Missions Department gradually clarified the goals of its overseas endeavors. This was largely achieved through its growing concern for missionary preparation and the publication of *The Indigenous Church* by Melvin L. Hodges, a missionary to Central America and later (1954–1973) field secretary for Latin America and the West Indies.

The 1943 Missionary Conference in Springfield had recommended that further educational preparation be available for missionary candidates. The General Council chose Central Bible Institute to provide such training under the instruction of Robert W. Cummings because of its location (near the Foreign Missions Department offices), its status as a General Council school, and the many missionary candidates it graduated. New courses the institute added to its curriculum included church and missions relations; Christian approach to non-Christians; first aid; French I, II, III; Hindustani for beginners; Hindustani advanced; linguistics and phonemics; phonetics; Spanish-beginners and Spanish-advanced.[1]

Though initially slanted toward missionary service in India because of Cummings' experience there, the training nevertheless represented a significant advance in missionary education among Assemblies of God schools.

The precedent of gathering furloughed missionaries at the 1943 and 1948 Missionary Conferences showed the value of continuing such events. From May 30 to June 9, 1950, about 100 missionaries and candidates assembled for another conference, or "seminar," at Central Bible Institute to receive instructions and discuss problems related to missionary life and activities. A variety of subjects dealt with the spiritual life of the missionary and relationships with his peers, the home office, and the local supporting Assemblies of God churches. Conference speakers also taught the principles of setting up and implementing indigenous churches. Other topics included "Planning Our Missionary Program," "Race Prejudices," "Comity," "Guidance of the Holy Spirit," "Problems Related to Polygamy," "Language Problems," "Publications," "The Missionary on Furlough," and so forth.[2]

The convention exhibited the spiritual nature of missionary work. Devotional time with guest speakers and periods of prayer were scheduled for twice a day.

The missionaries paid for their travel expenses and lodging at the seminar. In its report to the Executive Presbytery, the Foreign Missions Department stated that it had paid Central Bible Institute "one dollar per day for each missionary so that the cost of entertainment to the missionary was only one dollar per day which was for room and board."[3]

The seminars continued and the General Council formally approved a "School of Missionary Orientation" in 1957.[4] The First Annual School of Orientation took place from July 14 to 24, 1959, at Central Bible Institute. Noel Perkin directed the school, which drew 115 missionaries: 43 veterans on furlough and 72 new appointees.[5] Plans for the future called for extending the Schools of Missionary Orientation to 6 weeks.

The life and work of an Assemblies of God missionary had become considerably more complex since the days when individuals—sensing a call from God and believing He would provide their needs—went overseas without definite financial support, knowledge of the host culture or language, or a clear strategy for action. A sign of the increasing complexity of missionary work during the period after World War II is the growing size of *The Missionary Manual*: from 28 pages in 1931 to 48 pages in 1949 to 77 pages in 1956.[6] The Schools of Missionary Orientation assisted the missionaries with the increased departmental regulations and procedures.

Insurance for missionaries and education for their children caused growing concern during this period. Adequate housing for missionaries on furlough also received attention. In 1950, the Foreign Missions Department purchased the 20-acre Wilhoit property, adjoining Central Bible Institute, for $35,000. Although the purchase was made in the corporate name of CBI, the Foreign Missions Department drew up an agreement with them for the development of the property. Wooden-framed houses purchased from the O'Reilly Army Hospital in Springfield were placed on the land. The property became known as Mission Village and for many years housed missionaries home on furlough.[7]

Missionary applications became more demanding during this period. Besides wanting references, a medical examination, district approval, and interviews, the Foreign Missions Department required personality and general aptitude tests. These were administered and analyzed by Dr. Harry Goldsmith, a psychologist and member of the faculty of Evangel College, an Assemblies of God liberal arts college in Springfield. He analyzed the tests and submitted a confidential report to the Foreign Missions Committee.[8]

During this period—as indicated by the concern for the missionary's mental well-being, housing needs, insurance coverage, and advanced training—greater care of the missionary family was taken to ensure long-range effectiveness of both the missions program and the family. This did not, however, lessen the leadership's sense of urgency about evangelism and belief in the imminent return of Christ.[9]

By 1959, the missionaries of the Assemblies of God possessed clearer, more articulate goals for overseas evangelism and implementation of indigenous church principles than ever before. To a marked degree, this growing understanding and acceptance of indigenous church principles owed its success to the work of Melvin L. Hodges. Without doubt, the most significant Assemblies of God publication on missionary strategy to that point in the history of the enterprise was *The Indigenous Church*, written by Hodges and published in 1953. Having been associated with Ralph D. Williams, an indigenous church pioneer missionary in Central America, and strongly influenced by Roland Allen's *The Spontaneous Expansion of the Church and the Causes Which Hinder It,* Hodges became the most prominent Assemblies of God exponent for the implementation of the principles overseas. [10] The book was based on a series of lectures given at the 1950 missionary conference in Springfield. Hodges expanded his treatment of the subject and Gospel Publishing House printed the work in 1953. The following year, when Moody Press of Chicago received permission to reprint the book, it gained wider publicity. *The Indigenous Church* became famous for its clear exposition of these principles. Perkin considered its publication to be a trial balloon and hoped that it would be well received by the Assemblies of God missionary personnel. It was the only book of its kind by a Pentecostal author.

In 11 chapters, Hodges discussed the nature of a New Testament church, the implementation of the "three selfs": self-government, self-propagation, and self-support. He also gave advice on how to change over to these methods and to handle the problems that might arise. According to him, "New Testament preaching and practice will produce a New Testament church in any place where the gospel is preached." [11]

In many respects, Hodges repeated principles advocated by Rufus Anderson, Henry Venn, John Nevius, Roland Allen, and others at the turn of the century. However, the book's uniqueness lay not only with his successful experiences at applying these principles and his easy-to-read writing style, but also with his underlying Pentecostal theology. The New Testament church, as restored, would be characterized by "signs and wonders," just as its first-century predecessor had been. Thus it cannot be restored without the authenticating work of the Holy Spirit. To the author, "the mechanics of a successful church on the mission field are the New Testament methods; the dynamics are the power and ministries of the Holy Spirit. Either factor alone is incomplete and inadequate." [12] Thus, Hodges added to the works of Anderson, et al., the pneumatological dynamic of the Early Church.

Another important feature of the book, which accurately portrays the way many Assemblies of God missionaries worked over the years, was its concern for Biblical instruction and evangelism. To

Hodges, the emphasis on each believer receiving the Pentecostal baptism, that is, a personal "infilling" of the Holy Spirit, had produced many earnest believers.[13] The accompanying working of miracles and healing of the sick were significant factors in the growth of the Assemblies of God abroad. Benjamin P. Shinde, an Assemblies of God missiologist and leader in India, wrote:

> One of the important features of Pentecostal work has been prayer for the sick and their subsequent healing. Many illustrations can be cited to show that because of healings, a family became Christian, or an individual became a Christian. Not only the healing of the physical body, but in Pentecostal churches prayers are offered for the deliverance of the demon possessed.[14]

Finally, Hodges saw the filling in of "the artificial gap" between clergy and laity as a key to restoring the New Testament church. He maintained that "the faith which Pentecostal people have in the ability of the Holy Spirit to give spiritual gifts and supernatural abilities to the common people, even to those who might be termed 'ignorant and unlearned,' has raised up a host of lay preachers and leaders of unusual spiritual ability—not unlike the rugged fishermen who first followed the Lord."[15] This statement accurately reflects the thinking and hopes of many Assemblies of God missionaries.

Although Hodges explained the indigenous church principles simply and clearly in his book, its actual implementation by Assemblies of God missionaries took a good deal of effort at times. The leadership hoped that increased missionary training would reduce the problems for the missionary. Perkin lamented that some missionaries, for example, had exhibited racial prejudice: "There are many things that we have to learn to overcome when we enter into our life in Christ. There are some things that are so deeply rooted in us that we are hardly conscious of them. One of these is an innate feeling of white superiority. . . . I have seen difference of treatment by our missionaries of those who are colored."[16] One national minister charged that the Assemblies of God mission enterprise in his country was based on "unscriptural ground which has produced a set of spoon-fed workers who have learned to look only to the missionary for their support and not to the living God from whom every good and perfect gift cometh, and thus we have become spiritually and financially crippled."[17] However, the mere fact that this minister's letter of complaint could receive hearing in *The Missionary Forum* testifies to the seriousness with which the missions department worked to foster overseas indigenous churches.

The department tried to avoid forcing a western-type, or North American pattern, of organization on the national churches. It attempted instead to "encourage the type readily understood and easily operated by the nationals of the country."[18] Nevertheless, the department did advocate a democratic representative church government for indigenous church organizations. Accordingly, Hodges and others thought that this approach to church government best represented the ideal of the New Testament church.

In spite of occasional failures and problems facing the implementation of overseas indigenous churches, the Assemblies of God proved to be remarkably successful in this venture. Nicholas Nikoloff, an early missionary to Europe, reported that the work in Eastern Europe since 1926 had successfully followed that approach.[19] Everett L. Phillips, field secretary for Africa (1954-1971), wrote:

> An African saved and filled with the Holy Spirit is invariably a better witness of the gospel to his own people than the missionary can ever be. We have fourteen Bible Schools in Africa training Africans for the ministry among their own people of many languages. What is accomplished by these trained Africans could never be accomplished by missionaries.[20]

By 1959 virtually every Assemblies of God mission field had moved toward the eventual implementation of an indigenous church structure. In new fields, missionaries laid the groundwork for such a structure by evangelizing and then training a national leadership. Other established fields moved rapidly toward electing their own leaders and becoming self-governing. Occasionally, where the old paternalistic mission station approach had been followed, this proved to be difficult and slow. Many others, however, had already become indigenous bodies and were now in fraternal association with the Assemblies of God in the United States.

Upon the dismantling of the overseas district councils and the establishment of national church organizations, the missionaries then formed field fellowships to assist the continuing development of the indigenous church. These bodies advised the department on policy and missionary personnel. They were also meant to maintain harmonious relationships with the overseas national churches without encroaching on their activities and independence.[21] As a consequence, the national organizations successfully weathered the storms that nationalistic aspirations brought about on many fields. Because of their indigenous makeup, they were not considered foreign organizations.[22]

Significant in the training of an indigenous leadership was the overseas Bible institute. By 1959, the Assemblies of God led all Protestant missions agencies in the number of such institutes, operating twice as many as any other agency. The department's leadership had been unaware of this achievement until a member of the Southern Baptist Convention brought it to their attention. Carl Malz, a missionary who conducted a study of these overseas institutions along with Melvin L. Hodges and Maynard L. Ketcham, reported that the number of new schools opened in the 1930s more than doubled in the 1940s and then doubled again in the following decade. Half of the Bible institutes abroad were founded in the 1950s.[23] Malz also noted the higher number of national ministers (60 percent) serving on the boards of directors of these institutions.[24] In addition, he estimated that about half of the overseas missionary personnel and half of the departmental budget were focused on Bible institute programs.

In the late 1950s the Foreign Missions Department expressed its resolve to support the growth of indigenous churches by slowly eliminating financial assistance for national ministers from the undesignated fund.[25] It underscored the resolve by stressing that it could not meet the expenses of benevolent institutions overseas when they exceeded their revenues. Nevertheless, those missionaries engaged in such activities could receive approval for publicizing their needs in the missionary publications. However, since "all available missionary funds could readily be absorbed in such work . . . the missionary should seek to restrict his obligations within his vision and degree of faith."[26] The department aimed at directing all possible resources toward building national church organizations. In spite of this, the Assemblies of God constituency in the United States, having a concern for orphans, lepers, and other dependent persons, usually responded to appeals on their behalf, though not necessarily to other kinds of appeals.

Cooperative Relationships

The size of the Assemblies of God foreign missions program did not permit it to skirt the tensions of the period with other organizations, including the Foreign Missions Conference of North America and the newly formed Evangelical Foreign Missions Association. Even other Pentecostal groups had to be reckoned with.

During the early 1950s, after the appearance of the salvation-healing movement in America, many evangelistic crusades were conducted overseas by both independent and Assemblies of God evangelists who focused on the role of faith healing in their ministries.[27] Some of these crusades had long-lasting effects on the growth of Assemblies of God constituencies abroad. For example, thousands attended the evangelistic campaigns held by evangelist Clifton O. Erickson in Chile in 1951. Hundreds were converted and professed being healed of various ailments. Local assemblies grew as a result.[28] Erickson, along with Lester F. Sumrall, held another noteworthy campaign 2 years later in Manila, the Philippines.[29]

A spectacular crusade under the direction of evangelist Tommy Hicks took place in Buenos Aires, Argentina, in 1954. Tens of thousands attended these meetings. Missionary Louie W. Stokes reported that over 3 million people attended the services during the 2 months they were held. As a result, thousands were converted and many reported being healed. He added that "many of our young pastors are now praying for the sick with increased faith, new churches are being opened, and people everywhere are asking for literature and Bibles."[30]

Although some of these efforts resulted in overseas growth for the Assemblies of God, numerous problems arose by the mid-1950s over some healing evangelists' financial policies, spectacular claims (with negative effects overseas), and promotion of direct support to sympathetic national pastors and evangelists. It should be noted that these conflicts arose precisely when the missions department had become most aware of its responsibility to plant self-governing, self-propagating, and self-supporting national churches overseas.

In 1954, the Foreign Missions Committee determined to grant publicity only to those evangelists who had worked in harmony with the missionaries overseas.[31] Noel Perkin openly questioned the positive results of some evangelistic campaigns:

In numbers of instances healings that have been reported have not been lasting and the number of souls actually saved and added to the church in such meetings has frequently been quite small in comparison with the magnitude of the meeting. The adverse reaction in the thinking of many who crowd to these meetings for healing when disappointed in their hopes is impossible to calculate. We cannot help but wonder if we have not reversed things. Our commission is to preach the gospel. It is the Lord's work to confirm the Word with signs following. The gospel basically is that Christ died for our sins and has risen for our justification. As this message is preached in the power of the Spirit and souls are added to Christ and His Church we believe the life also of Jesus will be made manifest in and through His body in physical benefit as we exercise faith to this end.[32]

To capitalize on the benefits of such campaigns, the Foreign Missions Department set up in 1955 a Division for Overseas Evangelism, naming Glenn Horst secretary. The efforts of approved evangelists abroad were to be assisted by this new agency.[33]

The policy of some overseas evangelists who raised funds to finance national pastors and evangelists received strong denunciation from the leadership of the missions program. J. Philip Hogan wrote that no church at home or abroad "can progress very far down the road toward being a stable, witnessing church until it assumes, sometimes at great sacrifice, the support of its own ministry and leadership."[34] Hogan's statement strongly reflected the leadership's growing concern about the speedy implementation of the indigenous church ideal.[35]

Relationships with other Pentecostal organizations that were more positive came with the formation of the World Pentecostal Fellowship in 1947 (now known as the Pentecostal World Conference) and the Pentecostal Fellowship of North America (P.F.N.A.) the following year.[36] The latter body adopted seven criteria for missionary cooperation and pledged itself to "the promotion of spiritual fellowship and co-ordination of missionary and evangelistic effort throughout the world."[37] The P.F.N.A. serves as a body for consultation and cooperation; it does not govern the missions program of any of its member organizations.

In one notable case, the Foreign Missions Department helped the Pentecostal (mostly Assemblies of God) and evangelical believers in Italy to gain religious liberty. The Supreme Council of Italy ruled in favor of religious freedom by setting aside an old law from the regime of Benito Mussolini. This act opened the way for the eventual recognition of the Assemblies of God in Italy as a church body.[38]

Affiliation with missionary service agencies proved to be a problem following the war. For many years the department had been associated with the Foreign Missions Conference of North America, benefiting from its services for the missionary enterprise. The department nevertheless denounced the continuing move toward liberal, or modernistic, theology among its constituent members. When the Evangelical Foreign Missions Association (E.F.M.A.), an arm of the newly formed National Association of Evangelicals (1942), came into existence in 1945, the Foreign Missions Department joined the following year.[39] This missionary agency represented distinctly conservative evangelical and Pentecostal missionary agencies.

When the Foreign Missions Conference became affiliated with the National Council of Churches, the Executive Presbytery and the department's leadership felt compelled to drop their affiliation in 1950. In spite of this, they were allowed to attend the conferences, join any of the subcommittees, and speak to issues on the floor, but without a vote. This arrangement was accepted and utilized. The Assemblies of God received listing as a "consultative body" and continued to make small financial contributions to the support of this organization. Benefits continued from this contact.[40]

Even the early affiliation with the Evangelical Foreign Missions Association did not prove to be tranquil. Several conservative evangelical missions agencies refused to join the E.F.M.A. because of the existing membership of several Pentecostal organizations. In view of the developing resentment, the new association's unproved record of assistance, and the cost of supporting contributions, Noel Perkin reluctantly recommended withdrawal from the agency in late 1950.[41] Three years later the department responded positively to the request of Dr. Clyde Taylor, executive director of the E.F.M.A., to reaffiliate with the agency. Since then, the relationship of the Foreign Missions Department and the E.F.M.A. has been warm and cordial. Noel Perkin was elected to serve as its president in 1959 for a 1-year term. He had the honor of being the first Pentecostal elected to this post.[42]

Conclusion

From the 1943 Missionary Conference to the retirement of Noel Perkin in 1959, the Assemblies of God witnessed dramatic changes and growth in its overseas missions program. In the final year of this period, it supported 753 missionaries with a budget of $6,734,780 and reported 61 foreign Bible institutes, 11,338 national ministers, 13,795 churches, and 627,443 converts.[43]

Notable changes came with the addition of the Promotions Division, several support agencies, and improvements in missionary training. Nevertheless, the most important thrust of the endeavor came with the implementation of strategic planning to achieve world evangelization and the firm resolve to plant indigenous churches overseas, the ideal toward which the Assemblies of God had committed itself from its beginning.

The success of the foreign missions program caught the attention of church leaders at home and abroad, liberal and conservative.[44] The election of Noel Perkin as president of the Evangelical Foreign Missions Association in 1959 represented a milestone in the recognition of the program. When Perkin's farsighted leadership ended in the same year, the Assemblies of God foreign missions program had entered a new era of cooperation with its daughter organizations abroad.

Evangelist Tommy Hicks conducted a salvation/healing crusade (1954) in Buenos Aires, Argentina, that made a major impact on the growth of the Assemblies of God and other Pentecostal bodies in that country. Standing with supporting ministers is Evangelist Tommy Hicks (at the microphone) and Assemblies of God missionary Louie W. Stokes (without suit jacket).

Thousands attended the overseas crusades of Assemblies of God evangelist Clifton O. Erickson. Pictured above is a crowd assembling to hear him in Rio de Janiero, Brazil, in 1956.

Discussing the future plans for Global Conquest were (left to right) Wesley R. Hurst, promotions secretary; Everett Phillips, secretary for Africa; V. G. Greisen, secretary for Europe, the Middle East, and Southern Asia; Melvin L. Hodges, secretary for Latin America and the West Indies. Maynard L. Ketcham, secretary for the Far East, was in the Far East when the photo was taken.

J. Philip Hogan (left), executive director of the Division of Foreign Missions since 1959, is pictured with his predecessor, Noel Perkin, who directed the agency from 1927 to 1959.

12

Concluding Observations

Organized during the last year of the Great Century in Christian missions, the Assemblies of God foreign missions program represented a fresh and vigorous thrust in world evangelization. Although other missions agencies were soon wracked by discord over the finality of the Christian message and the fundamentalist/modernist controversy, the Assemblies of God missions enterprise maintained a conservative theological posture. Indeed, its belief that it had been raised up for evangelism in the last days reinforced its confidence in Biblical authority and the validity of its message. The premillennial concern of rescuing the perishing and preparing them for the coming kingdom of God on earth motivated many to engage in overseas ministry. They saw the outpouring of the Holy Spirit around the turn of the century as the fulfillment of an Old Testament prophecy (Joel 2:28,29). Like other Pentecostals, Assemblies of God church members believed that the spiritual dynamic of the early Christian church had been restored.

In the early days of the Pentecostal movement some had promoted the missionary use of speaking in tongues, but Assemblies of God missionaries looked upon this experience as an avenue of power for Christian witness. In their view, miraculous healings and deliverances from sinful practices would follow the preaching of the gospel. This expectancy never waned even though the foreign missions program changed in other ways.

From the beginning, the enterprise's ideal was the establishment of self-supporting, self-governing, and self-propagating (i.e., indigenous) churches. Although influenced by the new concern for indigenous works already in some missions circles and being taught in the Christian and Missionary Alliance, Assemblies of God leaders and many of its early missionaries were also markedly impressed by the church planting accompanied by signs and wonders of the Holy Spirit portrayed in the Book of Acts.

However, because of primitive conditions, poverty, and reluctance of some personnel, it took many years to implement indigenous churches. Nevertheless, many missionaries worked toward that end. As the Assemblies of God missions program grew and actively began to direct the efforts of its missionaries, it strongly contributed to the fulfillment of the ideal. The 1921 General Council's formal adoption of indigenous church principles for its foreign missions program served to provide direction for the future. Many years passed, however, before this approach to church order was linked to Pentecostal pneumatology. Melvin L. Hodges, a veteran missionary, educator, and field secretary, clearly explained the indigenous strategy and fused it with Pentecostal theology in his book *The Indigenous Church.* Throughout the years, however, charitable institutions were also founded abroad, illustrating the humanitarian concerns of the missionaries and their supporting constituency.

The Pentecostal revivals had a leveling effect among the early participants. The sharp distinction between clergy and laity was almost nonexistent during the beginning years. The Pentecostal baptism was believed to equip all Christians for an aggressive witness, at home and abroad. Scores of early Pentecostals traveled overseas to tell of their new spiritual experiences and preach the gospel. Most of these efforts ended in disillusionment due to inadequate training and financial support.

The wide participation accorded to women, particularly single women, also reflected the leveling effect of the Pentecostal movement. Single women often became pastors, evangelists, and missionaries. Although playing an important role in Assemblies of God missions, they rarely served in administrative capacities. As more men enlisted in missionary service, the influence of women declined.

With the establishment of Pentecostal organizations, the Assemblies of God in particular, distinctions arose between clergy and laity. Endorsement and ordination for missionaries followed. Many viewed such changes in a positive light since church order could be found in the New Testament and achievement of the goal of world evangelism in the last days seemed to demand a professional clergy.

Contrary to the general distrust of educational preparation for ministers and missionaries that marked some early Pentecostals, four early Bible institutes founded in the northeastern region of the United States strongly influenced the course of the Assemblies of God and its missionary enterprise. A. B. Simpson's Missionary Training Institute at Nyack, New York, was possibly the most influential. The other three schools were all founded by women and distinctively Pentecostal: the Rochester (N.Y.) Bible Training School; Beulah Heights Bible and Missionary Training School, North Bergen, New Jersey; and Bethel Bible Training School, Newark, New Jersey. Although these three schools eventually closed or merged, they existed long enough to train many future leaders, pastors, and missionaries. The lasting influence of these schools on the denomination has never been adequately assessed in Assemblies of God historiography.

The founding fathers and mothers of the Assemblies of God were acutely aware of the need for coordination and direction of the scattered and disorganized missionary efforts abroad. Even with the establishment of the Missionary Department in 1919, directing the program eluded the organization for many years. In reality the department functioned primarily as a distribution center for missionary funds. It forwarded designated offerings to the missionaries and also equitably distributed undesignated contributions. Although many churches enthusiastically supported the missionaries, they were often reluctant to contribute to the operating expenses of the department. This caused its instability and forced it to be subsidized by Gospel Publishing House. In addition, many missionaries resented outside interference with their activities, preferring to be guided directly by the Holy Spirit. But Harold K. Needham's survey of the major Assemblies of God mission fields in 1920–1921 confirmed to the Council's leadership that more direction was imperative to fulfill the goals of the enterprise.

The permanent appointment of Noel Perkin as foreign missions secretary in 1927 inaugurated a long era of growth and stability. During his tenure, the financial support of the department began to increase and the General Council became better informed about its missions program. The issuance of the *Missionary Manual* in 1931 marked a milestone in the development of the program. Its policies signaled an increasing maturity in the organization and concern for efficiently achieving its objectives. Perkin and other Council leaders reiterated the essentially spiritual role of the program in spite of its growing structure.

World War II forced the department to plan for the future and precipitated its taking a stronger hand in directing its operation. The leadership, however, remained flexible in its response to new and more successful initiatives. At the 1943 Missionary Conference held in Springfield, Missouri, goals were set for the period following the war. Latin America became an important focus of missionary endeavor because the war hampered activities in the Far East and Europe. The appointment of field secretaries to coordinate the work in various regions of the world greatly strengthened the effectiveness of the program. The Assemblies of God became a leader in theological training for prospective national ministers on its fields of ministry. Through the long-term efforts of many missionaries and the development of strategic planning, national church organizations arose overseas that actualized the original ideal of the enterprise. This forced the traditional role of the missionary into a more fraternal, advisory one.

With the increasing developments in organization and governing policies of the department, a tension arose in some missionaries between their desire for personal direction by the Holy Spirit and adherence to departmental regulations. This problem had existed from the early years of the foreign missions program. But at that time missionaries were more closely attached to local supporting congregations than to the Department of Foreign Missions and enjoyed the freedom to travel to locations of their choice overseas. They claimed their locations of ministry were directed by the Holy Spirit. As the organizational structure increased and strategic planning occurred, this latitude was curbed but not eliminated. More and more the missionary became a person loyal to and guided by the policies of the department. Some wondered if the department and its leadership could be directed by the Spirit in the same manner an individual could. The leadership and many missionaries believed this was possible, for the enterprise had been raised up by God and the personnel were empowered by the Spirit at the end of history to fulfill the Great Commission of Christ. Hopefully the structure would assist in achieving the spiritual objectives of the enterprise instead of hampering them. During the years surveyed in this study, the department's leadership tried to maintain a balance between needed structure and freedom for individual action as directed by the Holy Spirit. While this approach largely resolved the issue, the tension has continued to exist.

To further promote the overseas program among the local churches, the department created a Promotions Division. This agency, coupled with the appointment of district council missionary secretaries in the 1950s, forged stronger links between the department, the districts, and local congregations in the United States.

Over the years, the zeal of the churches for the missions program never waned. The continual increases in financial contributions were accompanied by the creation of several important support agencies, such as the Women's Missionary Council (later the Women's Ministries Department) and Speed–the–Light, to expedite the work of the missionaries. Conventions in local churches featuring guest missionary speakers stirred the interest of many and proved to be fertile ground for recruiting potential missionaries. The Assemblies of God never lacked missionary candidates. Increasing departmental publications kept the successes and needs of the endeavor before the home constituency.

In the early years of the Assemblies of God, ecumenical contacts with other Pentecostals were strongly encouraged. The close association of the nondenominational Missionary Conferences with the meetings of the General Council illustrated this interest. Overseas, missionaries often cooperated with non-Council personnel in various endeavors. The long cooperative relationship with the Russian and Eastern European Mission was the most important of its kind.

As the foreign missions program grew and the number of its personnel increased, relationships with its daughter organizations became the preeminent concern. Interest in the activities of other Pentecostal missionaries gradually declined. The department slowly became self-reliant and ecumenical contacts eventually took the form of membership in the Pentecostal Fellowship of North America and the Evangelical Foreign Missions Association. It abandoned full membership with the Foreign Missions Conference of North America when that body became allied with the liberally oriented National Council of Churches. In this matter, the department reflected the tensions that had been produced by the fundamentalist/modernist controversy and the increasing alignment of the Assemblies of God with conservative evangelicals in the United States.

When Noel Perkin retired in 1959, the department had moved in other farsighted directions. Global Conquest, another strategic move for world evangelism, was introduced in the same year. The agency's relationship with its overseas churches had taken a more fraternal tone. Missionary education had advanced from an earlier course of instruction provided at Central Bible Institute to an annual School of Missionary Orientation.

The Assemblies of God foreign missions program adopted the indigenous church principles of earlier advocates and combined them with its unique Pentecostal theology. Implementation took many years to achieve, as did Pentecostal exposition of these principles. However, at the end of 45 years, the Assemblies of God had successfully established indigenous churches abroad and achieved a position of leadership in the Christian world mission.

Epilogue

Since this study has focused on the background and development of the Assemblies of God foreign missions enterprise from the turn of the century to 1959, it is important to mention that materials are available that provide some information on the events occurring after this period. William W. Menzies discusses the changes in the Division of Foreign Missions between 1960 and 1971 in *Anointed To Serve: The Story of the Assemblies of God* (Springfield, MO: Gospel Publishing House, 1971). A more recent survey by Joyce Wells Booze also provides valuable information: *Into All the World: A History of Assemblies of God Foreign Missions* (Springfield, MO: Assemblies of God Division of Foreign Missions, 1980). An excellent treatment of Assemblies of God missiological perspectives is provided by Melvin L. Hodges in *A Theology of the Church and Its Mission: A Pentecostal Perspective* (Springfield, MO: Gospel Publishing House, 1977).

For further historical study of Assemblies of God foreign missions, two other publications merit careful attention. *Mountain Movers,* a monthly periodical produced by the Assemblies of God Division of Foreign Missions, keeps members of the General Council and other interested readers informed about the overseas activities of the agency and occasionally includes accounts of missionary pioneers. In addition, the Assemblies of God Archives issues a quarterly publication, *Assemblies of God Heritage.* It frequently includes meaningful articles on various historical aspects of Assemblies of God foreign missions. Both of these periodicals are highly recommended for those interested in the history of the missions endeavor.

Endnotes

PART 1: BEGINNINGS

Chapter 1: American Protestant Missions by 1914

[1]Kenneth Scott Latourette, *A History of the Expansion of Christianity*, vol. 4: *The Great Century: Europe and the United States: A.D. 1800–A.D. 1914* (New York: Harper and Row, 1941), p. 7.

[2]R. Pierce Beaver, "Missionary Motivation Through Three Centuries," in *Reinterpretation in American Church History*, ed. Gerald H. Anderson (Chicago: University of Chicago Press, 1968), p. 115.

[3]Franklin H. Littell, "The Free Church View of Missions," in *The Theology of the Christian Mission*, ed. Gerald H. Anderson (New York: McGraw–Hill Book Co., 1969), p. 115.

[4]Paul A. Varg, *Missionaries, Chinese, and Diplomats: The American Protestant Missionary Movement in China 1890–1952* (New York: Octagon Books, 1977), p. 56.

[5]Beaver, "Missionary Motivation," pp. 147–148.

[6]Valentin H. Rabe, *The Home Base of American China Missions, 1880–1920* (Cambridge: Harvard University Press, 1978), pp. 15, 17–18.

[7]W. Richie Hogg, "The Rise of Protestant Missionary Concern, 1517–1914," in *The Theology of the Christian Mission*, ed. Gerald H. Anderson (New York: McGraw–Hill Book Co., 1961), pp. 110–111.

[8]W. Richie Hogg, "The Role of American Protestantism in World Mission," in *American Missions in Bicentennial Perspective*, ed. R. Pierce Beaver (South Pasadena: William Carey Library, 1977), p. 380. For analyses of the role of women in foreign missions, see R. Pierce Beaver, *American Protestant Women in World Mission: A History of the First Feminist Movement in North America* (Grand Rapids: Wm. B. Eerdmans Publishing Co., 1980) and Barbara Welter, "She Hath Done What She Could: Protestant Women's Missionary Careers in Nineteenth-Century" in *Women in American Religion*, ed. Janet Wilson James (Philadelphia: University of Pennsylvania Press, 1980).

[9]Charles W. Forman, "A History of Foreign Mission Theory in America," in *American Missions in Bicentennial Perspective,* ed. R. Pierce Beaver (South Pasadena: William Carey Library, 1977), p. 83.

[10]James S. Dennis, *The New Horoscope of Missions,* 2nd ed. (New York: Fleming H. Revell Co., 1908), p. 97.

[11]John P. Jones, *The Modern Missionary Challenge: A Study of the Present Day World Missionary Enterprise: Its Problems and Results* (New York: Fleming H. Revell Co., 1910), p. 344.

[12]William McKinley, "Address of the President of the United States of America," in *Ecumenical Missionary Conference, New York, 1900:* Report of the Ecumenical Conference on Foreign Missions, Held in Carnegie Hall and Neighboring Churches, April 21 to May 1 (New York: American Tract Society, 1900), 1:39.

[13]Latourette, *A History,* 4:65.

[14]John R. Mott, *The Evangelization of the World in This Generation* (New York: Student Volunteer Movement for Foreign Missions, 1900), pp. 3–4, 7. For Mott's defense of the watchword, see pp. 1–10. Objections may be found in Edward A. Lawrence's *Modern Missions in the East: Their Methods, Successes, and Limitations* (New York: Harper and Brothers, 1894), pp. 34–37.

[15]John R. Mott, "An Unprecedented World-Situation," in *Students and the World-Wide Expansion of Christianity:* Addresses Delivered Before the Seventh International Convention of the Student Volunteer Movement for Foreign Missions, Kansas City, Missouri, December 31, 1913, to January 4, 1914. ed. Fennell P. Turner (New York: Student Volunteer Movement for Foreign Missions, 1914), p. 85.

[16]Beaver, "Missionary Motivation," pp. 121, 126.

[17]Ibid., pp. 129–130.

[18]C. I. Scofield, ed. *The Scofield Reference Bible* (New York: Oxford University Press, 1909), p. 1170.

[19]William Owen Carver, *Missions in the Plan of the Ages: Bible Studies in Missions* (New York: Fleming H. Revell Co., 1909), pp. 254–257. Significantly, Carver's book was the first theology of missions offered for sale in the merchandising catalog (1929-1930) of Gospel Publishing House, the publishing arm of the Assemblies of God.

[20]Ibid., p. 257.

[21]In *The Church in an Age of Revolution,* vol. 5: *The Pelican History of the Church* (Baltimore: Penguin Books, 1961), p. 241, Alec R. Vidler defines *social gospel* as a "reaction against the individualism and pietism of the conservative evangelicals. Positively, it focused attention on the social implications of the Christian faith and the duty of churchmen to promote social justice in every area of the common life." For a more detailed account, see Sydney E. Ahlstrom, *A Religious History of the American People* (Garden City, N.Y.: Doubleday and Co., 1975), 2:250–273.

[22]Timothy P. Weber, *Living in the Shadow of the Second Coming: American Premillennialism: 1875–1925* (New York: Oxford University Press, 1979), p. 65.

[23]Ibid., p. 67.

[24]Nelson Hart Hodges, "The True and the False: The Worlds of an Emerging Evangelical Protestant Fundamentalism in America, 1890–1920" (Ph. D. dissertation, Michigan State University, 1976), p. 108.

[25]George M. Marsden, *Fundamentalism and American Culture: The Shaping of Twentieth Century Evangelicalism: 1870–1925* (New York: Oxford University Press, 1980), pp. 97–98.

[26]Weber, *Living in the Shadow,* p. 79.

[27]Carver, *Missions,* p. 258.

[28]Dennis, *The New Horoscope,* pp. 100–101.

[29]William R. Hutchinson, "Modernism and Missions. The Liberal Search for an Exportable Christianity, 1875–1935," in *The Missionary Enterprise in China and America,* ed. John R. Fairbank (Cambridge: Harvard University Press, 1974), p. 116.

[30]Augustus H. Strong, *A Tour of the Missions: Observations and Conclusions* (Philadelphia: The Griffith and Rowland Press, 1918), p. 193.

[31]Ibid., p. 191.

[32]Robert T. Handy, *A Christian America: Protestant Hopes and Historical Realities* (New York: Oxford University Press, 1971), p. 131.

[33]Rabe, *The Home Base,* p. 69.

[34]Handy, *A Christian America,* p. 132.

[35]Forman, "A History," p. 69.

[36]Ibid., p. 78.

[37]Ibid.

[38]R. Pierce Beaver, "The History of Mission Strategy," *Southwestern Journal of Theology* 12 (Spring 1970):22.

[39]Ibid., p. 23. For a historical interpretation that questions the value of Venn's methods in West Africa, see Stephen Neill, *A History of Christian Missions,* vol. 6: *The Pelican History of the Church* (Baltimore: Penguin Books, 1964), pp. 259–260, 377.

[40]Philip Schaff, "The English Language," *Literature and Poetry* (New York: Charles Scribner's Sons, 1890), pp. 1–62, quoted in James E. Wood, Jr., "Anglo-Saxon Supremacy and Protestant Missions in the Nineteenth Century," in *The Teacher's Yoke: Studies in the Memory of Henry Trantham,* eds. E. Jerry Vardaman and James Leo Garrett, Jr. (Waco, Tex.: Baylor University Press, 1964), p. 222.

[41]Ibid., pp. 230–231.

[42]For a discussion of the application of the Nevius Plan in Korea, see "The Nevius Methods: A Study and an Appraisal of Indigenous Mission

Methods" by Wi Jo Kang in the *Concordia Theological Monthly* XXXIX (June 1963): 335–342.

[43]Robert E. Speer, "Paul, The Great Missionary Example," in *The Student Missionary Enterprise:* Addresses and Discussions of the Second International Convention of the Student Volunteer Movement for Foreign Missions Held at Detroit, Mich., Feb. 28 to Mar. 4, 1894. ed. Max Wood Moorhead (New York: Fleming H. Revell Co., 1894), p. 7.

[44]Edward A. Lawrence, *Modern Missions in the East: Their Methods, Successes, and Limitations* (New York: Harper and Brothers, 1894), pp. 31–32.

[45]Edward Pfeiffer, *Missions Studies,* 3rd rev. ed. (Columbus: Lutheran Book Concern, 1920), p. 347. Forman contends that Pfeiffer "derived his ideas from Germany rather than from his American context" in "Evangelization and Civilization: Protestant Missionary Motivation in the Imperialist Era: II. The Americans," *International Bulletin* 6 (April 1982):56.

[46]Roland Allen, *Missionary Methods: St. Paul's or Ours?* (Grand Rapids: Wm. B. Eerdmans Publishing Co., 1962), pp. 141–150.

[47]Mott, *The Evangelization,* p. 16.

[48]Arthur Judson Brown, *The Foreign Missionary: An Incarnation of a World Movement* (New York: Fleming H. Revell Co., 1907), pp. 33–43, 291–318.

[49]Edwin Munsell Bliss, *The Missionary Enterprise: A Concise History of Its Objects, Methods and Extension* (New York: Fleming H. Revell Co., 1908), pp. 178–195.

[50]*Ecumenical Missionary Conference,* 2:289–324.

[51]*World Missionary Conference,* 1910, vol. 1: *Report of Commission 1: Carrying the Gospel to All the Non-Christian World* (Edinburgh: Oliphant, Anderson and Ferrier, n.d.), 1:312–313.

[52]Significantly, Roman Catholic missions were also moving toward the formation of an indigenous clergy. For the encyclical letter that expressed this, see Pope Benedict XV, "Maximum Illud," in *Catholic Missions: Four Great Missionary Encyclicals,* Incidental Papers of the Institute of Mission Studies, no. 1 (New York: Fordham University Press, 1957), pp. 9–23. For an interpretation of the significance of this document in Roman Catholic missiology, see Francis X. Clark, S.J., *The Purpose of Missions: A Study of Mission Documents of the Holy See, 1909–1946* (New York: The Missionary Union of the Clergy, 1948), pp. 28, 38–40.

[53]Kenneth Scott Latourette, *Missions Tomorrow* (New York: Harper and Brothers, 1936), pp. 94–96.

[54]Lawrence, *Modern Missions,* p. 241.

[55]Allen, *Missionary Methods,* p. 135.

[56]R. Pierce Beaver, *Ecumenical Beginnings in Protestant World Mission: A History of Comity* (New York: Thomas Nelson and Sons, 1962), pp. 31–32.

[57]Ibid., pp. 42–80.

[58]Rabe, *The Home Base,* p. 41.

[59]Kenneth Scott Latourette, "Ecumenical Bearings of the Missionary Movement and the International Missionary Council," in *A History of the Ecumenical Movement: 1517–1948,* 2nd ed., eds. Ruth Rouse and Stephen Charles Neill (Philadelphia: The Westminster Press, 1967), pp. 357–362.

[60]William Richie Hogg, *Ecumenical Foundations: A History of the International Missionary Council and Its Nineteenth-Century Background* (New York: Harper and Brothers, 1952), p. 130.

[61]Arthur P. Johnston, *The Battle for World Evangelism* (Wheaton, Ill.: Tyndale House Publishers, 1978), p. 43.

Chapter 2: The Pentecostal Revival Begins

[1]Henry P. Van Dusen, "The Third Force in Christendom," *Life,* June 9, 1958, pp. 113–124.

[2]J. Edwin Orr, *The Flaming Tongue: Evangelical Awakenings, 1900—* (Chicago: Moody Press, 1975), p. 184.

[3]George H. Williams and Edith Waldvogel, "A History of Speaking in Tongues and Related Gifts," in *The Charismatic Movement,* ed. Michael P. Hamilton (Grand Rapids: Wm. B. Eerdmans Publishing Co., 1975), pp. 61–113.

[4]Edith Lydia Waldvogel, "The 'Overcoming Life': A Study in the Reformed Evangelical Origins of Pentecostalism" (Ph. D. dissertation, Harvard University, 1977), p. 8.

[5]Premillennialism, according to Bernard Ramm, a well-known evangelical theologian, "is the belief that Christ will return and set up a glorious kingdom which will last a thousand years. This kingdom is the interim period between the return of Christ and the final judgment." See Ramm, *A Handbook of Contemporary Theology* (Grand Rapids: Wm. B. Eerdmans Publishing Co., 1966), p. 83. For further information, see Dwight Wilson, *Armageddon Now! The Pre-Millenarian Response to Russia and Israel Since 1917* (Grand Rapids: Baker Book House, 1977).

[6]Sarah E. Parham, *The Life of Charles F. Parham* (Joplin, Mo.: The Tri-State Printing Co., 1930); reprint ed. (Birmingham, Ala.: Commercial Printing Co., 1977), p. 51.

[7]Stanley H. Frodsham, *With Signs Following,* 2nd ed. (Springfield, Mo.: Gospel Publishing House, 1946), p. 20.

[8]Parham, *The Life,* p. 54.

[9]Ibid., pp. 51–52.

[10]John Thomas Nichol, *Pentecostalism* (New York: Harper and Row, 1966), p. 29.

[11]Cited in Parham, *The Life,* pp. 133–134.

[12]For further information, see Cecil M. Robeck, Jr., "The Earliest Pen-

tecostal Missions in Los Angeles," *Assemblies of God Heritage,* Fall 1983, pp. 3–4, 12.

[13] *The Apostolic Faith,* September 1907, p. 1.

[14] *The Apostolic Faith,* September 1906, p. 1.

[15] Ibid.

[16] Ibid.

[17] *The Apostolic Faith,* November 1906, p. 2.

[18] *The Apostolic Faith,* September 1907, p. 1.

[19] For evidence from a hostile perspective, see *The Eleventh Annual Report of the Christian and Missionary Alliance,* May 27, 1908, by A. B. Simpson, president and general superintendent, pp. 11–12; also, an untitled article in *The Independent* (Boston: Independent Publications), June 10, 1909, p. 1289. Significantly, in the report of his trip in 1909 to visit Pentecostal missionaries in China, India, Ceylon, Palestine, and Europe, Bishop Joseph H. King of the Pentecostal Holiness Church made no mention of the "missionary use" of tongues. Perhaps by this date many had abandoned that position. See King, *Yet Speaketh: Memoirs of the late Bishop Joseph H. King* (Franklin Springs, Ga.: The Publishing House of the Pentecostal Holiness Church, 1949), pp. 143–293. For further information, see Nils Bloch–Hoell, *The Pentecostal Movement* (Oslo: Universitetsforlaget, 1964), p. 87.

[20] For reports of Pentecostals speaking in distinct foreign languages unknown to them, see Ralph W. Harris, *Spoken by the Spirit: Documented Accounts of "Other Tongues" from Arabic to Zulu* (Springfield, Mo.: Gospel Publishing House, 1973). Broader views on the role of speaking in tongues in Pentecostalism are provided by Carl Brumback, *What Meaneth This?* (Springfield, Mo.: Gospel Publishing House, 1947); Stanley M. Horton, *What the Bible Says About the Holy Spirit* (Springfield, Mo.: Gospel Publishing House, 1976); and William G. McDonald, *Glossolalia in the New Testament* (Springfield, Mo.: Gospel Publishing House, 1964.) The following may be consulted for further discussion on the linguistic nature of speaking in tongues: Robert Mapes Anderson, *Vision of the Disinherited: The Making of American Pentecostalism* (New York: Oxford University Press, 1979), pp. 10–27; William J. Samarin, "The Linguisticality of Glossolalia," *The Hartford Quarterly* VIII, no. 4 (Summer 1968):49–75.

[21] J. Roswell Flower (untitled editorial), *The Pentecost,* August 1908, p. 4.

[22] Frank Bartleman, *What Really Happened at "Azusa Street"?* ed. John Walker (Northridge, Calif.: Voice Christian Publications, 1962; original printing, 1925), p. 34.

[23] *The Apostolic Faith,* October 1906, p. 1.

[24] Ibid., p. 2. Vinson Synan describes the failure of the A. G. Garrs to speak the native languages in India and China as "the outstanding attempt at carrying out Parham's teaching concerning the missionary use of tongues,

and it ended in failure." They afterwards studied Chinese. See Synan, *The Holiness-Pentecostal Movement in the United States* (Grand Rapids: Wm. B. Eerdmans Publishing Co., 1971), p. 111.

[25]For a discussion of the role of women in Pentecostalism, see Nichol, *Pentecostalism,* pp. 62–63. Joseph R. Flower, an executive officer of the Assemblies of God, has written a theological defense of the role of women in ministry entitled "Does God Deny Spiritual Manifestations and Ministry Gifts to Women?" (Springfield, Mo., 1979; mimeographed).

[26]*The Apostolic Faith,* May 1907, p. 2.

[27]*The Apostolic Faith,* September 1906, p. 3.

[28]*The Apostolic Faith,* October to January 1908, p. 1.

[29]*The Apostolic Faith,* February–March 1907, p.1.

[30]*The Apostolic Faith,* April 1907, p. 1; *Ecumenical Missionary Conference,* 2:400.

[31]Arthur T. Pierson, "Speaking in Tongues," *The Missionary Review of the World,* July 1907, p. 492.

[32]Arthur T. Pierson, "Speaking With Tongues"—II, *The Missionary Review of the World,* September 1907, p. 684.

[33]Donald Gee, *The Pentecostal Movement,* 2nd ed. (London: Elim Publishing Co., 1949), pp. 14–15.

[34]For an excellent discussion of Barratt's influence in Scandinavia and the rest of Europe, see Bloch–Hoell, *The Pentecostal Movement,* pp. 65ff.

Chapter 3: Revivals in the East

[1]Elizabeth V. Baker, et al., *Chronicles of a Faith Life,* 2nd ed. (Rochester, N.Y.: Elim Publishing Co., ca. 1926), p. 51.

[2]Ibid., pp. 106–107.

[3]William T. Ellis, "Pentecostal Revival Touches India," *Chicago Daily News,* January 14, 1908; reprinted in *Assemblies of God Heritage,* Winter 1982–83, pp. 1,5.

[4]Baker, *Chronicles,* p. 135.

[5]Ibid., p. 132.

[6]Carl Brumback, *Suddenly . . . From Heaven: A History of the Assemblies of God* (Springfield, Mo.: Gospel Publishing House, 1961), p. 229. The influence of the Rochester school on the General Council of the Assemblies of God is illustrated by the three buildings on the Evangel College campus (Springfield, Mo.) named for Rochester alumni: Gayle F. Lewis (general superintendent of the Assemblies of God: 1952–1953), Charles W. H. Scott, and Grace Walther.

[7]Virginia E. Moss, *Following the Shepherd: Testimony of Mrs. Virginia E. Moss* (North Bergen, N.J.: Beulah Heights Assembly and Bible Training School, ca. 1919), pp. 15–16.

[8]Ibid., p. 22.

[9]"Pentecostal Bible Schools," *The Latter Rain Evangel,* July 1912, p. 12.

[10]Moss, *Following,* pp. 44–45.

[11]See Nichol, *Pentecostalism,* p. 37.

[12]A. B. Simpson, *The Gospel of Healing,* 2nd ed. (Harrisburg, Pennsylvania: Christian Publications, Inc., 1915), p. 33.

[13]A. B. Simpson quoted in Daryl Westwood Cartmel, "Mission Policy and Program of A. B. Simpson" (M.A. thesis, The Hartford Seminary Foundation, 1962), p. 33.

[14]For the controversy surrounding Simpson's association of faith healing with foreign missions work, see Cartmel, "Mission Policy," pp. 64–68; a similar view was put forward by David Wesley Myland in *The Latter Rain Covenant and Pentecostal Power* (Chicago: Evangel Publishing House, 1910), pp. 70–72. Myland, a former officer with the Christian and Missionary Alliance, became Pentecostal and left the organization. He strongly influenced some of the early leaders of the Assemblies of God. For further information on Myland, see James K. Butcher, "The Holiness and Pentecostal Labors of David Wesley Myland: 1890–1918" (Th. M. thesis, Dallas Theological Seminary, 1983).

[15]Cartmel, "Mission Policy," p.89.

[16]*Annual Report of the Superintendent and Board of Managers,* by A. B. Simpson, superintendent (May 4, 1900), p. 32.

[17]A. B. Simpson, *When the Comforter Came* (Harrisburg, Penn.: Christian Publications, 1911), "Thirtieth Day."

[18]Cartmel, "Mission Policy," p. 89.

[19]For more information on William Taylor, a famed missionary bishop of the Methodist Church and advocate of self-supporting missions, see *The Encyclopedia of World Methodism,* s.v. "Taylor, William," by Marvin H. Harper.

[20]Cartmel, "Mission Policy," p. 62.

[21]"The Missionary Training Institute Catalog, 1918–1919," p. 5.

[22]"As opposed to the charity principle Taylor advocated strict application of self-support. Either the foreign missionaries and evangelists must find some source of income short of salary from a foreign society or else be sustained by the people they serve. It was his proud boast that he had not drawn a dollar from the mission society of his church." Cartmel, p. 163.

[23]Cartmel, "Mission Policy," p. 171.

[24]A. E. Thompson, *The Life of A. B. Simpson* (New York: Christian Alliance Publishing Co., 1920), pp. 105–106.

[25]*The Ninth Annual Report of the Christian and Missionary Alliance,* by A. B. Simpson, president and general superintendent (May 30, 1906), p. 147.

[26]*The Tenth Annual Report of the Christian and Missionary Alliance,* by

A. B. Simpson, president and general superintendent (March 31, 1907), p. 166.

[27]Ibid., p. 180.

[28]Mary E. Lewer, "50 Years of Pentecostal Blessing," *Pentecostal Evangel,* January 26, 1958, p. 7; also, David H. McDowell, "I Remember," *Pentecostal Evangel,* March 1, 1964, p. 13.

[29]*Tenth Annual Report,* p. 77. For more information, see Gary B. McGee, "Pentecostal Awakenings at Nyack," *Paraclete* 18 (Summer 1984):22–28.

[30]Brumback, *Suddenly,* p. 89.

[31]*The Eleventh Annual Report of the Christian and Missionary Alliance,* by A. B. Simpson, president and general superintendent (May 27, 1908), p. 10.

[32]*The Apostolic Faith,* November, 1906, p. 1.

[33]*Eleventh Annual Report,* pp. 41–42.

[34]Some had been veteran Alliance missionaries, such as Gottfried Bender, H. W. Cragin, Christian Schoonmaker, William W. Simpson, and Alice C. Wood. Others were trained at Nyack and later served for the Assemblies of God. The number of Nyack alumni entering the ranks of the Assemblies of God foreign missions program tapered off rapidly after 1920 due to the rise of a number of Pentecostal Bible schools training missionaries. A helpful source, though incomplete, for determining the number of Nyack graduates serving in the Assemblies of God is the *Alumni Directory* of Nyack College (Nyack, N.Y.: The Nyack Alumni Association, 1976).

[35]Brumback, *Suddenly,* p. 93.

[36]Kenneth Mackenzie quoted in Thompson, *The Life,* p. 253.

[37]Brumback discusses seven ways in which the Alliance influenced the Assemblies of God in *Suddenly,* p. 94.

[38]Alice Reynolds Flower, *Grace for Grace* (Springfield, Mo.: By the Author, n.d.), pp. 26–27.

[39]Brumback, *Suddenly,* p. 80.

[40]Myland, *The Latter Rain Covenant,* p. 79.

[41]Ibid, p. 71.

[42]General Council Minutes, 1921, pp. 60–61.

[43]*Dedicated Unto Our Lord: Bethel Assembly of God* (50th Anniversary: 1913–1963), (Newark, N.J.: Bethel Assembly of God, 1963), p. 4; Christian J. Lucas, "In Memoriam" (Minnie T. Draper), *Full Gospel Missionary Herald,* April 1921, pp. 3–5. The Bethel Pentecostal Assembly affiliated with the General Council of the Assemblies of God in 1953 and changed its name to Bethel Assembly of God. However, there is some disparity in the sources about the date for the founding of this church.

[44]"The Home-Going of Sister Minnie T. Draper of Ossining, N.Y.," *Pentecostal Evangel,* April 2, 1921, p. 7.

[45]Harlan P. Beach and Charles H. Fahs, eds., *World Missionary Atlas* (New York: Institute of Social and Religious Research, 1925), p. 24.

[46]The Pentecostal Holiness Church organized a foreign missions program in 1904 and the Church of God (Cleveland, Tenn.) followed suit in 1910. For further information, see *The Encyclopedia of Modern Christian Missions: The Agencies*, s.v. "Pentecostal Holiness Church, Department of Foreign Missions," by W. H. Turner, and "Church of God, World Missions Board," by Duran M. Palmertree.

[47]Telephone interview with Paul J. Emery, Sr., former president of Northeast Bible Institute (later, Valley Forge Christian College), Allentown, Pennsylvania, 27 June 1983; personal interview with John B. Richards, former missionary of the Assemblies of God to the Republic of South Africa, Springfield, Missouri, 11 July 1983; telephone interview with Harry J. Steil, retired Assemblies of God minister and faculty member at Bethel Bible Training School, Cardiff–By–the–Sea, California, 27 June 1983. For further information on Minnie T. Draper, see Lucas, "In Memoriam," pp. 3–5; also, "The Home-Going," p. 7. It is interesting to note that Minnie T. Draper claimed to have been miraculously healed, felt called by God to preach, and then established a school for the training of ministers and missionaries. The lives of Elizabeth V. Baker and Virginia E. Moss reflect the same pattern. The schools they founded, all in the East, were more influential on the General Council of the Assemblies of God than were any other institutions during the early years, with the notable exception of the Missionary Training Institute at Nyack.

[48]Beach and Fahs, *Atlas*, p. 24.

[49]Helen Calvert Boyd, "History of the Early Days of Bethel Bible Training Institute," in *Memoirs of Bethel: 1916–1929*, ed. Theresa LeDuc Hartshorn (Red Hill, Penn.: Paul and Dorothy Emery, 1979), pp. 3–4; interviews with Emery and Richards.

[50]*Ecumenical Missionary Conference*, 2:412.

[51]Some students attended more than one Bible institute. For example, John Burgess attended both the Rochester Bible Training School and the Bethel Bible Training School. For limited information on the association of Ralph M. Riggs, a graduate of the Rochester Bible Training School, with the South and Central African Pentecostal Mission, see Wayne Warner, ed., *Touched by the Fire: Patriarchs of Pentecost* (Plainfield, N.J.: Logos International, 1978), p. 141, and interview with Richards.

[52]For information on Anna Richards Scoble, see John B. Richards, "Anna," 1980. (Typewritten.)

[53]It is noteworthy that five of the main buildings on the campus of Central Bible College ("Institute" until 1965) are named for former members of the Alliance: Eleanor Bowie, Frank M. Boyd, William I. Evans, J. Roswell Flower, and John W. Welch.

Chapter 4: The Formation of the General Council

[1]For an excellent discussion of the events leading up to the organization of the General Council of the Assemblies of God, see William W. Menzies, *Anointed to Serve: The Story of the Assemblies of God* (Springfield, Mo.: Gospel Publishing House, 1971), pp. 80–105.

[2]"Notes," *The Latter Rain Evangel,* March 1911, p. 14. For more information about Mrs. Murray and her missionary service in India, see King, *Yet Speaketh,* pp. 173–176.

[3]The South and Central African Pentecostal Mission set up in 1910 by the Bethel Pentecostal Assembly of Newark, New Jersey, was a notable exception.

[4]*The Gospel Witness* vol. 1, no. 2, p. 13. For limited information about the brief operation (1909–1910) of the Pentecostal Missionary Union founded by Levi Lupton in Alliance, Ohio, see Gloria G. Kulbeck, *What God Hath Wrought* (Toronto: The Pentecostal Assemblies of Canada, 1958), p. 36.

[5]Alice Reynolds Flower, *Grace,* p. 58.

[6]J. Roswell Flower, "A Closer and Deeper Fellowship for the Pentecostal Assemblies in Indiana and the Central States," *Christian Evangel,* July 19, 1913, p. 1.

[7]"Things Missionary," *The Latter Rain Evangel,* March 1913, p. 15.

[8]"The Missionary Problem Again," *The Latter Rain Evangel,* September 1913, p. 14.

[9]"Missionary Problems That Confront Us," *The Latter Rain Evangel,* January 1913, p. 18.

[10]George Mueller was a 19th-century Christian philanthropist in Bristol, England. Lacking the support of any governmental or social agency, he earnestly prayed and believed that God would supply the resources to support his large orphanage. His fame spread with the remarkable success of this institution and a later extended evangelistic tour around the world. He became a model of "living by faith" for many Christians. See Elgin S. Moyer, ed. *Who Was Who in Church History,* s.v. "George Muller." ("George Muller" is a variant spelling.)

[11]"Missionary Problems," *The Latter Rain Evangel,* p. 17.

[12]Ibid., p. 19.

[13]E. N. Bell, "A Word to Foreign Missionaries," *Word and Witness,* October 20, 1913, p. 3.

[14]E. N. Bell, "God's Work in Foreign Lands," *Word and Witness,* November 20, 1913, p. 4.

[15]E. N. Bell, "Missionary Opportunity," *Word and Witness,* October 20, 1913, p. 2.

[16]After Bell's death was mentioned at the 1923 General Council's memorial service for "those . . . who had been called home to glory," the missionaries who were present requested permission "to stand as an ap-

preciation of their love for Brother Bell for his sacrifices for the mission fields. The permission was gladly given." General Council Minutes, (Combined Minutes), 1914–1923, p. 64.

[17]General Council minutes, 1914, pp. 4–5.

[18]E. N. Bell, "God's Work in Foreign Fields," *Word and Witness,* April 20, 1914, p. 4.

[19]"A Missionary Movement," *Pentecostal Evangel,* November 13, 1920, p. 8. Welch was referring to both home and foreign missionary efforts when he made this statement.

PART II: THE EARLY YEARS OF ASSEMBLIES OF GOD FOREIGN MISSIONS (1914–1926)

Chapter 5: Missionaries and Missiology

[1]It is difficult to determine the exact number of missionaries who entered the Council that year. J. Roswell Flower, the elected secretary, listed on the rolls 17 persons with addresses outside the United States and Canada as missionaries. However, other individuals listed with addresses in the U.S. were probably also engaged in missionary activities at the time. Two possible explanations: home on furlough, they joined the Council and gave their current addresses, or their exact status at the time was unclear to Flower.

Later publications reflect the uncertainty over the precise number. Noel Perkin and John Garlock cited 15 missionaries at the first General Council (*Our World Witness: A Survey of Assemblies of God Foreign Missions.* Springfield, Mo.: Gospel Publishing House, 1963, p. 29); a year later Perkin enlarged this number to 32 ("Our First Five Years [1914–1919]," Missions Vignettes, no. 1, *Pentecostal Evangel,* October 25, 1964, p. 14). A more recent study by Joyce Wells Booze followed the later Perkin estimate (*Into All the World: A History of Assemblies of God Foreign Missions.* Springfield, Mo.: Assemblies of God Division of Foreign Missions, 1980, p. 12). A lower figure of 27 may be more precise.

[2]The General Council is the highest constitutional authority in the Assemblies of God and acts as a policy-making body. It is a legislative assembly composed of all ordained ministers and one delegate from each recognized assembly. This body met twice in 1914 and annually until 1921. After that the General Council meetings took place biennially. The denomination is sometimes referred to as the "General Council." For further information, see Klaude Kendrick, *The Promise Fulfilled: A History of the Modern Pentecostal Movement* (Springfield, Mo.: Gospel Publishing House, 1961), pp. 87–88.

[3]The early General Council lists of missionaries included those in the territory of Alaska as well as those in the continental United States ministering to American Indians and Hispanics (see note 1, chapter 8).

[4]H. B. Garlock, *Before We Kill and Eat You,* ed. Ruthanne Garlock (Dallas: Christ for the Nations, Inc., 1974), p. 12.

[5]By 1946, about 134 missionaries had been trained at Central Bible Institute; Southern California Bible School, 44; Bethel Bible Training School, 34; Glad Tidings Bible Institute, 33; North Central Bible Institute (founded in 1930 at Minneapolis, Minnesota), 30; Beulah Heights Bible and Missionary Training Institute, 27; Northwest Bible Institute (founded in 1934 at Seattle, Washington), 23; Southwestern Bible Institute (founded in 1927 at Enid, Oklahoma), 22; Rochester Bible Training School, 21. These statistics are only approximate since a small number of missionaries studied at more than one school. For further information, note the biographical data in *The Prayer Fellowship,* Springfield, Mo.: Foreign Missions Department, ca. 1946).

[6]"Opening of the Central Bible Institute," *Pentecostal Evangel,* October 25, 1924, p. 8.

[7]"Day by Day at Central Bible Institute," *Pentecostal Evangel,* December 20, 1924, p. 8.

[8]*First Annual Catalog, Central Bible Institute: 1922–1923.* (Springfield, Mo.: Assemblies of God, Inc.), p. 14.

[9]Garlock, *Before We Kill,* p. 24.

[10]"Modalistic monarchians . . . maintained that of the Godhead, 'Father,' 'Son,' and 'Spirit' were but descriptions of the successive modes or manifestations of God's coming to man, thus proclaiming the full divinity of Jesus, but doing so at the expense of individuality within the eternal God." *The Westminster Dictionary of Church History,* 1971 ed., s.v. "Monarchians." For the impact of this gathering on missions, see C. W. Doney, "Journal of Missionary Travels and Experiences," n.d., pp. 6–8. (Typewritten.)

[11]For further information, see Menzies, *Anointed,* pp. 106–121; Arthur L. Clanton, *United We Stand: A History of Oneness Organizations* (Hazelwood, Mo.: The Pentecostal Publishing House, 1970), p. 44; Frank J. Ewart, *The Phenomenon of Pentecost* (Hazelwood, Mo.: World Aflame Press, 1975), pp. 117–118.

[12]Personal interview with Noel Perkin, Executive Director Emeritus of the Assemblies of God Division of Foreign Missions, Springfield, Missouri, 16 August 1979; Noel Perkin, "Highlights of the 20's (1920–1924)," Missions Vignettes, no. 2, *Pentecostal Evangel,* November 29, 1964, pp. 17–18.

[13]For a brief history of the *Pentecostal Evangel,* see "Spreading the Pentecostal Message Across America and Around the World: A Brief History of 'The Pentecostal Evangel,' " n.d. (Typewritten.)

[14]W. W. Simpson, "Bro. W. W. Simpson's Plans," *Weekly Evangel,* January 5, 1918, p. 7.

[15]General Council Minutes, 1914, pp. 13–16; 1919, pp. 44–48; 1925, pp. 96–102.

[16]*Pentecostal Evangel,* December 5, 1925, p. 18; see also J. Roswell Flower, "Coming Home on Furlough," *Pentecostal Evangel,* October 1, 1921, p. 12.

[17]Executive Presbytery Minutes, November 23, 1914; also see "Rights and Offices of Women," General Council Minutes, (Combined Minutes), 1914–1917, p. 8.

[18]On May 6, 1935, the Foreign Missions Committee invited Eleanor Bowie, a former missionary to South Africa and then supervisor of women students at Central Bible Institute, to serve as an auxiliary member of the Committee "in order to assist in dealing with matters particularly pertaining to lady candidates." Foreign Missions Committee Minutes, May 6, 1935; "New Member of Missions Committee," *Pentecostal Evangel,* June 22, 1935, p. 9. For a limited study of the later problems of primarily married women missionaries in the Assemblies of God, see Eleanor Guynes, "The Place of Women in Assemblies of God Foreign Missions," 1977. (Typewritten.)

[19]J. Roswell Flower, "Men Wanted," *Pentecostal Evangel,* April 7, 1923, p. 12.

[20]Roger Robins, "Attitudes Toward War and Peace in the Assemblies of God: 1914–1918," 1982, p. 6 (Typewritten.); for a more comprehensive study of the changing attitudes of the General Council of the Assemblies of God toward war, see Jay Beaman, "Pentecostal Pacifism: The Origin, Development, and Rejection of the Pacific Belief Among the Pentecostals" (M. Div. thesis, North American Baptist Seminary, 1982).

[21]J. Roswell Flower, "Report of Missionary Treasurer for Year Ending September 1, 1920," *Pentecostal Evangel,* October 16, 1920, p. 9.

[22]Ibid., p. 8.

[23]J. Wilbur Taylor, "The Clarion Call for Reapers—Have You Kept Jesus Waiting?" *The Latter Rain Evangel,* September 1922, p. 2.

[24]Grace C. Agar, "Tibetan Border of Kansu Province," 1940, p. i. (Typewritten.)

[25]Letter from Walter Clifford, missionary to India, to Mrs. George Carmichael, 16 August 1950.

[26]Marie Stephany, *The Power of God in Shansi Province,* The Assemblies of God in Foreign Lands (Springfield, Mo.: Foreign Missions Department, ca. 1934), pp. 37–38.

[27]General Council Minutes, (Combined Minutes), 1914–1917, pp. 9–10.

[28]General Council Minutes, 1921, pp. 61–64.

[29]Alice E. Luce, "Paul's Missionary Methods," *Pentecostal Evangel,* January 8, 1921, pp. 6–7; January 22, 1921, pp. 6, 11; February 5, 1921, pp. 6–7.

[30]James E. Richardson, "A Study of the Leadership Training Programs of the Assemblies of God in Spanish America," 1974, p. 25. (Typewritten.)

³¹Alice E. Luce founded the Latin American Bible Institute in San Diego, California, in 1926 for the same purpose as Ball's school in Texas. For further information on Henry C. Ball, Alice E. Luce, and Assemblies of God missions to Hispanics, see Victor De Leon, *The Silent Pentecostals: A Biographical History of the Pentecostal Movement Among the Hispanics in the Twentieth Century* (Taylors, S.C.: Faith Printing Co., 1979); H. C. Ball and A. E. Luce, *Glimpses of Our Latin American Work in the United States and Mexico* (Springfield, Mo.: Foreign Missions Department, 1940); Inez Spence, *Henry C. Ball: Man of Action,* Heroes of the Conquest Series, no. 13 (Springfield, Mo.: Foreign Missions Department, n.d.).

³²Benjamin P. Shinde, "The Contributions of the Assemblies of God to Church Growth in India" (M.A. thesis, Fuller Theological Seminary School of World Mission, 1974), pp. 88, 184–192; see also Perkin and Garlock, *Our World Witness,* p. 29.

³³Esther B. Harvey, *The Faithfulness of God,* 2nd ed. (Battle Creek, Mich.: Grounds Gospel Press and Book Store, n.d.), p. 38.

³⁴For further information, see Beth Prim Howell, *Lady on a Donkey* (New York: E. P. Dutton and Co., 1960); Beverly Graham, ed., *Letters From Lillian* (Springfield, Mo.: Assemblies of God Division of Foreign Missions, 1983); Jerome Beatty, "Nile Mother," *American Magazine,* June 1939, pp. 55–56, 180; Lillian Trasher, *The Birth of Assiout Orphanage or Why I Came to Egypt in 1910,* (n.d.); Charles W. Conn, *Where the Saints Have Trod: A History of Church of God Missions* (Cleveland, Tenn.: Pathway Press, 1959), pp. 15–16.

³⁵Agar, "Tibetan Border," p. 14.

³⁶Violet Schoonmaker, *Christian Schoonmaker: A Man Who Loved the Will of God* (Landour, Mussoorie, India: Hyratt Press, 1959), pp. 37–39.

³⁷Personal interview with J. Philip Hogan, executive director of the Assemblies of God Division of Foreign Missions, Springfield, Missouri, 6 July 1983.

³⁸C. H. Schoonmaker, "God's Estimate of a Heathen Soul. What Is Yours?" *The Latter Rain Evangel,* November, 1917, p. 13; also, J. Roswell Flower, "A Missionary Spirit Necessary," *Pentecostal Evangel,* February 7, 1920, p. 12; E. N. Bell, "General Council Principles," *Evangel,* tract no. 914 (Springfield, Mo.: Gospel Publishing House, ca. 1922), pp. 12–13.

Chapter 6: Administrative and Structural Developments

¹John W. Welch, chairman in 1915, served as the first missionary treasurer. He was followed in this office by Stanley H. Frodsham.

²E. N. Bell, "Special Notice to Missionaries," *Christian Evangel,* August 22, 1914, p. 4.

³Mrs. W. P. Haynes, Rios, Wisconsin, "A Missionary Offering," *Christian Evangel,* January 11, 1919, p. 10.

⁴"Helping the Missionaries," *Weekly Evangel,* January 5, 1918, p. 8.

[5]E. N. Bell, "Complaints About Missionary Money," *Christian Evangel,* July 26, 1919, p. 4.

[6]This practice continued until the early 1960s when the policy was prohibited by the Internal Revenue Service. Even designated offerings to "Oneness" (modal monarchian) missionaries were faithfully sent overseas. Interview with Hogan.

[7]"Application Blank for Ordination Certificate," ca. 1917, p. 2.

[8]General Council Minutes, (Combined Minutes), 1914–1917, pp. 9–10.

[9]General Council Minutes, 1916, p. 14.

[10]The Executive Presbytery constituted an executive committee for the administration of the Council. To handle judicial and administrative matters between sessions of the General Council, a General Presbytery was formed, larger and more representative than the Executive Presbytery. For further information, see Menzies, *Anointed,* p. 121.

[11]General Council Minutes, 1917, pp. 21–22.

[12]General Council Minutes, 1917, pp. 21–24.

[13]Gerard A. Bailly, "Preparedness for Missionary Work," *Christian Evangel,* September 6, 1919, p. 9.

[14]Simpson returned as a missionary to China in 1918 and Eldridge pastored in California. General Council Minutes, 1918, p. 10.

[15]General Council Minutes, 1919, p. 22.

[16]Ibid., p. 14.

[17]General Council Minutes, 1920, p. 36.

[18]J. Roswell Flower, "Greetings From the New Treasurer," *Pentecostal Evangel,* November 1, 1919, p. 26.

[19]J. W. Welch, (editorial), *Pentecostal Evangel,* October 18, 1919, p. 9.

[20]J. Roswell Flower, "Report of Missionary Treasurer for Year Ending Sept. 1, 1920," *Pentecostal Evangel,* October 16, 1920, p. 9.

[21]Ibid., p. 10.

[22]Joyce Wells Booze, *Into All the World: A History of Assemblies of God Foreign Missions* (Springfield, Mo.: Division of Foreign Missions, 1980). p. 16.

[23]General Council Minutes, (Combined Minutes), 1914–1923, p. 54.

[24]Letter from Harold K. Needham, overseas representative for the General Council of the Assemblies of God, to W. T. Gaston, 5 December 1923.

[25]Stanley H. Frodsham, "The General Council Report," *Pentecostal Evangel,* October 15, 1921, p. 8.

[26]General Council Minutes, 1921, p. 61.

[27]J. Roswell Flower, "The Missionary Policy of the Assemblies of God," *Pentecostal Evangel,* July 7, 1923, p. 12.

[28]Cited in Booze, *Into All the World,* p. 18.

[29]For a more detailed account of the responsibilities of the district councils abroad, see General Council Minutes, 1921, pp. 61–64.

[30]Missionaries were occasionally recalled for various reasons. For examples, see: "Concerning Mrs. Anna S. Bush," *Pentecostal Evangel,* January 20, 1923, p. 12; "B. S. Moore Returning to Japan," *Pentecostal Evangel,* March 17, 1923, p. 12.

[31]William M. Faux, "Missionary Giving," *Pentecostal Evangel,* March 1, 1924, p. 10.

[32]General Council Minutes, 1925, pp. 47–52.

[33]William Milnes Faux, "My Impression of Missions," *Pentecostal Evangel,* January 2, 1926, p. 8.

[34]W. T. Gaston to the general presbyters, 26 January 1927; Foreign Missions Committee Minutes, January 17, 1927; "Change in Missionary Department," *Pentecostal Evangel,* December 18, 1926, p. 8; Interview with Noel Perkin.

Chapter 7: Cooperation and Popular Support

[1]Editor's Note, *Pentecostal Evangel,* August 10, 1918, p. 11.

[2]D. W. Kerr, "Third Missionary Conference," *Christian Evangel,* August 10, 1918, p. 11.

[3]Willa B. Lowther, "Approval of the Missionary Conference," *Weekly Evangel,* February 23, 1918, p. 11.

[4]Stanley H. Frodsham, "The World Wide Missionary Conference," *Christian Evangel,* June 1, 1918, p. 2.

[5](Advertisement), "A Barrel of Money for the Missionaries," *Christian Evangel,* August 10, 1918, p. 11.

[6]"The Third Missionary Conference," *Christian Evangel,* November 16, 1918, p. 2.

[7]Stanley H. Frodsham, "The Fourth Missionary Conference," *Pentecostal Evangel,* October 18, 1919, p. 1.

[8]*Concise Dictionary of the Christian World Mission,* s.v. "Foreign Missions Conference of North America, The," by F. W. Price.

[9]Foreign Missions Committee Minutes, February 12, 1925.

[10]John W. Welch, "The Present Great World Crisis," *Pentecostal Evangel,* March 28, 1925, p. 8.

[11]General Council Minutes, 1923, p. 61.

[12]For an examination of the motives behind this endeavor, see General Council Minutes, 1921, pp. 59–60.

[13]Elizabeth A. Galley Wilson, *Making Many Rich* (Springfield, Mo.: Gospel Publishing House, 1955), p. 12.

[14]Kulbeck, *What God Hath Wrought,* p. 211. A conference about comity overseas took place in Springfield, Missouri, in 1936 between officers of

the General Council and the Pentecostal Assemblies of Canada. For information about this meeting, see "Report of Conference Held at the Gospel Publishing House, May 13, 1936" in the Foreign Missions Committee Minutes, May 13, 1936.

[15]Schoonmaker, *Christian Schoonmaker,* pp. 34–35.

[16]"Report of Missionary Conference Held at Garraway, Liberia, W. A.," *The Bridegroom's Messenger,* September 1919, p. 3.

[17]General Council Minutes, 1916, p. 5.

[18]General Council Minutes, 1918, pp. 8–9.

[19]Ibid.

[20]General Council Minutes, 1925, p. 61.

[21]Elva Hoover, ed. *The WM Leader: Handbook of Leadership Training for Women's Ministries Leaders* (Springfield, Mo.: The Women's Ministries Department of the Assemblies of God, 1980), p. 9.

[22]General Council Minutes, 1925, p. 66.

[23]In 1975, the name was changed to the Women's Ministries Department. For further information about the history and role of the organization, see Anabel Manley, *WMC History: 1925–1975* (Houston: By the Author, 1975) and Hoover, *The WM Leader,* pp. 9–17.

PART III: THE MATURING YEARS (1927–1942)

Chapter 8: Noel Perkin and Departmental Changes

[1]General Council Minutes, 1927, pp. 48–49. In the early years of the missions program, both Hawaii and Alaska received classification as mission fields. For further information about these areas, their eventual change in classification, and the development of district councils there, see *Ka Malamalama No Ka Makahiki I Hala* ["Light on the Past"]: A History of the Assemblies of God in Hawaii (Hawaii: Hawaii Assemblies of God, ca. 1974) and B. P. Wilson, *The Assemblies of God in Alaska* (Anchorage, Alas.: Alaska District Council, 1980).

[2]General Council Minutes, 1927, pp. 38–39.

[3]Noel Perkin, "Personal Testimony," n.d., p. 3. (Typewritten.)

[4]For further information, see Noel Perkin, "Personal Testimony," pp. 5–6; interview with Perkin; missionary record for Harry L. Turner, Christian and Missionary Alliance Headquarters, Nyack, New York; Kulbeck, *What God Hath Wrought,* pp. 144, 222.

[5]Before 1927, the office of missionary secretary had been elective.

[6]For further insight into his thinking on missions, see *Facing Facts in Modern Missions: A Symposium,* ed. Noel Perkin (Chicago: Moody Press,

1963), pp. 130–141; also, Perkin, "To Whom Much is Given," n.d. (Type-written.)

⁷Melvin L. Hodges, "Noel Perkin Completes 33 Years of Service," *The Missionary Forum,* November–December 1959, p. 3.; for further information, see Inez Spence, *Mr. Missions, Director Emeritus: Noel Perkin,* Heroes of the Conquest Series, no. 7 (Springfield, Mo.: Foreign Missions Department, n.d.).

⁸For further information on Emory Ross and his distinguished missionary career, see *They Went to Africa,* (Indianapolis: The United Christian Missionary Society, 1952), pp. 52–53.

⁹Inez Spence, *Mr. Missions, Director Emeritus: Noel Perkin* Heroes of the Conquest Series, no. 7 (Springfield, Mo.: Foreign Missions Department, n.d.), p. 4.

¹⁰For further information about the controversy surrounding this, see Menzies, *Anointed,* pp. 142 143.

¹¹The title of chairman of the General Council had been changed to general superintendent.

¹²Foreign Missions Committee Minutes, February 14, 1928.

¹³For a brief time, beginning in 1923, Daniel W. Kerr had fulfilled a similar responsibility.

¹⁴The meetings of the General Council occurred biennially after 1921.

¹⁵Arthur F. Berg, "WORLD MISSIONS! How It Started—And WHY? [*sic*]" n.d., p. 2. (Typewritten.)

¹⁶"The Busy Bee World-Wide Missions Program," *Pentecostal Evangel,* November 9, 1929, p. 6.

¹⁷Noel Perkin, "Coordination and Advance (1925–1930)," Missions Vignettes, no. 3, *Pentecostal Evangel,* December 27, 1964, p. 11.

¹⁸General Council Minutes, 1929, pp. 40, 60–64.

¹⁹General Council Minutes, 1933, p. 57.

²⁰"A God-Blessed Convocation," *Pentecostal Evangel,* October 7, 1933, p. 2.

²¹General Council Minutes, 1929, pp. 60–61.

²²"A God-Blessed Convocation," p. 6.

²³Ibid., p. 7.

²⁴*Missionary Manual* (Springfield, Mo.: Foreign Missions Department, 1931), p. 6.

²⁵Ibid., p. 8.

²⁶Ibid., p. 23.

²⁷Noel Perkin, "The Missionary Secretary's Mail," *Pentecostal Evangel,* December 31, 1932, p. 6.

²⁸Noel Perkin, "Preparation for Missionary Service," *Pentecostal Evangel,* September 7, 1929, p. 10.

[29]Noel Perkin, "Missions in Practice," *Pentecostal Evangel,* October 12, 1935, p. 11.

[30]Noel Perkin, "Preparation for Missionary Service," *Pentecostal Evangel,* September 7, 1929, p. 10.

[31]One woman planning on missionary service in India during the early administration of Noel Perkin was a paralytic.

[32]Foreign Missions Committee Minutes, May 2, 1929.

[33]*Manual,* p. 14. "Praying through" was an expression used by many Pentecostals when referring to ardent prayer. One had "prayed through" when he became convinced that God had answered his prayer.

[34]Ibid., p. 22.

[35]Ibid., p. 16. For further information on the responsibilities of these agencies, see pp. 24–25.

[36]Ibid., p. 11.

[37]"Bible women" were converts engaged in literature distribution and evangelism. See the chapter "Lisu Leaders" in *China Call: Miracles Among the Lisu People* by Leonard Bolton (Springfield, Mo.: Gospel Publishing House, 1984).

[38]"The Hope of Foreign Missions," *Pentecostal Evangel,* September 24, 1938, p. 6.

[39]Foreign Missions Committee Minutes, February 20, 1928.

[40]*Manual,* p. 26.

[41]Menzies, *Anointed,* p. 252; also, Perkin and Garlock, *Our World Witness,* pp. 64–65.

[42]The manual (p. 7) does point out, however, that in places where property or the renting of preaching places was expensive, the policy could be modified to allow outside support.

[43]Ibid., p. 26; also Spence, *Mr. Missions,* pp. 4–5.

[44]*Manual,* p. 26; also, Perkin and Garlock, *Our World Witness,* pp. 65–67.

[45]Noel Perkin, "Assemblies of God Missions: First Things," n.d., p. 5. (Typewritten.)

[46]*Manual,* p. 28.

[47]Other publications from this period include *Progress of Evangelism in North India* (ca. 1935) by D. S. Mahaffey; *Daybreak in Malay* (1935, no author listed); *Light Along the Nile* (n.d., no author listed); *A Work of Faith and a Labor of Love* (1937, no author listed); *Gospel Rays in Manchoukuo* (ca. 1938) by Martin Kvamme; *Sowing and Reaping in Liberia* (ca. 1938, no author listed); *Nile Mother* (1939) by Jerome Beatty; *The Power of the Gospel in Shansi Province* (ca. 1939) by Marie Stephany; *Glimpses of Our Latin-American Work in the United States and Mexico* (1940) by H. C. Ball and A. E. Luce; and *A Call from Japan: An Opportunity for Practical Missionary Work* (n.d.) by Marie Juergensen.

[48]"A Great Missionary Rally," *Pentecostal Evangel,* September 30, 1939, p. 8. This statement probably was based on the number of churches contributing through the Missions Department. Since many continued to send offerings directly to the missionaries and not report them, the number actually contributing to missions would probably have been larger than the one cited. Nevertheless, a significant number of churches apparently did not contribute to missions for reasons unknown.

[49]General Council Minutes, 1939, p. 85.

[50]Spence, *Mr. Missions,* p. 6. In 1935, the department purchased its first motion picture projector for promotional uses in missions conventions. Many years passed, however, before some local assemblies would allow such a "worldly" medium to present the missionary interests of the Assemblies of God.

Chapter 9: Overseas Efforts and World War II

[1]General Council Minutes, 1937, p. 92.

[2]For further information, see David Plymire, *High Adventure in Tibet* (Springfield, Mo.: Gospel Publishing House, 1959).

[3]Elsie Bolton Ezzo, *Beyond the Mekong: Leonard Bolton,* Heroes of the Conquest Series, no. 6 (Springfield, Mo.: Foreign Missions Department, n.d.); Leonard Bolton, *China Call.*

[4]Everett Phillips and his wife received appointment as the first resident missionaries to Nigeria in 1939. For further information, see G. M. Alioha, *The History of Assemblies of God: Nigeria* (Aba, Nigeria: MacBlackson Press Publications, 1975).

[5]For further information, see Nora Blan, *Over Rugged Mountains: W. E. Simpson,* Heroes of the Conquest Series, no. 8 (Springfield, Mo.: Foreign Missions Department, n.d.); J. Philip Hogan, "China Church Growth—A Story of Danger and Dedication," *Mountain Movers,* November 1983, pp. 4–7; "Tribute to a Martyr," *Mountain Movers,* November 1983, p. 7.

[6]Louise Jeter Walker, *Peruvian Gold,* n.d., pp. 49–50. (Typewritten.)

[7]*To the Uttermost Parts of the Earth: A Survey of Assemblies of God in Foreign Lands* (Springfield, Mo.: Foreign Missions Department, 1938), p. 15.

[8]Perkin and Garlock, *Our World Witness,* pp. 51–52.

[9]The Hispanic work in the United States had been put on a sound indigenous footing through the efforts of Henry C. Ball and Alice E. Luce. It made an impact on Mexico, Puerto Rico, and other Spanish-speaking countries. The work in the United States was organized in 1918 as the Latin American Conference of the Assemblies of God. For an excellent historical treatment of the development of the Hispanic work in the United States, see De Leon, *The Silent Pentecostals;* also, Roberto Dominguez, *Pioneros de Pentecostes* (Miami: By the Author, 1977).

[10]Richardson, "A Study," pp. 26–27.

[11]Ralph D. Williams, "Adventuring With the Gospel in Central America," *Pentecostal Evangel,* May 11, 1935, p. 9.

[12]Ralph D. Williams, unpublished autobiography, 1981, p. 131. (Typewritten.)

[13]Personal interview with Melvin L. Hodges, former field secretary for Latin America of the Assemblies of God Division of Foreign Missions, Springfield, Missouri, 26 August 1983; Noel Perkin, "Sifting and Growth (1935–1939)," Missions Vignettes, no. 10, *Pentecostal Evangel,* August 22, 1965, p. 22. It is noteworthy that the Egyptian believers began to assume direction of their church and that as early as 1933 a national superintendent had directed practically every aspect of the work; see *Light Along the Nile,* The Assemblies of God in Foreign Lands (Springfield, Mo.: Foreign Missions Department, n.d.), p. 10.

[14]For an excellent treatment of this subject, see Melvin L. Hodges, *The Indigenous Church* (Springfield, Mo.: Gospel Publishing House, 1953).

[15]Wilson, *Making Many Rich,* p. 118.

[16]Arthur E. Wilson, *The Gospel Among the Mossi People, French West Africa* (Springfield, Mo.: Foreign Missions Department, ca. 1935), pp. 36–37. According to Raymond T. Brock, former editor-in-chief of Foreign Missions publications, "The More Bible of the Mossi tribe in Upper Volta [Burkina Faso] is a monument to A/G missionaries who opened the country to Protestant missions in 1924 and immediately began translation work. They completed the Old and New Testaments, which were later printed by the American Bible Society." *The Encyclopedia of Modern Christian Missions: The Agencies,* s.v. "Assemblies of God Foreign Missions Department," by Raymond T. Brock.

[17]Ibid., p. 38.

[18]Ibid., p. 22.

[19]Helen I. Gustavson, *Tsinan, China: The Opening of an Effectual Door* (By the Author, 1941), pp. 25–26; also see William W. Simpson, *Evangelizing West China,* The Assemblies of God in Foreign Lands (Springfield, Mo.: Foreign Missions Department, 1931), pp. 11–12.

[20]Noel Perkin, "Sifting and Growth (1935–1939)," Missions Vignettes, no. 10, *Pentecostal Evangel,* August 22, 1965, p. 22.

[21]Maynard L. Ketcham, *Pentecost in the Ganges Delta: Being an Account of the Birth and Development of the Assemblies of God Mission Work in Bengal, India* (By the Author, 1945), p. 52.

[22]Jerome Beatty, "Nile Mother," *American Magazine,* June 1939, pp. 55–56, 180.

[23]For further information on Florence Steidel and her work, see Inez Spence, *These Are My People: Florence Steidel,* Heroes of the Conquest Series, no. 4 (Springfield, Mo.: Foreign Missions Department, n.d.); Irvin Winehouse, *The Assemblies of God: A Popular Survey* (New York: Vantage Press, 1959), pp. 96–102.

[24]*To the Uttermost Parts,* pp. 29–30; Jacob J. Mueller, *With Our Missionaries in North India,* The Assemblies of God in Foreign Lands (Springfield, Mo.: Foreign Missions Department, 1937), pp. 14–17; also, Perkin and Garlock, *Our World Witness,* pp. 54–56.

[25]Mueller, *With Our Missionaries,* p. 17.

[26]Ruth V. Burgess, "Obeying the Great Commission: The Acts of Obedience of Ted and Estelle Vassar," 1983, p. 3. (Typewritten.)

[27]Louise Jeter Walker, "A Team Effort—Then and Now," *Mountain Movers,* August, 1980, pp. 6–7.

[28]Noel Perkin, "Missionary Secretary's Mail," *Pentecostal Evangel,* February 4, 1933, p. 10.

[29]Perkin and Garlock, *Our World Witness,* p. 44.

[30]Noel Perkin, "The Missionary Secretary's Mail," *Pentecostal Evangel,* September 3, 1932, p. 9.

[31]"Prayer Band Still Growing," *Pentecostal Evangel,* February 11, 1933, p. 10.

[32]General Council Minutes, 1929, p. 60; 1937, p. 94; 1939, pp. 79–80.

[33]"The North China Bible School," *Pentecostal Evangel,* April 23, 1932, p. 9.

[34]For further information, see *The Encyclopedia of Modern Christian Missions: The Agencies,* s.v. "Eastern European Mission," by Paul B. Peterson.

[35]Frodsham, *With Signs Following,* pp. 93–104; also Jeff Henderson, "Pentecostal Missions in Eastern Europe: 1919–1940," 1981. (Typewritten.)

[36]Noel Perkin, "Report on Russian and Eastern European Mission," January 29, 1940, p. 5.

[37]Ibid., p. 3.

[38]Foreign Missions Committee Minutes, August 29, 1940. For further information, see "Europe at War—and the Gospel at Work," *Pentecostal Evangel,* March 1, 1941, p. 8.

[39]Ralph M. Riggs, "Missionary Enterprise in the Light of the Soon Coming of Christ," *Pentecostal Evangel,* September 28, 1940, p. 5.

[40]"A Great Missionary Home-Coming," *Pentecostal Evangel,* September 23, 1939, p. 8.

[41]General Council Minutes, 1941, p. 88. The four sailed on the *S. S. Zam Zam* which was torpedoed by a German submarine. Held hostage briefly, they had returned to the United States by the time of Perkin's report.

[42]For example, see Harry Downey and Leonard Angerman, *It Was Really a Miracle* (Corvallis, Oregon: By the Author, n.d.), pp. 159–160. Downey served as a missionary in the Belgian Congo at the time. See also *Assemblies of God Heritage.* Articles on Philippine Internment and Liberation. Spring 1985, pp. 6-13; Summer 1985, pp. 7-11.

[43]Noel Perkin, "War and Missions," *Pentecostal Evangel,* July 20, 1940, p. 8.

[44]Noel Perkin, "War and Missions," *Pentecostal Evangel,* December 27, 1941, p. 6.

[45]Booze, *Into All the World,* p. 21.

[46]Booze, *Into All the World,* pp. 21–22; Leland Johnson, *I Was a Prisoner of the Japs* (Los Angeles: By the Author, ca. 1945); "China Missionaries in U.S. After Japanese Internment," *Pentecostal Evangel,* September 12, 1942, pp. 8–9; "Repatriated on the M. S. Gripsholm," *Pentecostal Evangel,* January 1, 1944, pp. 6–7, 11; for the account of a British Assemblies of God missionary held captive and tortured by the Japanese, see "The Revival in North China," *Pentecostal Evangel,* October 16, 1943, p. 11; and Alan Benson, *A "Guest" of the Japanese Military* (Inglewood, Calif.: Calvary Assembly, n.d.). Additional information about missionaries who suffered as a result of the conflict may be found in Inez Spence, *With a Song in Her Heart: Blanche Appleby,* Heroes of the Conquest Series, no. 1 (Springfield, Mo.: Foreign Missions Department, n.d.); Margaret Carlow, *The King's Daughter: Jessie Wengler,* Heroes of the Conquest Series, no. 19 (Springfield, Mo.: Foreign Missions Department, n.d.); and Wayne E. Warner, "1945 Philippine Liberation Creates Emotional Scenes," *Assemblies of God Heritage,* Spring 1985, pp. 6–11.

Marie Juergensen, a long-time missionary to Japan, remained in the United States during much of the war. Even so, she continued her missionary work in an internment camp for American citizens of Japanese ancestry at Eden, Idaho. "Ministering to Japanese-Americans in the Northwest," *Assemblies of God Heritage,* Spring 1985, pp. 7, 12–13.

[47]Noel Perkin, "War and Missions," *Pentecostal Evangel,* December 27, 1941, p. 6.

[48]"Latin America—The Land of the Dark Ages," *The Pentecostal Evangel,* November 13, 1920, p. 12.

PART IV: THE ERA OF STRATEGIC PLANNING (1943–1959)

Chapter 10: Strategy, Structure, and Promotions

[1]Noel Perkin, "Progress in Crisis (1940–1944)," Missions Vignettes, no. 11, *Pentecostal Evangel,* September 19, 1965, p. 11.

[2]Noel Perkin, "War and Missions," *Pentecostal Evangel,* December 27, 1941, p. 6.

[3]"Twenty-eight Added to Our Missionary Force in 1942," *Pentecostal Evangel,* March 6, 1943, p. 8; "The Diary of a Delegate," *Pentecostal Evangel,* September 18, 1943, p. 3; General Council Minutes, 1943, pp. 43–44.

[4]"Wishing You a Happy, *Missionary* New Year!" *Pentecostal Evangel,* January 1, 1944, p. 9.

[5]*To the Uttermost Parts,* p. 45.

[6]Melvin L. Hodges, "Religion Without Light," *Pentecostal Evangel,* December 23, 1939, p. 9; for a further treatment of the subject by Hodges' predecessor as field secretary, see H. C. Ball, "Latin America and the Evangelical Church," *Pentecostal Evangel,* July 22, 1944, pp. 1, 8–9.

[7]Melvin L. Hodges, *A Theology of the Church and Its Mission: A Pentecostal Perspective* (Springfield, Mo.: Gospel Publishing House, 1977), pp. 96–97; William W. Menzies, "Lessons From Great Revivals," in *Live in the Spirit: A Compendium of Themes on the Spiritual Life as Presented at the Council on Spiritual Life,* ed. Harris Jansen (Springfield, Mo.: Gospel Publishing House, 1972), pp. 159–164; Joseph R. Flower, "The Charismatic Movement," in *Live in the Spirit,* ed. Jansen, pp. 200–215; Executive Presbytery of the Assemblies of God, "Official Statement on the Charismatic Movement," in *Live in the Spirit,* ed. Jansen, pp. 335–336; Executive Presbytery of the Assemblies of God, "Is Mary a Mediatrix?" in *Pentecostal Evangel,* March 28, 1982, p. 13. For recent views by some conservative evangelical missiologists and theologians on the Roman Catholic Church overseas, see *Theology and Mission: Papers and Responses Prepared for the Consultation on Theology and Mission,* ed. David J. Hesselgrave (Grand Rapids: Baker Book House, 1978), pp. 131–170, 331–332.

[8]Noel Perkin, "Onward to Victory," *Pentecostal Evangel,* April 10, 1943, pp. 1, 6; also, "Progress in Crisis (1940–1944)," Missions Vignettes, no. 11, *Pentecostal Evangel,* September 19, 1965, pp. 11–12.

[9]According to the General Council Reports, 74 percent of the missionary personnel from 1914 to 1949 had received training in Bible institutes; this figure increased to 93 percent by 1953. General Council Reports, 1949, p. 19; 1953, p. 34.

[10]The proposal itself is vague. See General Council Minutes, 1943, p. 45.

[11]Ibid., pp. 45–46.

[12]"Special Training for Certain Missionaries and Prospective Missionaries," Foreign Missions Committee Minutes, March 18, 1943.

[13]At that time, Central Bible Institute offered a 3-year diploma. The courses in missionary education included history of missions, missionary construction, missionary principles and practice, obstetrics, nursing, religions of mission fields, and survey of world missions. *Central Bible Institute Catalog, 1941–1942,* pp. 35–36.

[14]*Central Bible Institute Catalog, 1944–1945,* p. 19. Central Bible Institute later became the focus of intense controversy when it became eligible for Bible college accreditation in 1947. For further information, see Menzies, *Anointed,* pp. 357–358.

[15]For more information on Cummings, see Marion Craig, *Prepared by*

God: Robert Cummings, Heroes of the Conquest Series, no. 10 (Springfield, Mo.: Foreign Missions Department, n.d.).

[16]Previously, the Foreign Missions Conference of North America had selected Cummings to teach a special course of instruction to first-term missionaries of numerous denominations at the language school in Landour, India. General Council Minutes, 1943, p. 46.

[17]"The Diary of a Delegate," *Pentecostal Evangel,* September 18, 1943, p. 2.

[18]Noel Perkin, "Onward to Victory," *Pentecostal Evangel,* April 10, 1943, p. 1. Some missionaries went overseas at the close of the war without pledged support from local churches, relying solely on this fund. When the fund was depleted, some returned home; others continued and eventually gained pledged support. The results of this procedure were mixed. Interview with Hogan; interview with Maynard L. Ketcham, former field secretary for the Far East of the Assemblies of God Division of Foreign Missions, 13 July 1983.

[19]General Council Minutes, 1945, p. 67.

[20]"The Missionary Conference," *Pentecostal Evangel,* July 10, 1948, p. 8. The All-China Conference of Assemblies of God missionaries took place in September 1948 in Wuchang, China, under the direction of Howard C. Osgood, field secretary for China. Since many of the missionaries had returned to China after the war, this conference looked forward to the future in a country wracked by devastation and civil war. At this conference, a national Assemblies of God organization in China came into being. By 1952, most of the missionaries had been forced out of China. Personal interview with Howard C. Osgood, former field secretary for China and the Far East of the Assemblies of God Division of Foreign Missions, Springfield, Missouri, 4 January 1984.

[21]Noel Perkin, "Foreign Missions Secretary's Report to the 1953 General Council," *Pentecostal Evangel,* September 27, 1953, p. 11.

[22]Ralph M. Riggs, "Pentecost and Christ's Return," *Pentecostal Evangel,* September 30, 1951, p. 16.

[23]Stanley M. Horton, *Bible Prophecy, Teacher's Manual* (Springfield, Mo.: Church School Literature Department, 1963), pp. 57–58.

[24]Frank M. Boyd, *Prophetic Light,* Book 2 (Springfield, Mo.: Correspondence School of the General Council of the Assemblies of God, 1948), pp. 12–17, 49–57.

[25]According to Bernard Ramm, a prominent conservative evangelical Biblical scholar, "The basic thesis of dispensationalism is that there are seven distinct economies of God in which God specifies certain conditions or terms and tests man for his obedience to these terms. This thesis in turn becomes a principle of hermeneutics according to which one cannot properly interpret the Scriptures unless one knows the dispensation to which the given passage refers or belongs. . . . Israel forms a distinct group of

redeemed people separate from the Church. If one pushes the principle further, a distinct eschatology develops. It is an eschatology that centers itself upon the future of Israel, her national conversion, her return to the Promised Land, and her millennial bliss." Bernard L. Ramm, *A Handbook of Contemporary Theology* (Grand Rapids: Wm. B. Eerdmans Publishing Co., 1966), pp. 36–37. For information by dispensationalist writers, see Lewis Sperry Chafer, *Systematic Theology,* 8 vols. (Dallas: Dallas Seminary Press, 1947–1948), vol. 7: *Doctrinal Summarization,* pp. 223–225; W. C. Stevens, *Mysteries of the Kingdom* (San Francisco: M. G. McClinton and Co., 1904), pp. 129–130. Stevens, a professor of theology at The Missionary Training Institute at Nyack, probably taught several future Assemblies of God leaders, including Frank M. Boyd and William I. Evans.

[26]"A Great Move Forward," *Pentecostal Evangel,* May 1, 1926, p. 3.

[27]Ibid.

[28]Ernest S. Williams, *Systematic Theology,* 3 vols. (Springfield, Mo.: Gospel Publishing House, 1953), 3:95; for a recent interpretation, see Paul Anthony Pomerville, "Pentecostalism and Missions: Distortion or Correction? The Pentecostal Contribution to Contemporary Mission Theology" (Ph. D. dissertation, Fuller Theological Seminary School of World Mission, 1982).

[29]Stanley M. Horton, *Panorama of the Bible* (Springfield, Mo.: Church School Literature Department, 1961), p. 52.

[30]"What Do You Think?" *The Missionary Forum,* no. 20, n.d., p. 3.

[31]Letter from Martha Schoonmaker to Maynard L. Ketcham and members of the Executive Committee, 29 July 1950. For Perkin's point of view on this issue, see interview with Perkin, and Perkin and Garlock, *Our World Witness,* pp. 51–52.

[32]Africa, 143; China, 53; India and Ceylon, 101; Latin America and the West Indies, 149; various smaller fields of endeavor, such as Europe, 29; 35 ministers of the Council serving abroad without regular appointment; 11 associated Canadian and 17 retired missionaries. General Council Minutes, 1945, p. 59. The highest number of missionaries could now be found in Africa and Latin America, a significant shift from earlier years when the number of missionaries to China and India had dwarfed the number serving in Latin America.

[33]*Pentecostal Evangel,* May 31, 1947, p. 9.

[34]Maynard L. Ketcham, "Information Please!" *World Challenge,* December 1955, p. 4. For further information about departmental personnel and their years of service, see "Division of Foreign Missions Personnel," n.d. (Typewritten.)

[35]General Council Minutes, 1947, p. 10.

[36]General Council Minutes, 1955, p. 28.

[37]Ruby M. Enyart, "Operation Headquarters: The Story of the Foreign

Missions Department Office—Its Staff and Work—Told in Two Parts," Part 2, *The Missionary Challenge,* April 1950, pp. 10–11.

[38]General Council Reports, 1955, pp. 19–20.

[39]Ibid., p. 18. Beginning in 1948, Christine Carmichael served as *deputational secretary,* which involved writing promotional literature and helping furloughed missionaries arrange their itineraries among the local churches. For further information about the structure, personnel, and office layout in 1950, see Enyart, "Operation Headquarters," Parts 1 (March 1950; pp. 15–21, 26) and 2 (April 1950; pp. 10–14, 31–33), *The Missionary Challenge.*

[40]Letter from W. Neil McDaniel, president of the Springfield Travel Service, Inc., to Gary B. McGee, 11 November 1983; personal interview with Robert T. McGlasson, former foreign missions secretary of the Assemblies of God Division of Foreign Missions, Springfield, Missouri, 17 November 1983.

[41]General Council Minutes, 1955, p. 23.

[42]For further information on the Foreign Missions Board and its Advisory Committee, see General Council Minutes, 1957, pp. 30–31, 51–52.

[43]General Council Minutes, 1955, p. 23.

[44]"Administrative Assistant Appointed," *World Challenge,* June 1958, p. 9; General Council Minutes, 1959, p. 40.

[45]General Council Minutes, 1957, p. 29.

[46]When J. Philip Hogan became assistant general superintendent in 1959 with the responsibility of administering the missions program, his new administrative assistant, Robert T. McGlasson, received the title of foreign missions secretary. General Council Minutes, 1959, pp. 24–25.

[47]For further information on the New York office, see "Missionaries Visit New York Office," *The Missionary Challenge,* August 1949, pp. 16–17; "The New York Office," *The Missionary Forum,* no. 14, n.d., pp. 3–4.

[48]General Council Minutes, 1959, p. 14. Among districts, the Southern California District Council led in giving during the biennium with $1,087,482.30. The Glad Tidings Tabernacle in New York City led all local churches by giving $94,975.67.

[49]The General Council in 1955 authorized the incorporation of the World Missions Plan into its bylaws. General Council Minutes, 1955, pp. 30–31.

[50]General Council Minutes, 1957, pp. 18–19.

[51]Noel Perkin, "Introduction to the Missions Seminar," *Key,* July–August 1956, p. 4. It should also be noted that in 1955, the Council recommended that missionaries support the operational expenses of the department with one half of their tithes. General Council Minutes, 1955, p. 24.

[52]*DFM PASSPORT: The Missions Manual.* Springfield: Assemblies of God Division of Foreign Missions, n.d., pp. 5–5, 5–6, 5–7.

[53]F. Wildon Colbaugh, "Can We Meet Today's Opportunities?" *Pentecostal Evangel,* June 25, 1949, p. 6.

[54]Noel Perkin, "Our Funds Are Gone, But Our Faith Is in God," *Pentecostal Evangel,* August 6, 1949, p. 8.

[55]For example, "The Story of a Missionary Dollar," *Pentecostal Evangel,* June 14, 1953, p. 11.

[56]"Questions and Answers," *Key,* March 1953, p. 5.

[57]"Development in Deputational Program," *Pentecostal Evangel,* July 1, 1944, p. 11.

[58]Foreign Missions Committee Minutes, March 24, 1943.

[59]Kenneth Short, "When the Doors Are Opened Again," *The Missionary Challenge,* January–March 1945, p. 21.

[60]Enyart, "Operation Headquarters," Part 2, pp. 12–13.

[61]Foreign Missions Committee Minutes, July 18, 1950.

[62]"1949 Missionary Advance," *Pentecostal Evangel,* January 1, 1949, p. 9.

[63]"Forward in '50—Double in '51," *The Missionary Challenge,* July 1950, p. 4.

[64]Foreign Missions Committee Minutes, August 2, 1949.

[65]"Missionary Representatives' Conference," *The Missionary Challenge,* April 1950, p. 3. For later important recommendations that were presented to the General Council, see General Council Minutes, 1951, pp. 12–13.

[66]"The District Missionary Secretary," *Key,* April 1953, p. 9.

[67]For more information about the expanding role of the Promotions Division, see J. Philip Hogan, "A Strong Arm of Missions," *The Missionary Challenge,* March 1954, pp. 9–11. At the 1956 District Missionary Secretaries Conference in Springfield, a recommendation to set up a new standard for awards for missionary giving received approval. Before this, awards were based only on total and per capita giving. For an explanation of the new program, see D. G. Foote, "Dear KEY Friends:" *Key,* July–August 1956, pp. 1–2.

[68]Glenn Horst, "National Missionary Day," *Key,* vol. 1, no. 1, 1953, p. 10.

[69]General Council Minutes, 1953, p. 21.

[70]"A Picture's Worth a Thousand Words," *Key,* February 1953, p. 11.

[71]J. Philip Hogan, "A Gentle Reminder," *Key,* March 1954, p. 3.

[72]For a brief biographical sketch, see Menzies, *Anointed,* pp. 166–168.

[73]"Where Does VISION Begin?" *World Challenge,* November 1955, p. 16.

[74]J. Philip Hogan, "Announcing 1956 World Missions Regional Conferences," *Pentecostal Evangel,* September 11, 1955, p. 7.

[75]The editors included Kenneth Short, Howard C. Osgood, Melvin L. Hodges, and F. Wildon Colbaugh.

[76]Leslie W. Smith and Cyril L. Carden served as editors.

[77]"Why the *Forum?*" *The Missionary Forum,* no.1, 1948, p. 2.

[78]General Council Minutes, 1957, p. 28.

[79]J. Philip Hogan, "Goals Set for New 'Crash' Program of World Evangelism," *Pentecostal Evangel,* July 26, 1959, p. 6; "Global Conquest . . ." *Global Conquest,* August 1959, pp. 2–3.

[80]Foreign Missions Committee Minutes, October 7, 1959.

[81]Paul Yonggi Cho, *Successful Home Cell Groups* (Plainfield, N.J.: Logos International, 1981); Maynard L. Ketcham, *Tigers That Talk* (Charlotte, N.C.: PTL Television Network, 1979), pp. 99–111; for a discussion of the results of Global Conquest in the 1960s and its eventual successor, Good News Crusades, see Menzies, *Anointed,* pp. 249–251.

[82]General Council Minutes, 1959, pp. 32, 40. For tributes to the work of Noel Perkin, see Melvin L. Hodges, "Noel Perkin Completes 33 Years of Service," *Missionary Forum,* November–December 1959, pp. 2–5; Adele Flower Dalton, "A Brother Beloved: Noel Perkin (January 15, 1893–October 3, 1979)," *Mountain Movers,* February 1980, pp. 6–7. In 1980, the Assemblies of God Theological Seminary, Springfield, Missouri, established the Noel Perkin Chair of World Missions in his honor. Dr. Melvin L. Hodges, former field secretary for Latin America and the West Indies and well-known Pentecostal missiologist (author of *The Indigenous Church*), received the first appointment to that post.

[83]Menzies, *Anointed,* pp. 274–275.

[84]Noel Perkin, "Our Missionary Transport," *Pentecostal Evangel,* October 9, 1948, p. 12.

[85]Menzies, *Anointed,* pp. 247–248.

[86]"Our First Missionary Plane," *The Missionary Challenge,* January–March 1945, p. 16. For further information, see Wayne Warner, "Flying *Ambassadors* of Good Will," *Assemblies of God Heritage,* Winter 1985-86, pp. 3, 4, 13, 14; "Missionary Yacht Is Dedicated," *Pentecostal Evangel,* June 16, 1945, p. 6; Ruby M. Enyart, "Our Missionary Transport Service," *Pentecostal Evangel,* July 15, 1950, pp. 6–7, 10; *Declare His Glory: Speed–the–Light—40th Anniversary* (Springfield, Mo.: Youth Department of the Assemblies of God, 1983).

[87]J. Philip Hogan, "S.T.L.," *World Challenge,* January 1959, p. 31.

[88]"First Offering to Boys and Girls Missionary Crusade," *Pentecostal Evangel,* September 10, 1949, p. 10.

[89]General Council Minutes, 1959, p. 18.

[90]"Our Radio Missionary to the Orient," *Pentecostal Evangel,* August 30, 1953, p. 13. For further information on the use of radio in missionary evangelism, see Hugh Preston Jeter (an Assemblies of God missionary), "Radio in World Evangelism" (M.A. thesis, Columbia Bible College Graduate School of Missions, 1963).

[91]General Council Minutes, 1945, pp. 60–61; for further information, see

Paul Finkenbinder, *Using Radio To Reach the World.* August 29, 1965, audiotape.

Chapter 11: Missiology and Cooperation

[1]*Central Bible Institute Catalog, 1944–1945,* p. 19. See also "Prepare for Missionary Service," *Pentecostal Evangel,* August 14, 1943, p. 11.

[2]For further information, see "The Missionary Seminar," *The Missionary Challenge,* August 1950, pp. 6–10, 14; "Seminar Profitable to Missionaries," *Pentecostal Evangel,* July 1, 1950, p. 5.

[3]"Report to the Executive Presbytery for Missionary Seminar: May 30–June 9th, 1950" in Foreign Missions Committee Minutes.

[4]General Council Minutes, 1957, p. 31. The name was later changed to the School of Missions.

[5]"School of Orientation Becomes Annual Event," *Pentecostal Evangel,* September 27, 1959, p. 7; "First Annual School of Orientation a Success," *Key,* September–October 1959, p. 9.

[6]*Missionary Manual* (Springfield, Mo.: Foreign Missions Department, 1931); *Missionary Manual* (Springfield, Mo.: Foreign Missions Department, 1949); *Missionary Manual* (Springfield, Mo.: Foreign Missions Department, 1956).

[7]Board of Administration, Central Bible College, Minutes, June 13, 1950; Noel Perkin, "Increasing Mobility (1950–1954)," Missions Vignettes, no. 13, *Pentecostal Evangel,* November 21, 1965, p. 20.

[8]Foreign Missions Committee Minutes, 1958, pp. 1613–1614.

[9]In 1947 the General Council reaffirmed its commitment to overseas evangelism and the establishment of indigenous churches. General Council Minutes, 1947, p. 32.

[10]Hodges became one of the few Assemblies of God writers on missions to publish outside the organization's periodicals. Among other articles are the following: "A Pentecostal's View of Mission Strategy," *International Review of Missions* 57 (July 1968):304–310; "Spiritual Dynamics in El Salvador," *Evangelical Missions Quarterly* 2 (Winter 1966):80–83.

[11]Melvin L. Hodges, *The Indigenous Church* (Springfield, Mo.: Gospel Publishing House, 1953; 1976 printing), p. 14.

[12]Ibid., p. 131.

[13]Ibid., p. 132; also, "Purpose of Pentecost," *The Missionary Challenge,* August 1951, p. 4.

[14]Benjamin P. Shinde, "The Contribution of the Assemblies of God to Church Growth in India" (M.A. thesis, Fuller Theological Seminary School of World Mission, 1974), p. 179. For further information, see Harry R. Boer, *Pentecost and Missions* (Grand Rapids: Wm. B. Eerdmans Publishing Co., 1961), pp. 225–226; C. Peter Wagner, *Look Out! The Pentecostals*

Are Coming (Carol Stream, Ill.: Creation House, 1973), p. 126, Chapter 9: "Praying for the Sick."

[15]Hodges, *Indigenous,* p. 132.

[16]Noel Perkin, "Racial Superiority," *The Missionary Forum,* no. 12, n.d., p. 3.

[17]"As Others See Us," *The Missionary Forum,* 1948, no. 1, p.1. For further information, see "Report on Meeting of North India Missionary Group" in Foreign Missions Committee Minutes, March 7, 1945.

[18]Foreign Missions Committee Minutes, November 7, 1958.

[19]Nicholas Nikoloff, "Report on Europe" at the 1943 Missionary Conference, Springfield, Mo., pp. 18–19.

[20]Everett L. Phillips, "The Africa Question," *World Challenge,* September 1955, p. 5. For further information about the successful application of indigenous church principles, see Christine Carmichael, "Where They Are Now" (Edgar and Mabel Pettenger, missionaries to South Africa), *The Missionary Forum,* 3rd Quarter, 1966, p. 16; Hilda C. Olsen and Peggy Anderson, *Triumphs and Tears—Basutoland: 1950–1960* (Maseru, Basutoland, South Africa, By the Authors, 1960), p. 27.

[21]For more information on the role of the field fellowships, see *Missionary Manual* (Springfield, Mo.: Foreign Missions Department, 1956), pp. 67–70.

[22]J. Philip Hogan, "Do We Have a National Worker's Program?" *World Challenge,* December 1956, p. 19; Melvin L. Hodges, "The Future and Missions," *The Missionary Forum,* no. 19, n.d., pp. 1–2.

[23]Carl Malz, *Foreign Bible School Survey Report: A Report of the Bible School Program of the Foreign Missions Department of the Assemblies of God* (Springfield, Mo.: The Assemblies of God, 1959), p. 3; see also *This We Believe: Selected Educational Philosophies of Our Assemblies of God Bible School Administrations on the Foreign Field,* ed. Malz (Springfield, Mo.: Foreign Missions Department, ca. 1959).

[24]Carl Malz, "The Crowning Missionary Method," *Pentecostal Evangel,* July 26, 1959, p. 4.

[25]Foreign Missions Committee Minutes, August 8, 1958. Some allowances were made, however, for the expenses of Bible school students and limited support for students who engaged in pioneer evangelism with the supervision of the national church or missionary field fellowship. See Perkin, "Introduction to the Missions Seminar," *Key,* July–August 1956, pp. 3–6.

[26]Noel Perkin, "Support of Benevolent Institutions," *The Missionary Forum,* no. 12, n.d., p. 2.

[27]Numerous evangelists, such as William Branham, Jack Coe, Clifton Erickson, T. L. Osborn, Oral Roberts, and A. A. Allen, attained prominence in the late 1940s and early 1950s. Engaging largely in mass crusades, often held in large tents, they preached the necessity of a born-again conversion experience and the sufficiency of Christ's atonement for the physical healing

of all believers. Many of these evangelists became associated with The Voice of Healing organization headed by Gordon Lindsay of Dallas, Texas. The movement peaked in the mid-1950s. Menzies provides an Assemblies of God perspective in *Anointed,* pp. 330–335. For an excellent treatment of the movement as a whole, see David Edwin Harrell, Jr., *All Things Are Possible: The Healing and Charismatic Revivals in Modern America* (Bloomington, Ind.: Indiana University Press, 1975).

[28]"Field Focus: Chile" (Springfield, Mo.: Assemblies of God Division of Foreign Missions, n.d.), p. 3.

[29]Lester F. Sumrall, *Modern Manila Miracles: The Story of the Great Philippine Revival* (Springfield, Mo.: Pub. by Rev. Clifton O. Erickson, 1954); *The True Story of Clarita Villanueva* (South Bend, Ind.: By the Author, 1955).

[30]Louie W. Stokes, *The Great Revival in Buenos Aires* (Buenos Aires: Casilla De Correo, 1954), p. 40.

[31]Foreign Missions Committee Minutes, May 4, 1954.

[32]Noel Perkin, "Introduction to the Missions Seminar," *Key,* July–August 1956, p. 6.

[33]For the criteria for endorsement of overseas evangelists, see "The Policy Governing the Ministry of Missionary Evangelists" in the Foreign Missions Committee Minutes, 1958, p. 1470A.

[34]J. Philip Hogan, "Harvest Hints," *World Challenge,* January 1957, p. 18. For the department's response to the direct support of national pastors and evangelists by evangelist T. L. Osborn, see "Information for District Officials Concerning Our Relationship With the Association for Native Evangelism," *Key,* January–February 1956, pp. 3–4.

[35]A resolution at the 1957 meeting of the General Council called for the Foreign Missions Department "to take such steps as may seem expedient to develop plans for the establishing of an International Assemblies of God Fellowship by which authorized representatives of national Assemblies of God groups may meet at regular intervals for fellowship and conference in the interests of world evangelism by the closer co-operation of national Assemblies of God groups." General Council Minutes, 1957, pp. 31–32. The Fellowship never came into being. Because of the desire of the Missions Department to avoid charges of dominating national churches, the idea of an organic fellowship was discarded in favor of fraternal relationships. Regional fellowships did come into being to enhance communication, cooperative efforts, and partnership. Interview with Hogan.

[36]See Menzies, *Anointed,* pp. 215–220.

[37]"Second Exploratory Conference of Pentecostal Leaders," *Pentecostal Evangel,* August 28, 1948, p. 6.

[38]Noel Perkin, "Increasing Mobility (1950–1954)," Missions Vignettes, no. 13, *Pentecostal Evangel,* November 21, 1965, p. 20; General Council Reports, 1953, pp. 17–18.

[39]Foreign Missions Committee Minutes, February 15, 1946; Menzies, *Anointed,* pp. 185–189, 192, 209.

[40]Foreign Missions Committee Minutes, May 26, 1950; November 7, 1951; January 9, 1953.

[41]Foreign Missions Committee Minutes, December 19, 1950.

[42]Letter from Wade T. Coggins to Gary B. McGee, 15 August 1983.

[43]Noel Perkin, "Our Missionary Advance Around the World," *Pentecostal Evangel,* October 4, 1959, pp. 12–13, 30.

[44]For assessments by two non-Assemblies of God observers, see James D. Crane, "What We Can Learn From the Assemblies of God in El Salvador," ca. 1962 (Typewritten.), and George W. Peters, "The Missionary Thrust and Dynamic of the Assemblies of God," n.d. (Mimeographed.)

Bibliography

PRIMARY SOURCES

Manuscript Collections

Nyack, N. Y.: The A. B. Simpson Historical Library
Springfield, Mo.: The Assemblies of God Archives
Springfield, Mo.: The Assemblies of God Collection, Central Bible College
  Library
Springfield, Mo.: Editorial Office Files, Assemblies of God Division of
  Foreign Missions
Springfield, Mo.: Editorial Office Files, *Pentecostal Evangel*
Springfield, Mo.: The General Secretary's Office Files

Periodicals

The Apostolic Faith (Los Angeles, Calif.)
Assemblies of God Heritage
The Bridegroom's Messenger (Atlanta, Ga.)
The Christian Evangel
Full Gospel Missionary Herald
Global Conquest
Good News Crusades
The Gospel Call
The Gospel Witness (Los Angeles, Calif.)
The Independent (Boston, Mass.)
International Bulletin
Key
The Latter Rain Evangel
The Missionary Challenge
The Missionary Forum
The Missionary Review of the World
Missionettes Memos
Mountain Movers

Paraclete
The Pentecost
Pentecostal Evangel
Pneuma
Pulpit
South and Central African Pentecostal Herald
Trust
Weekly Evangel
Word and Witness
World Challenge

Published Works

Adams, Charles V. *No Time for Furlough: Mabel Dean.* Heroes of the Conquest Series, no. 15. Springfield, Mo.: Foreign Missions Department, n.d.

"Administrative Assistant Appointed." *World Challenge,* June 1958, p. 9.

Alumni Directory. Nyack, N.Y.: The Nyack College Alumni Association, 1976.

Appleby, Blanche R. "Darkness and Dawn." *Pentecostal Evangel,* June 8, 1929, pp. 2–3, 6.

"As Others See Us." *The Missionary Forum,* 1948. Vol. 1, no. 1, n.d., p. 1.

The Assemblies of God in Foreign Lands. Springfield, Mo.: Foreign Missions Department, 1948.

Bailly, Gerard A. "Preparedness for Missionary Work." *Christian Evangel,* September 6, 1919, p. 9.

Baird, Mollie. *Of Whom the World Is Not Worthy: Stories of North India's Christians.* Springfield, Mo.: Gospel Publishing House, 1941.

Baker, Elizabeth V., et al. *Chronicles of a Faith Life.* 2nd ed. Rochester, N.Y.: Elim Publishing Co., ca. 1926.

Baker, H. A. *God in Ka Do Land.* Mokiang, Yunnan, China: The Adullam Reading Campaign, 1937.

Ball, H. C. "Healed for Service Among the Mexicans." *The Latter Rain Evangel,* January 1931, pp. 10–11.

————. "Latin America and the Evangelical Church." *Pentecostal Evangel,* July 22, 1944, pp. 1, 8–9.

Ball, H. C., and Luce, A. E. *Glimpses of Our Latin American Work in the United States and Mexico.* Springfield, Mo.: Foreign Missions Department, 1940.

Baltau, Loretta. *His Witness.* By the Author, 1968.

Bard, Ruth J. *In the Service of the King of Kings.* By the Author, ca. 1960.

Barratt, Thomas Ball. *When the Fire Fell and the Outline of My Life.* Oslo: Alfons Hansen & Soner, 1927.

"A Barrel of Money for the Missionaries." (Advertisement) *Christian Evangel,* August 10, 1918, p. 11.

Bartleman, Frank. *What Really Happened at "Azusa Street"?* Edited by John Walker. Northridge, Calif.: Voice Christian Publications, Inc., 1962.
—————. *Two Years Mission Work in Europe.* Los Angeles: By the Author, n.d.
—————. *Around the World by Faith.* Los Angeles: By the Author, n.d.
—————. *Another Wave Rolls In!* Edited by John Walker. Revised and Enlarged Edition by John G. Myers. Northridge, Calif.: Voice Publications, 1970.
Baugh, Edith E. " 'Upon the Handmaidens Will I Pour Out My Spirit': A Call to India Crystallized at the Convention." *The Latter Rain Evangel,* July 1909, pp. 4–6.
Beach, Harlan P. and Fahs, Charles H., eds. *World Missionary Atlas.* New York: Institute of Social and Religious Research, 1925.
Beatty, Jerome. "Nile Mother." *American Magazine,* June 1939, pp. 55–56, 180.
—————. *Nile Mother: The Story of Lillian Trasher.* Springfield, Mo.: Foreign Missions Department, ca. 1939.
Beckdahl, Agnes N. T. *A Witness of God's Faithfulness.* Lucknow, India: Lucknow Publishing House, ca. 1930.
Bell, E. N. *Questions and Answers.* Springfield, Mo.: Gospel Publishing House, n.d.
—————. "A Word to Foreign Missionaries." *Word and Witness,* October 20, 1912, p. 3.
—————. "God's Work in Foreign Lands." *Word and Witness,* November 20, 1913, p. 4.
—————. "Missionary Opportunity." *Word and Witness,* October 20, 1913, p. 2.
—————. "God's Work in Foreign Lands." *Word and Witness,* April 20, 1914, p. 4.
—————. "Complaints About Missionary Money." *Christian Evangel,* July 26, 1919, p. 4.
—————. "General Council Principles." *Evangel,* Tract no. 914. Springfield, Mo.: Gospel Publishing House, ca. 1922.
Benson, Alan. *A "Guest" of the Japanese Military.* Inglewood, Calif.: Calvary Assembly, n.d.
Berg, Arthur F. *African or Scriptural Brick: The Congo Call.* Minneapolis: By the Author, 1930.
—————. "WORLD MISSIONS! How It Started—And WHY? [*sic*]" n.d. (Typewritten.)
Bethel Bible Training School Catalog. n.d.
"Bible School Notes." *Trust,* April 1915, p. 2.
Blan, Nora. *Over the Rugged Mountains: W. E. Simpson.* Heroes of the Conquest Series, no. 8. Springfield, Mo.: Foreign Missions Department, n.d.
Bolton, Leonard. *China Call: Miracles Among the Lisu People.* Springfield, Mo.: Gospel Publishing House, 1984.

Boyd, Frank M. *Prophetic Light,* Book 2. Springfield, Mo.: Correspondence School of the General Council of the Assemblies of God, 1948.

Brumback, Carl. *What Meaneth This?* Springfield, Mo.: Gospel Publishing House, 1947.

Burgess, John. *Opportunities in South India and Ceylon.* Springfield, Mo.: Foreign Missions Department, ca. 1934.

"The Busy-Bee World-Wide Missions Program." *Pentecostal Evangel,* November 9, 1929, pp. 6–8.

Carlow, Margaret, *The King's Daughter: Jessie Wengler.* Heroes of the Conquest Series, no. 19. Springfield, Mo.: Foreign Missions Department, n.d.

Carmichael, Christine. "The New Africa." Missions Vignettes, no. 5. *Pentecostal Evangel,* March 21, 1965, pp. 25–26.

―――― . "Forward in the Far East." Missions Vignettes, no. 6. *Pentecostal Evangel,* April 25, 1965, pp. 13–14.

―――― . "Pentecost in Latin America." Missions Vignettes, no. 7. *Pentecostal Evangel,* May 23, 1965, pp. 19–20.

―――― . "Europe—A Strategic Mission Field." Missions Vignettes, no. 8. *Pentecostal Evangel,* June 20, 1965, pp. 13–14.

―――― . "Territory in Turmoil." Missions Vignettes, no. 9. *Pentecostal Evangel,* July 18, 1965, pp. 15–16.

―――― . "The Emerging National Church Needs a Steady Stream of Adequately Trained Leaders." Our Foreign Mission, no. 2: Assemblies of God Bible Schools. *Pentecostal Evangel,* April 10, 1966, pp. 19–20.

―――― . "Thirteen Thousand National Workers Form a Vibrant Missionary Force." Our Foreign Mission, no. 4: Assemblies of God National Workers. *Pentecostal Evangel,* June 19, 1966, pp. 13–14.

―――― . "Literature Is an Integral Part of the Assemblies of God Missions Enterprise." Our Foreign Mission, no. 6: Assemblies of God Missions Literature. *Pentecostal Evangel,* August 21, 1966, pp. 19–20.

―――― ."Where They Are Now." *The Missionary Forum,* 3rd Quarter, 1966, p. 16.

―――― . "Arise . . . Go to That Great City." Our Foreign Mission, no. 8: Assemblies of God Metropolitan Evangelism. *Pentecostal Evangel,* October 23, 1966, pp. 21–22.

―――― . "Radio Is Having Unprecedented Outreach." Our Foreign Mission, no. 9: Assemblies of God Radio Evangelism. *Pentecostal Evangel,* November 20, 1966, pp. 19–20.

Carmichael, Mrs. George. "Our Goal." *Key,* March 1953, p. 2.

Central Bible Institute Catalog. Springfield, Mo.: Assemblies of God, Inc. 1922–1923, 1923–1924, 1924–1925, 1925–1926, 1941–1942, 1944–1945.

"Change in Missionary Department." *Pentecostal Evangel,* December 18, 1926, p. 8.

Chawner, Charles, and Chawner, Emma. *Called to Zululand: A Story of God's Leading.* South Africa: By the Authors, n.d.

"China Missionaries in U.S. After Japanese Internment." *Pentecostal Evangel,* September 12, 1942, pp. 8–9.

Christie, Florence, and Burt, Karlene. *New Buildings on Old Foundations: Missionary Experiences in Egypt.* Los Angeles: By the Authors, n.d.

"A Conference of Pentecostal Workers and Missionaries: Boston, March 5–13, 1913." *The Latter Rain Evangel,* October 1912, p. 24.

Cook, Robert F. *Half a Century of Divine Leading and 37 Years of Apostolic Achievements in South India.* Cleveland, Tenn: Church of God Foreign Missions Department, 1955.

Coxe, Sara. "When Pentecost Came to India." *The Latter Rain Evangel,* June 1918, pp. 4–7.

Craig, Marion. *Prepared by God: Robert Cummings.* Heroes of the Conquest Series, no. 10. Springfield, Mo.: Foreign Missions Department, n.d.

Cummings, Robert. "The Spiritual Life of the Missionary." *The Missionary Forum,* no. 3, n.d., pp. 3–5, 8.

Dalton, Adele Flower. *Until the Resurrection: Frank Isensee.* Heroes of the Conquest Series, no. 3. Foreign Missions Department, n.d.

Davison, Eva. *They Two Went On.* London: Evangel Press, 1979.

Daybreak in Malay. The Assemblies of God in Foreign Lands. Springfield, Mo.: Foreign Missions Department, 1935.

"Day by Day at Central Bible Institute." *Pentecostal Evangel,* December 20, 1924, pp. 8–9.

Declare His Glory: Speed–the–Light—40th Anniversary. Springfield, Mo.: Youth Department of the Assemblies of God, 1983.

Dedicated Unto Our Lord: Bethel Assembly of God (50th Anniversary: 1913–1963). Newark, N.J.: Bethel Assembly of God, 1963.

"The District Missionary Secretary." *Key,* April 1953, p. 9.

Downey, Harry, and Angerman, Leonard. *It Was Really a Miracle.* Corvallis, Oreg.: By the Authors, n.d.

Ecumenical Missionary Conference, 1900: Report of the Ecumenical Conference on Foreign Missions Held in Carnegie Hall and Neighboring Churches, April 21 to May 1. New York: American Tract Society, 1900.

Edwards, Doris M. *The Good Fight: Robert Wade Edwards.* Shencottah, Madras State, India: A. G. Press, n.d.

Eldridge, George N. *Personal Reminiscences.* Los Angeles: The West Coast Publishing Co., n.d.

Enyart, Ruby M., ed. *Before Their Eyes: Missionary Plays for Church and Church Group Presentation.* Springfield, Mo.: Gospel Publishing House, 1956.

———. "Operation Headquarters," Part 1. *The Missionary Challenge,* March 1950, pp. 15–21, 26.

———. "Operation Headquarters," Part 2. *The Missionary Challenge,* April 1950, pp. 10–14, 31–33.

———. "Our Missionary Transport Service." *Pentecostal Evangel,* July 15, 1950, pp. 6–7, 10.

Erickson, Leif. *Beyond That Sunrise.* By the Author, ca. 1972.

"Europe at War—and the Gospel at Work." *Pentecostal Evangel,* March 1, 1941, p. 8.

Ewart, Frank J. *The Phenomenon of Pentecost.* Houston: Herald Publishing House, 1947.

Executive Presbytery of the Assemblies of God. "Is Mary a Mediatrix?" *Pentecostal Evangel,* March 28, 1982, p. 13.

Ezzo, Elsie Bolton. *Beyond the Mekong: Leonard Bolton.* Heroes of the Conquest Series, no. 6. Springfield, Mo.: Foreign Missions Department, n.d.

Faux, William M. "Missionary Giving." *Pentecostal Evangel,* March 1, 1924, p. 10.

————. "Our Mexican Work." *Pentecostal Evangel,* December 5, 1925, p. 18.

————. "A Forward Missionary Movement." *Pentecostal Evangel,* June 6, 1925, p. 11.

————. "My Impression of Missions." *Pentecostal Evangel,* January 2, 1926, p. 8.

"Fifteen Hundred Students Rejected Last Year." *Pentecostal Evangel,* May 10, 1947, p. 16.

"First Annual School of Orientation a Success." *Key,* September–October 1959, p. 9.

"First Offering to Boys and Girls Missionary Crusade." *Pentecostal Evangel,* September 10, 1949, p. 10.

Flower, Alice Reynolds. *Grace for Grace.* Springfield, Mo.: By the Author, ca. 1961.

Flower, J. Roswell. "A Closer and Deeper Fellowship for the Pentecostal Assemblies in Indiana and the Central States." *Christian Evangel,* July 19, 1913, p. 1.

————. "Greetings From the New Treasurer." *Pentecostal Evangel,* November 1, 1919, p. 26.

————. "Seven Reasons Why You Should Send Your Offerings for the Foreign Field Through the Missionary Department." *Pentecostal Evangel,* January 10, 1920, p. 12.

————. "A Missionary Spirit Necessary." *Pentecostal Evangel,* February 7, 1920, p. 12.

————. "Report of Missionary Treasurer for Year Ending Sept. 1, 1920." *Pentecostal Evangel,* October 16, 1920, pp. 8–10.

————. "Where the Money Goes." *Pentecostal Evangel,* April 30, 1921, p. 12.

————. "My Responsibility." *Pentecostal Evangel,* June 25, 1921, p. 12.

————. "Coming Home on Furlough." *Pentecostal Evangel,* October 1, 1921, p. 12.

————. "An Important Resolution Affecting Prospective Missionaries." *Pentecostal Evangel,* February 17, 1923, p. 12.

————. "Men Wanted." *Pentecostal Evangel,* April 7, 1923, p. 12.

――――― . "The Missionary Policy of the Assemblies of God." *Pentecostal Evangel,* July 7, 1923, p. 12.

――――― . "Co-operation and Fellowship in the Present World Crisis." *Pentecostal Evangel,* October 18, 1941, pp. 1, 6–7.

Foote, D. G. "Urgent Need in General Missions Fund." *The Missionary Challenge,* July 1954, pp. 3, 17.

――――― . "Dear KEY Friends:" *Key,* July and August 1956, pp. 1–2.

"Forward in '50—Double in '51." *The Missionary Challenge,* July 1950, p. 4.

Franklin, John L. "Latin America Calling." *Pentecostal Evangel,* June 5, 1943, pp. 1, 8–9.

Frodsham, Stanley H. "The World Wide Missionary Conference." *Christian Evangel,* June 1, 1918, pp. 2–3, 11.

――――― . "The 1918 General Council." *Christian Evangel,* October 5, 1918, pp. 2–3.

――――― . "The Fourth Missionary Conference." *Pentecostal Evangel,* October 18, 1919, pp. 1, 4.

――――― . "The Seventh General Council Meeting." *Pentecostal Evangel,* October 18, 1919, pp. 2–4.

――――― . "The General Council Report." *Pentecostal Evangel,* October 15, 1921, pp. 2–3, 6–10.

――――― . "General Presbyters Meet." *Pentecostal Evangel,* October 5, 1946, pp. 2–3.

――――― . *With Signs Following,* rev. ed. Springfield, Mo.: Gospel Publishing House, 1946.

Garlock, H. B. *Before We Kill and Eat You.* Edited by Ruthanne Garlock. Dallas: Christ for the Nations, Inc., 1974.

Garlock, Mrs. H. B. "The Social Life of the Missionary." *The Missionary Forum,* no. 3, n.d., pp. 1–2, 7–8.

Gee, Donald. *Upon All Flesh: A Pentecostal World Tour,* rev. ed. Springfield, Mo.: Gospel Publishing House, 1947.

――――― . *The Pentecostal Movement,* rev. ed. London: Elim Publishing Co., Ltd., 1949.

"General Council Missionary Meeting." *Pentecostal Evangel,* January 12, 1935, p. 6.

Goss, Ethel E. *The Winds of God: The Story of the Early Pentecostal Days (1901–1914) in the Life of Howard A. Goss.* New York: Comet Press Books, 1958.

Gustavson, Helen I. *Tsinan, China: The Opening of an Effectual Door.* By the Author, 1941.

Hall, John F. "O for the Life of a Missionary!" *The Missionary Forum,* no. 20, n.d., pp. 2–3.

Handbook for Leaders of Missionary Meetings. Springfield, Mo.: Department of Foreign Missions, n.d.

Harris, C. C. *Africa Has Me Hooked.* By the Author, n.d.

Harris, Ralph W. *Spoken by the Spirit: Documented Accounts of "Other*

Tongues" from Arabic to Zulu. Springfield, Mo.: Gospel Publishing House, 1973.

Hartshorn, Theresa LeDuc. "Bethel News: 1919–1971." Pinellas Park, Fla.: By the Author, n.d.

_____, ed. Memoirs of Bethel: 1916–1929. Red Hill, Penn.: Paul and Dorothy Emery, 1979.

Harvey, Esther B. The Faithfulness of God, 2nd ed. Battle Creek, Mich.: Grounds Gospel Press and Book Store, n.d.

Haynes, Mrs. W. P. "A Missionary Offering." Christian Evangel, January 11, 1919, p. 10.

"Help Bring Back the King." (Advertisement) Pentecostal Evangel, January 10, 1948, p. 13.

Hicks, Tommy. Millions Found Christ. Los Angeles: Manifest Deliverance and Worldwide Evangelism, Inc., 1956.

Hill, Elton G. "India Remains One of the Most Needy Mission Fields." Our Foreign Mission, no. 7: The Indigenous Church in India. Pentecostal Evangel, September 18, 1966, pp. 21–22.

Hodges, Melvin L. "Religion Without Light." Pentecostal Evangel, December 23, 1939, p. 9.

_____. "Missionaries Without Portfolio." The Missionary Challenge, March 1949, pp. 14–15, 32.

_____. "Missions and Bible Prophecy," The Missionary Challenge, April 1950, pp. 6–7, 27.

_____. The Indigenous Church. Springfield, Mo.: Gospel Publishing House, 1953.

_____. "We Believe in Missions." Pentecostal Evangel, September 23, 1956, pp. 14–15.

_____. Build My Church. Springfield, Mo.: Foreign Missions Department, 1957.

_____. "The World Mission of the Assemblies of God." Pentecostal Evangel, November 29, 1959, pp. 2–3, 28.

_____. Grow Toward Leadership. Chicago: Moody Press, 1960.

_____. "We Are Following New Testament Principles." Our Foreign Mission, no. 1: The Indigenous Church in Latin America. Pentecostal Evangel, February 20, 1966, pp. 11–12.

_____. "Spiritual Dynamics in El Salvador." Evangelical Missions Quarterly 2 (Winter 1966):80–83.

_____. "A Pentecostal's View of Mission Strategy." International Review of Missions 57 (July 1968):304–310.

_____. "Are Indigenous Church Principles Outdated?" Evangelical Missions Quarterly 9 (Fall 1972):43–46.

_____. The Indigenous Church and the Missionary. South Pasadena, Calif.: Wm. Carey Library, 1977.

_____. A Theology of the Church and Its Mission. Springfield, Mo.: Gospel Publishing House, 1977.

————. "The Future and Missions." *The Missionary Forum*, no. 19, n.d., pp. 1–2.

Hodges, Serena M., ed. *Look on the Fields: A Missionary Survey.* Springfield, Mo.: Gospel Publishing House, 1956.

Hogan, J. Philip. "Uncle Dudley's Debut." *Key*, Vol. 1, no. 1, 1953, pp. 4, 9.

————. "D. M. S. Sectional Conferences." *Key*, Vol. 1, no. 1, 1953, pp. 8–9.

————. "A Strong Arm of Missions." *The Missionary Challenge*, March 1954, pp. 9–11.

————. "A Gentle Reminder." *Key*, March 1954, p. 3.

————. "Announcing 1956 World Missions Regional Conferences." *Pentecostal Evangel*, September 11, 1955, p. 7.

————. "We Lead the Parade!" *World Challenge*, October 1955, p. 19.

————. "Do We Have a National Workers' Program?" *World Challenge*, December 1956, p. 19.

————. "W–E Day Builds Churches." *World Challenge*, August 1957, p. 19.

————. "S. T. L." *World Challenge*, January 1959, p. 31.

————. "Global Conquest Day." *Pentecostal Evangel*, June 28, 1959, p. 7.

————. "Goals Set for New 'Crash' Program of World Evangelism." *Pentecostal Evangel*, July 26, 1959, p. 6.

————. "Global Conquest. . . ." *Global Conquest*, August 1959, pp. 2–3.

————. "Dear Key Friends:" *Key*, September–October 1959, pp. 1–2.

————. "Global Conquest Report." *Pentecostal Evangel*, November 29, 1959, p. 7.

"The Home-Going of Sister Minnie T. Draper of Ossining, N.Y." *Pentecostal Evangel*, April 2, 1921, p. 7.

Hoover, Elva J., ed. *The WM Leader: Handbook of Leadership Training for Women's Ministries Leaders.* Springfeld, Mo.: The Women's Ministries Department of the Assemblies of God, 1980.

Horst, Glenn. "National Missionary Day." *Key*, Vol. 1, no. 1, 1953, p. 10.

Horton, Stanley M. *Panorama of the Bible.* Springfield, Mo.: Church School Literature Department, 1961.

————. *Bible Prophecy,* Teacher's Manual. Springfield, Mo.: Church School Literature Department, 1963.

————. *What the Bible Says About the Holy Spirit.* Springfield, Mo.: Gospel Publishing House, 1976.

Howell, Beth Prim. *Lady on a Donkey.* New York: E. P. Dutton and Co., 1960.

Hurst, Wesley R. "To Be New Testament the Indigenous Church Must Be Missionary." Our Foreign Mission, no. 11: The Missionary Dimension of the Indigenous Church. *Pentecostal Evangel*, January 15, 1967, pp. 19–20.

Jansen, Harris, ed. *Live in the Spirit: A Compendium of Themes on the Spiritual Life as Presented at the Council on Spiritual Life.* Springfield, Mo.: Gospel Publishing House, 1972.

Johnson, Elva. *Through Deepest Waters: Oren Munger.* Heroes of the Conquest Series, no. 17. Springfield, Mo.: Foreign Missions Department, n.d.

Johnson, Leland E. *I Was a Prisoner of the Japs.* Los Angeles: By the Author, ca. 1945.

Jones, Mair E. *The Merry Missionary.* By Richard Jarvis Specialties, 1955.

Jones, Wilma. *Called to the Congo: Ebba and Joseph Nilsen.* Heroes of the Conquest Series, no. 14. Springfield, Mo.: Foreign Missions Department, n.d.

Juergensen, Marie. *A Call From Japan: An Opportunity for Practical Missionary Work.* Springfield, Mo.: Foreign Missions Department, n.d.

——— . "Reaching Interned Japanese in Idaho." *Pentecostal Evangel,* March 13, 1943, p. 11.

——— . *Foundation Stones: Carl F. Juergensen.* Heroes of the Conquest Series, no. 11. Springfield, Mo.: Foreign Missions Department, n.d.

Keller, Marian. *Twenty Years in Africa: 1913–1933: Retrospect and Prospect.* Toronto: Full Gospel Publishing Co., n.d.

Kerr, D. W. "Third Missionary Conference." *Christian Evangel,* August 10, 1918, p. 11.

Kerr, D. W., and Reynolds, Zella H. "Announcement, Fourth Missionary Conference." *The Bridegroom's Messenger,* September 1919, p. 2.

Ketcham, Maynard L. *Pentecost in the Ganges Delta: Being an Account of the Birth and Development of the Assemblies of God Mission Work in Bengal, India.* By the Author, 1945.

——— . "Information Please!" *World Challenge,* December 1955, pp. 4–5.

——— . "New Churches Are Being Developed Constantly." Our Foreign Mission, no. 3: The Indigenous Church in the Far East. *Pentecostal Evangel,* May 22, 1966, pp. 19–20.

——— . "All the Far East Fields Have Forged Ahead." Our Foreign Mission, no. 10: Assemblies of God Far East Conferences. *Pentecostal Evangel,* December 11, 1966, pp. 13–14.

——— . *Tigers That Talk.* Charlotte, N.C.: PTL Television Network, 1979.

King, Joseph H. *Yet Speaketh: Memoirs of the late Bishop Joseph H. King.* Franklin Springs, Ga.: The Publishing House of the Pentecostal Holiness Church, 1949.

Kvamme, Martin. *Gospel Rays in Manchoukuo.* Springfield, Mo.: Foreign Missions Department, ca. 1937.

La Berge, Agnes N. O. *What God Hath Wrought: Life and Work of Mrs. Agnes N. O. La Berge, Nee Miss Agnes N. Ozman.* Chicago: Herald Publishing Co. Press, n.d.

"Latin America—The Land of the Dark Ages." *Pentecostal Evangel,* November 13, 1920, p. 12.

Lawrence, B. F. *The Apostolic Faith Restored.* St. Louis: Gospel Publishing House, 1916.

Light Along the Nile. The Assemblies of God in Foreign Lands. Springfield, Mo.: Foreign Missions Department, 1942.

Loomis, Marjorie L. *With All My Love: The Story of Marguerite Flint Based on Her Letters Home.* Springfield, Mo.: Gospel Publishing House, 1963.

Lowther, Willa B. "Approval of the Missionary Conference." *Weekly Evangel,* February 23, 1918, p. 11.

Lucas, Christian J. "In Memoriam." *Full Gospel Missionary Herald,* April 1921, pp. 3–5.

Luce, Alice E. "Paul's Missionary Methods," Part 1. *Pentecostal Evangel,* January 8, 1921, pp. 6–7.

————. "Paul's Missionary Methods," Part 2. *Pentecostal Evangel,* January 22, 1921, pp. 6, 11.

————. "Paul's Missionary Methods," Part 3. *Pentecostal Evangel,* February 5, 1921, pp. 6–7.

————. "Scriptural Methods in Missionary Work." *Pentecostal Evangel,* May 9, 1931, pp. 8–9.

Lupton, Levi R. " 'Wilt Thou Go With This Man?' A Strong Plea for Heathen Evangelization." *The Latter Rain Evangel,* June 1910, pp. 18–24.

McDowell, David H. "Earmarks of the Early Church." *Pentecostal Evangel,* April 15, 1939, pp. 1, 9.

Mahaffey, D. S. *Progress of Evangelism in North India.* The Assemblies of God in Foreign Lands. Springfield, Mo.: Foreign Missions Department, n.d.

Maloney, Doris. *Clarence T. Maloney: Ready To Go.* By the Author, n.d.

Malz, Carl. *Foreign Bible School Survey Report: A Report of the Bible School Program of the Foreign Missions Department of the Assemblies of God.* Springfield, Mo.: The Assemblies of God, 1959.

————. "The Crowning Missionary Method." *Pentecostal Evangel,* July 26, 1959, p. 4.

————, ed. *This We Believe: Selected Educational Philosophies of Our Assemblies of God Bible School Administrators on the Foreign Field.* Springfield, Mo.: Foreign Missions Department, ca. 1959.

Manley, Anabel. *WMC History: 1925–1975.* Houston: By the Author, 1975.

McLean, Sigrid. *Over Twenty Years in China.* Minneapolis: By the Author, ca. 1927.

Melching, A. Ruth. *Pearls by the Way.* Taipei, Taiwan, R.O.C.: Dixon Press, Ltd., 1976.

Mintle, Harold. "Missionaries Meet in Biennial Seminar." *Pentecostal Evangel,* July 27, 1958, p. 12.

"Missionaries Visit New York Office." *The Missionary Challenge,* August 1949, pp. 16–17.

"Missionary Conference." *Weekly Evangel,* February 2, 1918, p. 4.

Missionary Manual. Springfield, Mo.: Foreign Missions Department, 1931.

————— . Springfield, Mo.: Department of Foreign Missions, n.d.

————— . Springfield, Mo.: Department of Foreign Missions, 1956.

"A Missionary Movement." *Pentecostal Evangel,* November 13, 1920, p. 8.

"The Missionary Problem Again." *The Latter Rain Evangel,* September 1913, pp. 13–15.

"Missionary Problems That Confront Us; What Is Our Responsibility?" *The Latter Rain Evangel,* January 1913, pp. 17–19.

"Missionary Representatives Conference." *The Missionary Challenge,* April 1950, p. 3.

"Missionary Seminar." *The Missionary Forum,* no. 18, p. 2.

"The Missionary Seminar." *The Missionary Challenge,* August 1950, pp. 6–10, 14.

The Missionary Training Institute Catalog for 1918–1919. Nyack–on–Hudson, N.Y.: The Missionary Training Institute.

"Missionary Yacht Is Dedicated." *Pentecostal Evangel,* June 16, 1945, p. 6.

Moss, Virginia E. *Following the Shepherd: Testimony of Mrs. Virginia E. Moss.* North Bergen, N.J.: Beulah Heights Assembly and Bible and Missionary Training School, ca. 1919.

Moy, Agnes. *He Leadeth Me: My Life Story and Testimony for My Lord and Savior Jesus Christ.* Tokyo: Missionary Field Fellowship of the Assemblies of God, 1976.

Mueller, J. J. *With Our Missionaries in North India.* The Assemblies of God in Foreign Lands. Springfield, Mo.: Foreign Missions Department, 1937.

Myland, D. Wesley. *The Latter Rain Covenant and Pentecostal Power,* 2nd ed. Chicago: The Evangel Publishing House, 1911.

"New Member of Missions Committee." *Pentecostal Evangel,* June 22, 1935, p. 9.

"The New York Office." *The Missionary Forum,* no. 14, pp. 3–4.

Nichols, Nettie D., and Bang, Joshua. *God's Faithfulness in Ningpo.* The Assemblies of God in Foreign Lands. Springfield, Mo.: Foreign Missions Department, 1938.

Nicholson, George P. *Light-Bearers of Shan Tung.* Chicago: Word and Witness Publishing Co., n.d.

"The North China Bible School." *Pentecostal Evangel,* April 23, 1932, p. 9.

Norton, Mary Courtney. *Pilgrims in India.* Benares, U.P., India: The Pilgrim's Mission, n.d.

The Nyack Schools Catalog for 1913–1914. Nyack–on–Hudson, N.Y.: The Nyack Schools.

Olsen, Hilda C., and Anderson, Peggy. *Triumphs and Tears—Basutoland: 1950–1960.* Basutoland, South Africa: By the Authors, 1960.

"Opening of the Central Bible Institute." *Pentecostal Evangel,* October 25, 1924, p. 8.

"Our First Missionary Plane." *The Missionary Challenge,* January–March 1945, pp. 16–17.

"Our Missionary Funds." *The Missionary Challenge,* August 1950, p. 4.

"Our Radio Missionary to the Orient." *Pentecostal Evangel,* August 30, 1953, p. 13.

Parham, Charles F. *The Everlasting Gospel.* Baxter Springs, Kans.: Apostolic Faith Bible College (reprint ed.), n.d.

_____ . *A Voice Crying in the Wilderness,* 2nd ed. Baxter Springs, Kans.: Apostolic Faith Bible College (reprint ed.), 1910.

Payne, Joseph, and Payne, Wilhelmine. *I Beheld the Mountains,* 2nd ed. New York: Vantage Press, 1969.

"Pentecostal Bible Schools." *The Latter Rain Evangel.* July 1912, p. 12.

Perkin, Noel. "Have You Got Your Native Worker?" *Pentecostal Evangel,* June 11, 1927, p. 11.

_____ . "An Appeal for Help." *Pentecostal Evangel,* January 28, 1928, p. 11.

_____ . "Preparation for Missionary Service." *Pentecostal Evangel,* September 7, 1929, p. 10.

_____ . "Preparation for Missions Service." *Pentecostal Evangel,* September 14, 1929, p. 10.

_____ . "Are the Assemblies of God Missionaries Faith Missionaries?" *Pentecostal Evangel,* November 14, 1931, p. 14.

_____ . "Shall We Be Disobedient to the Heavenly Vision?" *Pentecostal Evangel,* April 16, 1932, p. 11.

_____ . "The Missionary Secretary's Mail." *Pentecostal Evangel,* September 3, 1932, p. 9.

_____ . "The Missionary Secretary's Mail." *Pentecostal Evangel,* December 31, 1932, p. 6.

_____ . "Missionary Secretary's Mail." *Pentecostal Evangel,* February 4, 1933, pp. 10–11.

_____ . "Notes From Missionary Secretary." *Pentecostal Evangel,* July 29, 1933, p. 8.

_____ . "Fulfilling the Master's Great Missionary Commission." *Pentecostal Evangel,* November 18, 1933, pp. 2–3, 10–11.

_____ . "Missions in Practice." *Pentecostal Evangel,* October 12, 1935, pp. 1, 10, 11, 13.

_____ . "Recollections of Liberia." *Pentecostal Evangel,* March 11, 1939, pp. 7, 12.

_____ . "The Growth of Missionary Interests." *Pentecostal Evangel,* September 9, 1939, pp. 7, 10.

_____ . "War and Missions." *Pentecostal Evangel,* July 20, 1940, p. 8.

_____ . "War and Missions." *Pentecostal Evangel,* November 2, 1940, p. 6.

_____ . "War and Missions." *Pentecostal Evangel,* December 7, 1940, p. 6.

_____ . "Occupy Till I Come." *Pentecostal Evangel,* September 20, 1941, pp. 4–7.

_____ . "War and Missions." *Pentecostal Evangel,* December 27, 1941, p. 6.

_____ . "Onward to Victory." *Pentecostal Evangel,* April 10, 1943, pp. 1, 6.

_____ . "What's New in the Missions Department?" *Pentecostal Evangel,* April 8, 1944, p. 10.

_____ . "We Press Forward." *Pentecostal Evangel,* December 23, 1944, p. 6.

_____ . "The Program of God." *Pentecostal Evangel,* December 20, 1947, pp. 2, 12–13.

_____ . "Our Missionary Transport." *Pentecostal Evangel,* October 9, 1948, p. 12.

_____ . "Our Funds Are Gone, But Our Faith Is in God." *Pentecostal Evangel,* August 6, 1949, p. 8.

_____ . "Biennial Report of Foreign Missions Department," Part 1. *Pentecostal Evangel,* September 2, 1951, pp. 8–9.

_____ . "Biennial Report of Foreign Missions Department," Part 2. *Pentecostal Evangel,* September 9, 1951, pp. 9, 13.

_____ . "Dear KEY Friends:" *Key,* Vol. 1, no. 1, 1953, pp. 1–2.

_____ . "Foreign Missions Secretary's Report to the 1953 General Council." *Pentecostal Evangel,* September 27, 1953, p. 11.

_____ . "A Word From Noel Perkin." *Pentecostal Evangel,* April 4, 1954, p. 11.

_____ . "Foreign Missions Calls Another Division Into Action." *Key,* July–August 1955, p. 6.

_____ . "Foreign Missions Secretary's Report to the 1955 General Council Meeting." *Pentecostal Evangel,* September 11, 1955, p. 6.

_____ . "Introduction to the Missions Seminar." *Key,* July–August 1956, pp. 3–6.

_____ . "Our World-Wide Missionary Advance." *Pentecostal Evangel,* September 29, 1957, pp. 12–15.

_____ . "Our Missionary Advance Around the World." *Pentecostal Evangel,* October 4, 1959, pp. 12–13, 30.

_____ . "The Secret of Successful Missions." *Pentecostal Evangel,* December 27, 1959, p. 5.

_____ . "Support of Benevolent Institutions." *The Missionary Forum,* no. 12, n.d., p. 2.

_____ . "Racial Superiority." *The Missionary Forum,* no. 12, p. 3.

_____ . "God's Purpose in Missions." *Pulpit,* March 1962, pp. 4–6.

_____ . "Missions—Why? Who? When?" *Pulpit,* January 1964, pp. 11–13.

_____ , ed. *Facing Facts in Modern Missions: A Symposium.* Chicago: Moody Press, 1963.

Perkin, Noel, and Garlock, John. *Our World Witness: A Survey of Assem-*

blies of God Foreign Missions. Springfield, Mo.: Gospel Publishing House, 1963.

Phillips, Everett L. "The Africa Question." *World Challenge,* September 1955, pp. 4–6.

———. "The Only Source of Manpower Sufficient To Accomplish the Task of Evangelizing a Nation Is the People of That Nation." Our Foreign Mission, no. 5: The Indigenous Church in Africa. *Pentecostal Evangel,* July 17, 1966, pp. 19–20.

"A Picture's Worth a Thousand Words." *Key,* February 1953, pp. 8–9, 11.

Pierson, Arthur T. "Speaking With Tongues." *The Missionary Review of the World,* July 1907, pp. 487–492.

———. "Speaking With Tongues—II." *The Missionary Review of the World,* September 1907, pp. 682–684.

Planter, Josephine. *Book of Remembrance or Led by the Spirit,* 3rd ed. Los Angeles: D. C. Welty, Printer, 1936.

Plotts, Morris. *Bwana Tembo: A Prince With God.* Baton Rouge: Jimmy Swaggart Evangelistic Association, 1980.

Plymire, David. *High Adventure in Tibet.* Springfield, Mo.: Gospel Publishing House, 1959.

Plymire, V. G. *Pioneering in Tibet.* The Assemblies of God in Foreign Lands. Springfield, Mo.: Foreign Missions Department, ca. 1931.

Pottorff, Bernice. "My Heart Is Set Down Good for Africa." *The Latter Rain Evangel,* July 1921, pp. 22–23.

The Prayer Fellowship. Springfield, Mo.: Foreign Missions Department, ca. 1946.

"Promotions Division Expanding." *Pentecostal Evangel,* October 26, 1952, pp. 9, 11.

"Purpose of Pentecost." *The Missionary Challenge,* August 1951, p. 4.

"The Question Box." *The Missionary Forum,* no. 2, n.d., p. 4.

"Questions and Answers." *Key,* March 1953, p. 5.

Ramabai, Pandita. "Showers of Blessing at Mukti, India, 39 Years Ago." *Pentecostal Evangel,* May 4, 1946, pp. 1, 12–13.

"Repatriated on the M. S. Gripsholm." *Pentecostal Evangel,* January 1, 1944, pp. 6–7, 11.

Reynolds, Zella H. "A Missionary Rest Home Now Certain." *Christian Evangel,* September 6, 1919, p. 8.

Riggs, Ralph M. "Missionary Enterprise in the Light of the Soon Coming of Christ." *Pentecostal Evangel,* September 28, 1940, pp. 4–5.

———. "Pentecost and Christ's Return." *Pentecostal Evangel,* September 30, 1951, pp. 3–4, 14, 16.

———. "The Doctrine of Divine Healing Is Being Wounded in the House of Its Friends." *Pentecostal Evangel,* November 4, 1956, p. 6.

Sanders, Raymond Ira. *Meet the Mossi.* Edited by Ruby M. Enyart. Springfield, Mo.: Gospel Publishing House, 1953.

Schaeffer, Sue. *Africa Is Waiting.* Grand Rapids: Baker Book House, 1970.

"School of Orientation Becomes Annual Event." *Pentecostal Evangel,* September 27, 1959, p. 7.

Schoonmaker, C. H. "God's Estimate of a Heathen Soul. What Is Yours?" *The Latter Rain Evangel,* November 1917, pp. 13–17.

Schoonmaker, Violet. *Christian Schoonmaker: A Man Who Loved the Will of God.* Landour, Mussoorie, India: Hyratt Press, ca. 1959.

―――― . *Light in India's Night.* Springfield, Mo.: Gospel Publishing House, 1957.

"Second Exploratory Conference of Pentecostal Leaders." *Pentecostal Evangel,* August 28, 1948, pp. 6–7.

"Seminar Profitable to Missionaries." *Pentecostal Evangel,* July 1, 1950, p. 5.

Shelton, Lois. *Tell Me.* Mattoon, Ill.: By the Author, 1949.

Short, Kenneth. "When the Doors Are Opened Again." *The Missionary Challenge,* January–March 1945, pp. 4–5, 21.

Simpson, A. B. *The New Testament Standpoint of Missions.* n.p., n.d.

―――― . *When the Comforter Came.* Harrisburg, Pa.: Christian Publications, 1911.

―――― . *Missionary Messages.* The Alliance Colportage Series. New York: The Christian Alliance Publishing Co., 1925.

―――― . *The Challenge of Missions.* New York: The Christian Alliance Publishing Co., 1926.

Simpson, W. W. "Bro. W. W. Simpson's Plans." *Weekly Evangel,* January 5, 1918, pp. 7, 13.

―――― . (Letter to the Editor) *The Missionary Forum,* no. 2, n.d., p. 3.

―――― . *Evangelizing West China.* The Assemblies of God in Foreign Lands. Springfield, Mo.: Foreign Missions Department, ca. 1934.

Sowing and Reaping in Liberia. Springfield, Mo.: Foreign Missions Department, n.d.

Specter, Ruth Rachel. *Mission to Haiti: Life and Letters of Rev. and Mrs. Homer Specter and Family in Haiti.* By the Author, 1956.

Spence, Inez. *With a Song in Her Heart: Blanche Appleby.* Heroes of the Conquest Series, no. 1. Springfield, Mo.: Foreign Missions Department, n.d.

―――― . *On the Plains of Mongolia: Mr. and Mrs. Thomas Hindle.* Heroes of the Conquest Series, no. 2. Springfield, Mo.: Foreign Missions Department, n.d.

―――― . *These Are My People: Florence Steidel.* Heroes of the Conquest Series, no. 4. Springfield, Mo.: Foreign Missions Department, n.d.

―――― . *Together They Served: Mr. and Mrs. Fred Merian.* Heroes of the Conquest Series, no. 5. Springfield, Mo.: Foreign Missions Department, n.d.

―――― . *Mr. Missions. Director Emeritus: Noel Perkin.* Heroes of the Conquest Series, no. 7. Springfield, Mo.: Foreign Missions Department, n.d.

———— . *Dark Is This Land: Grace Agar.* Heroes of the Conquest Series, no. 9. Springfield, Mo.: Foreign Missions Department, n.d.

———— . *Woman of Courage: Marie Stephany.* Heroes of the Conquest Series, no. 12. Springfield, Mo.: Foreign Missions Department, n.d.

———— . *Henry C. Ball: Man of Action.* Heroes of the Conquest Series, no. 13. Springfield, Mo.: Foreign Missions Department, n.d.

———— . *On the Borders of Nepal: Agnes and Christian Beckdahl.* Heroes of the Conquest Series, no. 16. Springfield, Mo.: Foreign Missions Department, n.d.

———— . *The Finished Task: Beulah Buchwalter.* Heroes of the Conquest Series, no. 18. Springfield, Mo.: Foreign Missions Department, n.d.

———— . *"I Must Go Back": J. W. Tucker.* Heroes of the Conquest Series, no. 20. Springfield, Mo.: Foreign Missions Department, n.d.

Stephany, Marie. *The Power of the Gospel in Shansi Province.* Springfield, Mo.: Foreign Missions Department, ca. 1934.

———— . *The Dragon Defeated: A Life Story of Divine Deliverances.* Milwaukee: Word and Witness Publishing Co., n.d.

Stokes, Louie W. *The Great Revival in Buenos Aires.* Buenos Aires: Casilla De Correo, 1954.

Stokes, Louie and Stokes, Lillian. *The Pentecostal Movement in Argentina.* Buenos Aires: By the Author, n.d.

"The Story of a Missionary Dollar." *Pentecostal Evangel,* June 14, 1953, p. 11.

Sumrall, Lester. *Lillian Trasher, Nile Mother.* Springfield, Mo.: Gospel Publishing House, 1951.

———— . *Modern Manila Miracles: The Story of the Great Philippine Revival.* Springfield, Mo.: by Rev. Clifton O. Erickson, 1954.

———— . *The True Story of Clarita Villaneuva.* South Bend, Ind.: By the Author, 1955.

———— . *The Real Manila Story.* South Bend, Ind.: Lester Sumrall Evangelistic Association, 1964.

Taylor, J. Wilbur. "The Clarion Call for Reapers—Have You Kept Jesus Waiting?" *The Latter Rain Evangel,* September 1922, pp. 2–5.

"The Tale of Totals Told." *Pentecostal Evangel,* March 14, 1936, pp. 12–13.

"The Third Missionary Conference." *Christian Evangel,* November 16, 1918, pp. 2–3.

Thompson, A. E. *The Life of A. B. Simpson.* New York: The Christian Alliance Publishing Co., 1920.

Trasher, Lillian. *The Birth of Assiout Orphanage or Why I Came to Egypt in 1910,* n.d.

Tucker, Angeline. *He Is in Heaven.* New York: McGraw–Hill Book Co., 1965.

Turnbull, Josephine E. "Women and Missions." *The Missionary Forum,* no. 19, n.d., pp. 2–4.

"Twenty-eight Added to Our Missionary Force in 1942." *Pentecostal Evangel*, March 6, 1943, pp. 8–9, 13.

Urshan, Andrew. *The Story of My Life*. St. Louis: Gospel Publishing House, n.d.

To the Uttermost Parts of the Earth: A Survey of the Assemblies of God in Foreign Lands. Springfield, Mo.: Foreign Missions Department, 1938.

Walker, Louise Jeter. "A Team Effort—Then and Now." *Mountain Movers*, August 1980, p. 6.

Webb, Ethel V. "Training in the Faith Life: How God Calls and Provides for a Missionary." *Weekly Evangel*, March 10, 1917, pp. 2–3.

Wegner, Adah Winger. *Think . . . What About South America?* Chicago: Word and Witness Publishing Co., 1941.

Welch, John W. (Editorial) *Pentecostal Evangel*, October 18, 1919, p. 9.

———. "The Present Great World Crisis." *Pentecostal Evangel*, March 28, 1925, pp. 2–3, 8.

Wengler, Jessie. *Letters From Japan*. Pasadena, Calif.: By the Author, n.d.

"What Do You Think?" *The Missionary Forum*, no. 20, n.d., p. 3.

"Why the *Forum?*" *The Missionary Forum*, no. 1, 1948, p. 2.

Williams, Ernest S. *Systematic Theology*. 3 vols. Springfield, Mo.: Gospel Publishing House, 1953.

———. "After Twenty-five Years." *Pentecostal Evangel*, April 8, 1939, p. 5.

Williams, Ralph D., and Arbizu, Francisco. *Standard of Christian Doctrine and Practice; For the Membership of Local Assemblies of God*. n.p., 1932.

Wilson, A. E. *A Visit to Mossi Land (French West Africa)*. Springfield, Mo.: Foreign Missions Department, ca. 1932.

———. *The Gospel Among the Mossi People. French West Africa*. The Assemblies of God in Foreign Lands. Springfield, Mo.: Foreign Missions Department, ca. 1935.

———. *Mining Black Diamonds in Upper Ivory Coast, French West Africa*. The Assemblies of God in Foreign Lands. Springfield, Mo.: Foreign Missions Department, 1942.

Wilson, Elizabeth A. Galley. *Making Many Rich*. Springfield, Mo.: Gospel Publishing House, 1955.

A Work of Faith and Labor of Love: The Assiout Orphanage, Assiout, Egypt. The Assemblies of God in Foreign Lands. Springfield, Mo.: Foreign Missions Department, 1937.

World Missions Convention Digest. Springfield, Mo.: Assemblies of God, n.d.

Unpublished Works

Agar, Grace C. "Tibetan Border of Kansu Province." 1940. (Typewritten.)

———. "Yunnan Province, China: A Glimpse of the Chinese, Tibetan and Tribal Work." ca. 1940. (Typewritten.)

Barrick, J. Edgar. "The Story of My Life." 1983. (Typewritten.)

Burgess, Ruth V. "Obeying the Great Commission: The Acts of Obedience of Ted and Estelle Vassar." 1983. (Typewritten.)

Christian and Missionary Alliance. Missionary record for Harry L. Turner. Nyack, N.Y.: Christian and Missionary Alliance Headquarters.

Dalton, Adele Flower. "Division of Foreign Missions Personnel." n.d. (Typewritten.)

Doney, C. W. "Journal of Missionary Travels and Experiences." n.d. (Typewritten.)

Ezzo, Elsie Bolton. "Watchman, What of the Night?" n.d. (Typewritten.)

Flint, M. Marguerite. "Biographical Sketch." n.d. (Typewritten.)

Flower, Joseph R. "Does God Deny Spiritual Manifestations and Ministry Gifts to Women?" 1979. (Mimeographed.)

Flower, J. Roswell. Lecture Notes on the History of the Assemblies of God. 1943. (Typewritten.)

_____ . "History of the Assemblies of God." (Class notes at Central Bible Institute) 1949. (Typewritten.)

Guynes, Eleanor. "The Place of Women in Assemblies of God Foreign Missions." 1977. (Typewritten.)

Ketcham, Maynard L. "How Pentecost Came to Eastern India." n.d. (Typewritten.)

Metaxatos, Mary Orphan. "I Am My Father's Child." 1973. (Typewritten.)

Perkin, Noel. "A Biblical Appraisal of World Missions." n.d. (Typewritten.)

_____ . "An Overall Plan." n.d. (Typewritten.)

_____ . "Books Recommended by the Foreign Missions Department." n.d. (Mimeographed.)

_____ . "Developing New Missionary Attitudes." ca. 1964. (Typewritten.)

_____ . "Extracts From Diary: Jan. 1, 1949–Oct. 23, 1951." (Typewritten.)

_____ . "Has the World Been Reached?" n.d. (Typewritten.)

_____ . "Missionary Administration." n.d. (Typewritten.)

_____ . "Our Commission . . . To Teach." n.d. (Typewritten.)

_____ . "Personal Testimony." n.d. (Typewritten.)

_____ . "Preparation and Orientation of the Missionary Candidate." n.d. (Typewritten.)

_____ . "Qualifications for Missionary Service." n.d. (Typewritten.)

_____ . "Redefine Our Objectives." n.d. (Typewritten.)

_____ . "The Crisis in Missions." Address Before the National Conference of District Missionary Representatives, 1950.

_____ . "The Goal of Missions." n.d. (Mimeographed.)

_____ . "The Motive for Missions." n.d. (Typewritten.)

_____ . "The World's Need and How It May Be Met." n.d. (Typewritten.)

_____ . "To Care Means To Share." n.d. (Typewritten.)

_____ . "To Whom Much Is Given." n.d. (Typewritten.)

_____ . "Use of Missionary Personnel." n.d. (Typewritten.)

————— . "Why Should the Church Engage in Missions or World Evangelization?" n.d. (Typewritten.)

Plymire, Wardella, ed. "A History of the Assemblies of God in China." 1980. (Typewritten.)

Richards, John B. "Anna." 1980. (Typewritten.)

"Spreading the Pentecostal Message Across America and Around the World: A Brief History of 'The Pentecostal Evangel.'" n.d. (Typewritten.)

Williams, Ernest S. "The Life Story of Reverend Ernest S. Williams." Edited by Dick D. Merrifield. n.d. (Typewritten.)

Williams, Ralph D. (Untitled autobiography), 1981. (Typewritten.)

Winters, Gail Petrena. "Twenty-five Years and a Day in the Congo or Saints and Simbas." n.d. (Typewritten.)

Wood, Alice Cristi. (Untitled autobiographical memoir), n.d. (Typewritten.)

————— . Diary, Entries: 1902–1910.

Minutes and Reports

Beck, Ida. *Problems and Opportunities in Palestine.* Report to the Missionary Conference, March 16–18, 1943. Springfield, Mo.: n.p., 1943.

Blakeney, A. A. *The Full Gospel in North India.* Report to the Missionary Conference, March 16–18, 1943. Springfield, Mo.: n.p., 1943.

Central Bible College. Board of Administration Minutes, June 13, 1950.

Christian and Missionary Alliance. Annual Reports, 1897–1916.

Division of Foreign Missions. Foreign Missions Committee Minutes, 1925–1959.

————— . Special Activities Reports: Africa, Europe, the Middle East, 1939–1959.

————— . Special Activities Reports: Southern Asia and Miscellaneous, 1936–1959.

General Council of the Assemblies of God. Minutes, 1914–1959.

————— . Reports and Financial Statements, 1945–1959, 1967.

————— . Executive Presbytery Minutes, November 23, 1914, November 24, 1919, April 20, 1920, January 3, 1923, January 5, 1923, December 4, 1923, February 24, 1925, October 12, 1925, October 21, 1925, December 30, 1925.

Maloney, C. T. *Report on South India and Ceylon.* Report to the Missionary Conference, March 16–18, 1943. Springfield, Mo.: n.p., 1943.

McKinney, L. O. *Glimpses of Malaya.* Report to the Missionary Conference, March 16–18, 1943. Springfield, Mo.: n.p., 1943.

Nikoloff, N. *Report on Europe.* Report to the Missionary Conference, March 16–18, 1943. Springfield, Mo.: n.p., 1943.

Perkin, Noel. "Report on Russian and Eastern European Mission." January 29, 1940. (Typewritten.)

Short, Kenneth G. *Report of the Dutch East Indies.* Report to the Missionary Conference, March 16–18, 1943. Springfield, Mo.: n.p., 1943.

Pamphlets

Assemblies of God Division of Foreign Missions. A series of pamphlets under no general heading were published that provided information about the geography, history, government, economy, etc., of each of the countries in which Assemblies of God missionaries were stationed. The pamphlets also contained brief histories and surveys of Assemblies of God missions activities in each country. Pamphlets were published on the following countries: Argentina (2 eds.), Basutoland, Belgian Congo, Belgium, Bolivia (2 eds.), Botswana, Brazil (2 eds.), British Guiana (2 eds.), British Honduras (2 eds.), Burma, Chile (2 eds.), Colombia, Costa Rica (2 eds.), Cuba, Dominican Republic (2 eds.), Ecuador, Egypt (2 eds.; a special pamphlet was devoted entirely to the Assiout Orphanage), El Salvador (2 eds.), Fiji, Formosa, Germany, Ghana (2 eds.), Greece, Guatemala (3 eds.), Guyana, Haiti, Hawaii, Honduras (3 eds.), Hong Kong (2 eds.), India (2 eds.), Indonesia (3 eds.), Italy (2 eds.), Jamaica, Japan (2 eds.), Jordan, Korea (2 eds.), Liberia (3 eds.; special pamphlets were devoted entirely to New Hope Town and New Hope Leprosy Mission), Malawi (2 eds.), Malaya–Singapore (2 eds.), Mexico, Nicaragua (2 eds.), Nigeria (4 eds.), North India, Nyasaland (2 eds.), Pakistan (2 eds.), Paraguay (2 eds.), Peru (2 eds.), Philippines (3 eds.), Republic of Congo, Samoa, Senegal (3 eds.), Sierra Leone, South Africa (2 eds.), Spain (2 eds.), Taiwan, Tanganyika (2 eds.), Tanzania, Togo and Dahomey, (2 eds.), Upper Volta (2 eds.), Uruguay (2 eds.), and Venezuela (2 eds.).

Field Focus. A series of pamphlets under this heading has been published by the Assemblies of God Division of Foreign Missions. Each one briefly describes the geography, history, government, and economy of, and provides a history and survey of Assemblies of God foreign missions activities in, one of the following countries: Bahamas, Bangladesh, Belgium, Bharat (Union of India), Bolivia, Brazil, Canary Islands, Chile, Egypt, Federation of Malaysia, Ghana, Greece, Guatemala, Israel, Ivory Coast, Jamaica, New Caledonia, Nigeria, Nippon (Japan), Philippines, Poland, Portugal, South Africa, South Korea, Taiwan, Thailand, Togo, and Zaire.

Audiotapes

Crouch, Philip A., and Gatlin, David. *History of A/G Missions in Egypt.* 2 Tapes. 1976.

Finkenbinder, Paul. *Using Radio To Reach the World.* Sermon, 29 August 1965.

Perkin, Noel. *Favorite Missionary Stories.* Springfield, Mo.: A/G Audio-visual Services, 1964.

Letters

Arminio, Roberta Y. Director of the Ossining (N.Y.) Historical Society. Letters, 22 July 1983, 20 November 1983.

Barrick, J. Edgar, Missionary to India, to Maynard L. Ketcham, 1 November 1959.

Clifford, Walter, Missionary to India, to Mrs. George Carmichael, 16 August 1950.

Coggins, Wade T. Executive Director of the Evangelical Foreign Missions Association. Letter 15 August 1983.

Doney, C. W., Missionary to Egypt, to "My Dear Brother" (W. T. Gaston?), 10 September 1925.

Flower, Joseph R. General Secretary of the General Council of the Assemblies of God. Letters, 16 March 1983, 25 May 1983.

Gaston, W. T., General Superintendent of the General Council of the Assemblies of God (1925–1929), to the General Presbyters, 26 January 1927.

Harris, Ralph W. National Secretary of the Youth Department and Editor of Church School Literature, retired. Letter, 13 May 1983.

King, Louis, President of the Christian and Missionary Alliance. Letter, 22 November 1985.

McDaniel, W. Neil. President of the Springfield Travel Service, Inc. Letter, 11 November 1983.

Needham, Harold K., Overseas Representative for the General Council of the Assemblies of God: 1920–1921, to W. T. Gaston, 5 December 1923.

Schoonmaker, Martha, Missionary to India, to Maynard L. Ketcham and the Executive Committee, 29 July 1950.

Personal Interviews

Ball, Henry C. Field Secretary for Latin America and the West Indies, retired. Interview with author. San Antonio, Texas, 8 July 1981.

Beckdahl, Samuel T. Former missionary to India and Africa; Assistant Professor in Bible and General Education, Central Bible College. Interview with author. Springfield, Missouri, 30 November 1983.

Berg, Anna C. Missionary to Africa, retired. Interview with author. Springfield, Missouri, 20 June 1983.

Bloom, Eva. Missionary to China and Hawaii, retired. Interview with author. Springfield, Missouri, 2 March 1984.

Booze, Joyce Wells. Former Foreign Missions Editor for the Assemblies of God Division of Foreign Missions; Assistant Professor in English, Central Bible College. Interview with author. Springfield, Missouri, 29 November 1983.

Burgess, John H. Missionary to India, retired. Interview with author. Springfield, Missouri, 10 May 1983.

Carmichael, Christine, C. Deputational Secretary for the Assemblies of God Division of Foreign Missions, retired. Interview with author. Springfield, Missouri, 18 January 1984.

Crouch, Philip A. Former missionary to Egypt and President of Central Bible College (1963–1980). Interview with author. Springfield, Missouri, 26 December 1979.

Dalton, Adele Flower. Former missionary to Latin America and Spain; senior editorial assistant for the Assemblies of God Division of Foreign Missions. Interview with author. Springfield, Missouri, 29 November 1983.

Drake, David B. Former Director of Admissions and Records; Associate Professor of Bible and English, Central Bible College. Interview with author. Springfield, Missouri, 7 November 1983.

Flokstra, Gerard J. Jr., Former Director of the Library; Associate Professor of Theology, Central Bible College. Interview with author. Springfield, Missouri, 1 September 1983.

Flower, Joseph R. General Secretary of the General Council of the Assemblies of God. Interview with author. Springfield, Missouri, 29 March 1983.

Harvey, Esther B. Missionary to India, retired. Interview with author. Springfield, Missouri, 21 June 1983.

Hodges, Melvin L. Field Secretary for Latin America and the West Indies, retired; Nocl Perkin Professor of World Missions, Assemblies of God Theological Seminary. Interview with author. Springfield, Missouri, 26 August 1983.

Hogan, J. Philip. Former missionary to China and Taiwan; Executive Director of the Assemblies of God Division of Foreign Missions. Interview with author. Springfield, Missouri, 6 July 1983.

Hogan, Virginia L. Former missionary to China and Taiwan. Interview with author. Springfield, Missouri, 1 March 1981.

Hoover, Elva J. Secretary for the Women's Ministries Department of the General Council of the Assemblies of God. Interview with author. Springfield, Missouri, 19 August 1983.

Horton, Stanley M. Professor of Old Testament, Assemblies of God Theological Seminary. Interview with author. Springfield, Missouri, 12 September 1983.

Ketcham, Maynard L. Field Secretary for the Far East, retired. Interview with author. Springfield, Missouri, 13 July 1983.

Lindgren, G. Arvid. Former student at the Rochester Bible Training School. Interview with author. Springfield, Missouri, 1 May 1983.

McGlasson, Robert T. Eastern Representative and Foreign Missions Secretary, retired. Interview with author. Springfield, Missouri, 17 November 1983.

Nikoloff, Martha. Former missionary to Eastern Europe. Interview with author. Springfield, Missouri, 19 August 1983.

Osgood, Howard C. Field Secretary for China and the Far East, retired. Interview with author. Springfield, Missouri, 1 November 1983.

Perkin, Noel. Executive Director Emeritus of the Assemblies of God Division of Foreign Missions. Interview with author. Springfield, Missouri, 16 August 1979.

Phillips, Everett L. Field Secretary for Africa, retired. Interview with author. Springfield, Missouri, 12 February 1984.

Richards, John S. Missionary to South Africa, retired. Interview with author. Springfield, Missouri, 11 July 1983.

Walegir, Stephen A. Office Manager for the Division of Home Missions of the General Council of the Assemblies of God. Interview with author. Springfield, Missouri, 19 August 1983.

Walker, Louise Jeter. Former missionary to Latin America, retired; writer and editor for the International Correspondence Institute. Interview with author. Springfield, Missouri, 1 June 1983.

Walther, Grace L. Missionary to India, retired; Associate Professor Emeritus, Evangel College. Interview with author. Springfield, Missouri, 9 December 1983.

Telephone Interviews

Eide, Frederick D. Former Pastor of the Bethel Pentecostal Assembly, Newark, New Jersey. Interview with author. Mountainhome, Pennsylvania, 27 June 1983.

Emery, Paul J. Sr., Former President of Northeast Bible Institute (later, Valley Forge Christian College). Interview with author. Allentown, Pennsylvania, 27 June 1983.

Steil, Harry J. Former teacher at Bethel Bible Training School, Newark, New Jersey. Interview with author. Cardiff–By–the–Sea, California, 27 June 1983.

SECONDARY SOURCES

Ahlstrom, Sydney E. *A Religious History of the American People.* 2 vols. Garden City, N.Y.: Doubleday and Co., 1975.

Alioha, G. M. *The History of Assemblies of God: Nigeria.* Aba, Nigeria: MacBlackson Press Publications, 1975.

Allen, Roland. *Missionary Methods: St. Paul's or Ours?* 2nd ed. Grand Rapids: Wm. B. Eerdmans Publishing Co., 1962.

Anderson, Gerald H., ed. *The Theology of the Christian Mission.* New York: McGraw–Hill Book Co., 1961.

Anderson, Robert Mapes. *Vision of the Disinherited: The Making of American Pentecostalism.* New York: Oxford University Press, 1979.

Assemblies of God—Ghana: 1931–1981. n.d.

Atter, Gordon F. *The Third Force.* Peterborough, Ontario, Canada: The College Press, 1962.

Barton, James L. *Human Progress Through Missions.* New York: Fleming H. Revell Co., 1912.

Bateman, Doris, ed. *History of Liberia Assemblies of God Mission.* Bath, England: H. Sharp, Printer and Stationer, 1968.

Beaman, Jay. "Pentecostal Pacifism: The Origin, Development, and Rejection of the Pacific Belief Among the Pentecostals." M. Div. thesis, North American Baptist Seminary, 1982.

Beaver, R. Pierce. "North American Thought on the Fundamental Principles of Missions During the Twentieth Century." *Church History* XXI (December 1952):345–364.

—————. "Eschatology in American Missions." In *Basileia: Walter Freytag zum 60: Geburtstag,* pp. 60–75. Edited by Jan Hermelink and Hans Jochen Margull. Stuttgart: Evang. Missionsverlag, 1959.

—————. *Ecumenical Beginnings in the Protestant World Mission: A History of Comity.* New York: Thomas Nelson and Sons, 1962.

—————. "Missionary Motivation Through Three Centuries." In *Reinterpretation in American Church History,* pp. 113–151. Edited by Jerald C. Brauer. Chicago: University of Chicago Press, 1968.

—————. "History of Mission Strategy." *Southwestern Journal of Theology* 12 (Spring 1970):7–28.

—————. *American Protestant Women in World Mission: A History of the First Feminist Movement in North America.* Grand Rapids: Wm. B. Eerdmans Publishing Co., 1980.

—————, ed. *To Advance the Gospel: Selections From the Writings of Rufus Anderson.* Grand Rapids: Wm. B. Eerdmans Publishing Co., 1967.

—————, ed. *American Missions in Bicentennial Perspective.* South Pasadena, Calif.: William Carey Library, 1977.

Bliss, Edwin Munsell. *The Missionary Enterprise: A Concise History of Its Objects, Methods and Extension.* New York: Fleming H. Revell Co., 1908.

Bloch–Hoell, Nils. *The Pentecostal Movement.* Oslo: Universitetsforlaget, 1964.

Boer, Harry R. *Pentecost and Missions.* Grand Rapids: Wm. B. Eerdmans Publishing Co., 1961.

Booze, Joyce Wells. *Into All the World: A History of Assemblies of God Foreign Missions.* Springfield, Mo.: Division of Foreign Missions, 1980.

Brenda, Albert W. *I Heard From Heaven.* A Biography of J. P. Kolenda. Turlock, Calif.: By the Author, n.d.

Brown, Arthur Judson. *The Foreign Missionary: An Introduction of a World Movement.* New York: Fleming H. Revell Co., 1907.

Brumback, Carl. *Suddenly From Heaven: A History of the Assemblies of God.* Springfield, Mo.: Gospel Publishing House, 1961.

Buckley, James M. *Theory and Practice of Foreign Missions.* New York: Easton and Mains, 1911.

Carmichael, Christine. "Spreading the Gospel in the Sixties." Missions Vignettes, no. 15. *Pentecostal Evangel,* January 16, 1966, pp. 19–20.

Cartmel, Daryl Westwood. "Mission Policy and Program of A. B. Simpson." M.A. thesis, The Hartford Seminary Foundation, 1962.

Carver, William Owen. *Missions in the Plan of the Ages.* New York: Fleming H. Revell Co., 1909.

—————. *Missions and Modern Thought.* New York: The Macmillan Co., 1910.

Christian and Missionary Alliance. *Report and Retrospect of the Work of the Christian and Missionary Alliance.* Nyack, N.Y.: The Christian Alliance Publishing Co., 1897.

————— . *Story of the Christian and Missionary Alliance.* Nyack, N.Y.: The Christian Alliance Publishing Co., 1900.

————— . *Christian and Missionary Alliance in South China.* n.p., 1917.

Clanton, Arthur L. *United We Stand: A History of Oneness Organizations.* Hazelwood, Mo.: The Pentecostal Publishing House, 1970.

Concise Dictionary of the Christian World Mission. S.v. "Foreign Missions Conference of North America, The," by F. W. Price.

Conn, Charles W. *Where the Saints Have Trod: A History of Church of God Missions.* Cleveland, Tenn.: Pathway Press, 1959.

Crane, James D. "What We Can Learn From the Assemblies of God in El Salvador." ca. 1962. (Typewritten.)

Dayton, Donald W. "From 'Christian Perfection' to the 'Baptism of the Holy Ghost.' " n.d. (Typewritten.)

————— . "Theological Roots of Pentecostalism." *Pneuma* 2 (Spring 1980):3–21.

De Leon, Victor. *The Silent Pentecostals: A Biographical History of the Pentecostal Movement Among the Hispanics in the 20th Century.* Taylors, S.C.: Faith Printing Co., 1979.

Dennis, James S. *Foreign Missions After a Century.* New York: Fleming H. Revell Co., 1893.

————— . *The New Horoscope of Missions,* 2nd ed. New York: Fleming H. Revell Co., 1908.

Dominguez, Roberto. *Pioneros de Pentecostes.* Miami, Fla.: By the Author, 1977.

Early History of . . . the Assemblies of God. Edited by C. C. Burnett. Springfield, Mo.: Assemblies of God, 1959.

The Encyclopedia of Modern Christian Missions: The Agencies. S.v. "Assemblies of God Foreign Missions Department," by Raymond T. Brock.

————— . S.v. "Church of God, World Missions Board," by Duran M. Palmertree.

————— . S.v. "Eastern European Mission," by Paul B. Peterson.

————— . S.v. "Pentecostal Holiness Church, Department of Foreign Missions," by W. H. Turner.

Fairbank, John K., ed. *The Missionary Enterprise in China and America.* Cambridge: Harvard University Press, 1974.

Frodsham, Stanley H. *Wholly for God.* A Call to Complete Consecration Illustrated by the Story of Paul Bettex, a truly consecrated soul. Springfield, Mo.: Gospel Publishing House, n.d.

————— . *With Signs Following,* 2nd ed. Springfield, Mo.: Gospel Publishing House, 1946.

Gordon, Adoniram Judson. *The Holy Spirit in Missions.* London: Hodder and Stoughton, 1896.

Hamilton, Michael P., ed. *The Charismatic Movement.* Grand Rapids: Wm. B. Eerdmans Publishing Co., 1975.

Handy, Robert T. *A Christian America: Protestant Hopes and Historical Realities.* New York: Oxford University Press, 1971.

Harrell, David Edwin. Jr., *All Things Are Possible: The Healing and Charismatic Revivals in Modern America.* Bloomington, Ind.: Indiana University Press, 1975.

Harrison, Irvin John. "A History of the Assemblies of God." Th. D. dissertation, Berkeley Baptist Divinity School, 1954.

Hawaii Assemblies of God. *Ka Malamalama No Ka Makahiki I Hala: A History of the Assemblies of God in Hawaii.* Hawaii: Hawaii Assemblies of God, 1975.

Henderson, Jeff. "Pentecostal Missions in Eastern Europe: 1919–1940." 1981. (Typewritten.)

————. "J. Roswell Flower: An Essay on Practical Spirituality." 1981. (Typewritten.)

History of Liberia Assemblies of God Mission. Zwedru, Liberia: By Annie Cressman, 1972.

Hodges, Nelson Hart. "The True and the False: The World of an Emerging Evangelical Protestant Fundamentalism in America, 1890–1920." Ph. D. dissertation, Michigan State University, 1976.

Hogg, William Richie. *Ecumenical Foundations: A History of the International Missionary Council and Its Nineteenth-Century Background.* New York: Harper and Brothers, 1952.

Hollenweger, Walter J. *The Pentecostals: The Charismatic Movement in the Church.* Minneapolis: Augsburg Publishing House, 1972.

Hoover, Mario G. "Origin and Structural Development of the Assemblies of God." M.A. thesis, Southwest Missouri State University, 1968.

In the Last Days: An Early History of the Assemblies of God. Springfield, Mo.: General Council of the Assemblies of God, 1973.

James, Janet Wilson, ed. *Women in American Religion.* Philadelphia: University of Pennsylvania Press, 1980.

Jeter, Louise. *Peruvian Gold.* n.d. (Typewritten.)

Johnston, Arthur P. *The Battle for World Evangelism.* Wheaton, Ill.: Tyndale House Publishers, Inc., 1978.

Jones, John P. *The Modern Missionary Challenge: A Study of the Present Day World Missionary Enterprise: Its Problems and Results.* New York: Fleming H. Revell Co., 1910.

Kang, Wi Jo. "Nevius' Methods: A Study and an Appraisal of Indigenous Mission Methods." *Concordia Theological Monthly* 34 (June 1963):335–342.

Kendrick, Klaude. "History of the Assemblies of God." M.A. thesis, Texas Christian University, 1948.

————. *The Promise Fulfilled: A History of the Modern Pentecostal Movement.* Springfield, Mo.: Gospel Publishing House, 1961.

Kulbeck, Gloria G. *What God Hath Wrought: A History of the Pentecostal Assemblies of Canada.* Toronto: The Pentecostal Assemblies of Canada, 1958.

Latourette, Kenneth Scott. *Missions Tomorrow.* New York: Harper and Brothers, Publishers, 1936.

_____ . *A History of the Expansion of Christianity,* Vol. 4: *The Great Century: Europe and the United States.* New York: Harper and Row, 1941.

_____ . *A History of the Expansion of Christianity,* Vol. 6: *The Great Century: North Africa and Asia.* New York: Harper and Row, 1944.

_____ . *A History of the Expansion of Christianity,* Vol. 7: *Advance Through Storm.* New York: Harper and Row, 1945.

Lawrence, Edward A. *Modern Missions in the East: Their Methods, Successes, and Limitations.* New York: Harper and Brothers, Publishers, 1895.

Lee, Randy H. "Robert W. Cumming's Perception of the Spiritual Life." 1981. (Typewritten.)

Marsden, George M. *Fundamentalism and American Culture: The Shaping of Twentieth-Century Evangelicalism: 1870-1925.* New York: Oxford University Press, 1980.

Menzies, William W. *Anointed To Serve: The Story of the Assemblies of God.* Springfield, Mo.: Gospel Publishing House, 1971.

Mott, John R. *The Evangelization of the World in This Generation.* New York: Student Volunteer Movement for Foreign Missions, 1900.

_____ . *The Present World Situation.* New York: Student Volunteer Movement, 1914.

Moyer, Elgin S., ed. *Who Was Who in Church History.* S.v. "George Muller."

Neill, Stephen, *A History of Christian Missions.* The Pelican History of the Church, no. 6. Baltimore: Penguin Books, 1964.

Nelson, Douglas J. "For Such a Time as This: The Story of Bishop William J. Seymour and the Azusa Street Revival." Ph. D. dissertation, University of Birmingham, 1981.

Nevius, John L. *The Planting and Development of Missionary Churches.* Shanghai, China: Presbyterian Press, 1886; reprint ed., Grand Rapids: Baker Book House, 1958.

Nichol, John Thomas. *Pentecostalism.* New York: Harper and Row, 1966.

Orr, J. Edwin. *The Flaming Tongue: Evangelical Awakenings, 1900—.* Chicago: Moody Press, 1975.

Parham, Sarah E. *The Life of Charles F. Parham: Founder of the Apostolic Faith Movement.* Joplin, Mo.: The Tri-State Printing Co., 1930.

Perkin, Noel. "Our First Five Years (1914–1919)." Missions Vignettes, no. 1. *Pentecostal Evangel,* October 25, 1964, pp. 13–14.

_____ . "Highlights of the 20's (1920–1924)." Missions Vignettes, no. 2. *Pentecostal Evangel,* November 29, 1964, pp. 17–18.

_____ . "Coordination and Advance (1925–1930)." Missions Vignettes, no. 3 *Pentecostal Evangel,* December 27, 1964, pp. 11–12.

_____ . "Call to Advance (1930–1934)." Missions Vignettes, no. 4 *Pentecostal Evangel,* January 24, 1965, pp. 9–10.

————. "Sifting and Growth (1935–1939)." Missions Vignettes, no. 10. *Pentecostal Evangel,* August 22, 1965, pp. 21–22.

————. "Progress in Crisis (1940–1944)." Missions Vignettes, no. 11. *Pentecostal Evangel,* September 19, 1965, pp. 11–12.

————. "Postwar Expansion (1945–1949)." Missions Vignettes, no. 12. *Pentecostal Evangel,* October 24, 1965, pp. 21–22.

————. "Increasing Mobility (1950–1954)." Missions Vignettes, no. 13. *Pentecostal Evangel,* November 21, 1965, pp. 19–20.

————. "The Building Grows (1955–1959)." Missions Vignettes, no. 14. *Pentecostal Evangel,* December 19, 1965, pp. 19–20.

Peters, George W. "The Missionary Thrust and Dynamic of the Assemblies of God." n.d. (Mimeographed.)

Pfeiffer, Edward, *Mission Studies,* 3rd ed. Columbus: Lutheran Book Concern, 1920.

Pomerville, Paul Anthony. "Pentecostalism and Missions: Distortion or Correction? The Pentecostal Contribution to Contemporary Mission Theology." Ph. D. dissertation, Fuller Theological Seminary School of World Mission, 1982.

Rabe, Valentin H. *The Home Base of American China Missions, 1880–1920.* Cambridge: Harvard University Press, 1978.

Ramm, Bernard. *A Handbook of Contemporary Theology.* Grand Rapids: Wm. B. Eerdmans Publishing Co., 1966.

Richardson, James E. "A Study of the Leadership Training Programs of the Assemblies of God in Spanish America." 1974. (Typewritten.)

Robeck, Cecil M. Jr., "The Earliest Pentecostal Missions in Los Angeles." *Assemblies of God Heritage,* Fall 1983, pp. 3–4, 12.

Robins, Roger. "Attitudes Toward War and Peace in the Assemblies of God: 1914–1918." 1982. (Typewritten.)

The Romance of the Missionary Institute at Nyack–on–Hudson, New York. n.p., n.d.

Rouse, Ruth, and Neill, Stephen Charles, eds. *A History of the Ecumenical Movement: 1517–1948,* 2nd ed. Philadelphia: The Westminster Press, 1967.

Rupert, Marybeth. "The Emergence of the Independent Missionary Agency as an American Institution: 1860–1917." Ph. D. dissertation, Yale University, 1974.

Sandeen, Ernest R. *The Roots of Fundamentalism: British and American Millenarianism: 1800–1930.* Chicago: University of Chicago Press, 1970.

Scofield, C. I., ed. *The Scofield Reference Bible.* New York: Oxford University Press, 1909.

Shinde, Benjamin P. "The Contribution of the Assemblies of God to Church Growth in India." M.A. thesis, Fuller Theological Seminary School of World Mission, 1974.

Shumway, Charles William. "A Critical History of Glossolalia." Ph. D. dissertation, Boston University, 1919.

Speer, Robert E. *Christianity and the Nations.* New York: Fleming H. Revell Co., 1910.

Stotts, George Raymond. "The History of the Modern Pentecostal Movement in France." Ph. D. dissertation, Texas Tech University, 1973.

Strong, Augustus Hopkins. *A Tour of the Missions: Observations and Conclusions.* Philadelphia: The Griffith and Rowland Press, 1918.

Sturgeon, Inez. *Give Me This Mountain.* Oakland, Calif: By the Author, 1960.

Synan, Vinson. *The Holiness–Pentecostal Movement in America.* Grand Rapids: Wm. B. Eerdmans Publishing Co., 1971.

_____, ed. *Aspects of Pentecostal–Charismatic Origins.* Plainfield, N.J.: Logos International, 1975.

Turner, Fennell P., ed. *Students and the World-Wide Expansion of Christianity:* Addresses Delivered Before the Seventh International Convention of the Student Volunteer Movement for Foreign Missions, Kansas City, Missouri, December 31, 1913 to January 4, 1914. New York: Student Volunteer Movement for Foreign Missions, 1914.

Van Dusen, Henry P. "The Third Force in Christendom." *Life,* June 9, 1958, pp. 113–124.

Vardaman, E. Jerry, and Garrett, James Leo, Jr., eds. *The Teacher's Yoke: Studies in the Memory of Henry Trantham.* Waco, Tex.: Baylor University Press, 1964.

Varg, Paul A. *Missionaries, Chinese, and Diplomats: The American Protestant Missionary Movement in China. 1890–1952.* New York: Octagon Books, 1977.

Vidler, Alec R. *The Church in an Age of Revolution.* The Pelican History of the Church, no. 5. Baltimore: Penguin Books, 1961.

Wagner, C. Peter *Look Out! The Pentecostals Are Coming.* Carol Stream, Ill.: Creation House, 1973.

Waldvogel, Edith Lydia. "The 'Overcoming Life': A Study in the Reformed Evangelical Origins of Pentecostalism." Ph. D. dissertation, Harvard University, 1977.

Weber, Timothy P. *Living in the Shadow of the Second Coming: American Premillennialism: 1875–1925.* New York: Oxford University Press, 1979.

The Westminster Dictionary of Church History. S.v. "Monarchians."

Wilson, B. P. *The Assemblies of God in Alaska.* Anchorage, Alaska: Alaska District Council, 1980.

Wilson, Dwight. *Armageddon Now! The Premillenarian Response to Russia and Israel Since 1917.* Grand Rapids: Baker Book House, 1977.

Winehouse, Irwin. *The Assemblies of God: A Popular Survey.* New York: Vantage Press, 1959.

Index

277